Send Lazarus

CATHOLIC PRACTICE IN NORTH AMERICA

SERIES EDITOR:

John C. Seitz, Associate Professor, Theology Department, Fordham
University; Associate Director for Lincoln Center, Curran Center
for American Catholic Studies

This series aims to contribute to the growing field of Catholic
studies through the publication of books devoted to the historical
and cultural study of Catholic practice in North America, from the
colonial period to the present. As the term "practice" suggests, the
series springs from a pressing need in the study of American
Catholicism for empirical investigations and creative explorations
and analyses of the contours of Catholic experience. In seeking to
provide more comprehensive maps of Catholic practice, this series is
committed to publishing works from diverse American locales,
including urban, suburban, and rural settings; ethnic, postethnic,
and transnational contexts; private and public sites; and seats of
power as well as the margins.

Send Lazarus

CATHOLICISM AND THE CRISES
OF NEOLIBERALISM

Matthew T. Eggemeier and Peter Joseph Fritz

FORDHAM UNIVERSITY PRESS
New York 2020

Visit us online at www.fordhampress.com.

Library of Congress Cataloging-in-Publication Data available online at https://catalog.loc.gov.

Printed in the United States of America

22 21 20   5 4 3 2 1

First edition

Contents

Abbreviations

CA John Paul II, *Centesimus Annus* (1991)
CV Benedict XVI, *Caritas in Veritate* (2009)
DC Benedict XVI, *Deus Caritas Est* (2005)
DM John Paul II, *Dives in Misericordia* (1980)
EA John Paul II, *Ecclesia in America* (1999)
EG Francis, *Evangelii Gaudium* (2013)
LE John Paul II, *Laborem Exercens* (1981)
LS Francis, *Laudato Si'* (2015)
MM John XXIII, *Mater et Magistra* (1961)
PP Paul VI, *Populorum Progressio* (1967)
QA Pius XI, *Quadragesimo Anno* (1931)
RH John Paul II, *Redemptor Hominis* (1979)
RN Leo XIII, *Rerum Novarum* (1891)
SRS John Paul II, *Sollicitudo Rei Socialis* (1987)
SS Benedict XVI, *Spe Salvi* (2007)
VS John Paul II, *Veritatis Splendor* (1993)

All references to the Bible, unless otherwise noted, are from the *New American Bible*, the translation used in the worship and prayer of US Catholics, available on the US Conference of Catholic Bishops website at http://usccb.org/bible/index.cfm.

Send Lazarus

Introduction

Pope Francis's message for Lent from 2016 has as its epigraph Jesus's saying, "I desire mercy, not sacrifice" (Mt 9:13; cf. Hos 6:6).[1] He explicates this saying by making a plea to Catholics to turn toward God and to evangelize through the spiritual and corporal works of mercy. He proceeds to discuss the reality of this mercy, which is made incarnate in Jesus Christ, which changes hearts and "enables us . . . to become merciful in turn."[2] Francis exhorts his readers to practice this mercy, especially toward the poor, in whom Christ's tortured flesh becomes visible.[3] In doing so, they oppose people with great power and wealth, in whom a temptation often becomes overwhelming, to "the point of being blind to Lazarus at their doorstep" (see Lk 16:19–31).[4] Such blindness, Francis contends, may be "seen in the sinful structures linked to a model of false development based on the idolatry of money, which leads to a lack of concern for the fate of the poor on the part of wealthier individuals and societies; they close their doors, refusing even to see the poor."[5] The implication of Francis's Lenten message is clear: Lent, often seen as a season of sacrifice, should be a time of mercy—prophetic mercy proclaiming the Gospel to a world that idolizes "knowledge, power, and riches," and that risks refusing Christ and "plunging into the eternal abyss of solitude that is Hell."[6] Francis expresses hope that a Lent defined by the works of mercy will bring conversion.[7]

Jesus's saying on which Francis reflects begins in noteworthy fashion. Jesus states, *"Go and learn the meaning of the words,* 'I desire mercy, not sacrifice.'" This book aims to facilitate such learning. It asks what mercy and sacrifice look like today. It does so by examining the dominant social order in today's world, which we call *neoliberalism.*

This book is a work of systematic theology aimed at elucidating the reality of mercy in a world marked by practices, social structures, and cultures of pathological sacrifice. It upholds the works of mercy as practices out of which new structures can be fashioned and cultures renewed. As a whole this book aims to enact the spiritual works of mercy. It admonishes sinners, or all of us—for all have been enlisted in some way, as subsequent chapters will show—who perpetuate an economic, political, legal, and cultural system founded on indifference toward the needs and desires of people and God's creation. It instructs the ignorant, bringing thematically to light this system that all of us know *notionally*, but most not *really*. It counsels the doubtful, by giving an account of Christian hope (1 Pet 3:15) to all of us who live in a period of obvious unrest and social upheaval. It comforts the sorrowful, namely, those who suffer the sorts of injustices discussed throughout the book. It bears wrongs patiently by carefully analyzing social crises and a culture of indifference and pathological sacrifice and pointing to theological and practical ingredients for alternatives. It forgives injuries by seeking conversion from those who perpetrate injustice, thus channeling Jesus's saying, "Go and sin no more" (Jn 8:11). All of this it does in a spirit of prayer for the living and the dead, meditating upon the scriptures, teachings of the popes, theories of theologians, practices of Christians, and ideas of all people of good will. Key, though, to addressing today's dominant sacrificial system, neoliberalism, is reimagining the corporal works of mercy. This will be the conclusive dimension of our theological proposal, discussed in the book's final chapter.

Introducing Neoliberalism

Neoliberalism is notoriously difficult to define, even to the point that some scholars claim that it is merely a label for "whatever I do not like."[8] It is true that the particular term *neoliberalism* is generally used by its critics on the left side of the political spectrum. This presents some difficulty for defining the term, given that those who describe neoliberalism could be dismissed for being biased. Also, given that in the United States, *liberalism* tends to be associated with "leftist," social welfare policies, it is difficult to figure how neoliberalism was originally a product of the Right.[9] Even worse, those who espouse the political-economic ethos that others call neoliberalism refuse to use that name.[10]

As we see it, the main difficulty is neither that neoliberalism does not exist nor that it exists only as a figment of a biased imagination. Instead, it is this: defining neoliberalism is like trying to define water to a fish. It is the political-economic-cultural order in which we live, move, and have our being—and for people younger than forty years old, they always have, since neoliberalism has been the dominant political and cultural ethos in our world since the 1980s. As Wendy Brown observes, neoliberalism is so pervasive that the relevant question is not who is a neoliberal today, but "who is *not* a neoliberal today?"[11] Ideas and practices that we will identify as indisputably neoliberal—such as the idea of freedom we tend to hold in the United States (lack of restrictions on our consumer and lifestyle choices and an unstated yet categorical imperative to "invest" well in all areas of existence)—pervade our lives. Nevertheless, as journalist George Monbiot points out, for many people neoliberalism remains anonymous, unnamed, and unidentified.[12] "So pervasive has neoliberalism become," Monbiot observes, "that we seldom ever recognize it as an ideology."[13]

Perhaps the best way of recognizing neoliberalism is to address it as "neo." A recent definition of neoliberalism can assist here. "Neoliberalism [is the] return to the principles of classical liberalism," writes Roger Scruton. "In particular, the defence of the free economy, free trade, and small government."[14] Indeed, neoliberals (especially in the line of Friedrich A. Hayek [1899–1992]) claim at times to be renewing classical liberalism in an age of socialist dominance or, after 1989, the threat of socialist resurgence. But in large measure this is deceiving. We will note as we go forward that neoliberalism makes at least two important innovations on the liberal tradition. First, the *free* in free economy and free trade is drastically relativized, inasmuch as neoliberalism consists *not* in unleashing the economy and allowing trade to transpire as it will but rather vigilantly cultivating, supporting, and sustaining the world economy through political and legal measures and structures. Second, in keeping with the first, government cannot be "small," but must be large and interventionist, not in the socialist mode of anticipating and providing for human needs but in a hypercapitalist mode of responding to the needs of capital as an abstract, inscrutable force.

With these preliminaries in place, let us provisionally define neoliberalism as follows: neoliberalism is a politicized mutation of capitalism, where the state's primary function is to foster market processes, each person's freedom in civil society is defined in terms of market logics of investment (which does not necessarily implicate direct monetization), and the needs of people and the earth are secondary to those of capital, because the world economy rules supreme as omniscient and unwaveringly just. Neoliberals purport that this redesigning of the state, reconfiguration of human freedom, and privileging of the market over personal demands represents, ultimately, the best means of serving human welfare and society.

This book raises a variety of theological objections to neoliberalism. We define neoliberalism theologically as a comprehensive program of market sacrifice. Our objections to this sacrificial system center on mercy, as we have already indicated. But the final clause of our longer definition of neoliberalism should suggest that we coordinate mercy with justice. Neoliberalism's "justice" cannot accord with God's justice because it leaves no room for God's mercy, and for God, justice and mercy always act together.[15] Obviously no human system will seamlessly comport with divine justice, but neither should any system close itself to or replace divine justice. We detail in this book how neoliberalism is a system that enables, expedites, and necessitates violations of the love of God, be they active idolatry (placing economic value at the center of life) or shaping people in such a way that true worship becomes undervalued and unpracticed. So, too, does neoliberalism form people who violate love of neighbor, or who are indifferent toward such violations. Perhaps worse, neoliberalism ingrains social structures predicated upon violations of love of neighbor and an attitude that insists that no one should, reasonably speaking, be neighbor to anyone else. The quintessential neoliberal question is Cain's: "Am I my brother's keeper?" (Gen 4:9). Put otherwise, neoliberalism enables and even encourages that Jesus's twofold formulation of the greatest commandment be violated by everyone everywhere.

Catholic Critique of Neoliberalism

Among other things, this book is a contribution to Catholic social thought, by which we mean a tradition of commentary on Catholic social teaching. This latter term designates official, magisterial teaching by popes, bishops, and other church leaders tasked with making official pronouncements on faith and morals regarding issues impinging upon people's lives (in groups, public, and so on). Chapter 1 examines specifically papal teaching on the economy.[16] This will provide some principles for further analysis.

Catholic social thought does not offer perfect models for society, and it remains ever suspicious of this-worldly utopias.[17] Catholic social thought does not offer ready-made answers to the questions the world raises; instead, it raises questions precisely to social systems that style themselves as answers. In our time, neoliberals proclaim that "there is no alternative" to a world that revolves around the market economy. There is, supposedly, no other "answer" that so suits human social order than the neoliberal one. Catholic social thought should, in the face of this answer, raise questions.[18] We do just this.

We have closely circumscribed our task. In this book, we put neoliberalism through a critique, in the etymological sense. As Wendy Brown notes, the Greek word at the root of "critique," "*krisis*," connotes the process of making distinctions in order to "rectify an alleged disorder."[19] Critique, in this sense, involves "distinguishing the true from the false, the genuine from the spurious, the beautiful from the ugly, and the right from the wrong, distinctions that involved weighing pros and cons of particular arguments—that is, evaluating and eventually judging evidence, reasons, or reasoning." For Brown, the goal of critique is not negative as it is often perceived, but rather restorative. It involves the attempt "to set the times right again by discerning and repairing a tear in justice."

This sense of critique defines our present undertaking, which is threefold.

First, an important dimension of critique is carefully defining terms and the proper bounds of the conversation. Here we do not engage in a totalizing criticism of capitalism—an approach that would not be supported by Catholic social teaching, which does not reject capitalism as such, but only unbridled, radical forms of it (e.g., the form that brought on the Great Depression). Instead, we focus on neoliberalism as its most recent and pernicious form. We acknowledge that there have been some positive outcomes to capitalism more generally, and even that Catholic arguments can be made in favor of different variants of capitalism.[20] But as we will show, the three most recent popes express critical reservations about the world's current dominant form of capitalism, which, on occasion, they name specifically as neoliberalism. We worry, too, that over the past four decades, capitalism generally has become increasingly neoliberalized.[21] Neoliberalization, as a term, is the key here. Obviously, there is no actual economy that is fully neoliberalized. At the same time, the trajectory in the majority of the world's economies has been toward increasing neoliberalization. Furthermore, over this relatively brief period of time, neoliberalism has widely become economic, political, legal, and even cultural common sense, and as common sense has an air of permanence and necessity.

Second, we raise questions about neoliberalism and judge it in light of the question of mercy. By raising questions, Catholic social thought follows the method set down by the great doctor of the church, Thomas Aquinas, who organized his most important writings around questions rather than preformed answers. In this book, we foreground the question of mercy as a divine reality that repairs a tear in justice. We place under scrutiny neoliberalism's (re)formation of human groups, individual human subjectivity, and the earth more widely. Our questioning leads us toward the theological assessment that neoliberalism undermines mercy. It does so by constructing a vast architecture of social exclusion and ecocide, sacrificing all but a few "winners" to the fictitious god of economic growth, and coaxing or coercing a growing global majority into corrupt ways of life.

Third and finally, we offer the works of mercy as concrete means of repairing the tear in justice that neoliberalism has made. We have already pointed out the role that the spiritual works of mercy play in our method (even as the works remain largely in the background in this text). We also argue that the corporal works of mercy represent not only concrete ways of responding to social crises (feeding the hungry, clothing the naked, visiting the sick, etc.), but practices that form people in a distinctive ethos contrary to the neoliberal ethos.

Here we invoke a category that is not necessarily theological and that does not appear (at least not as this specific word) in Catholic social teaching, but that we deploy theologically: *ethos*. As we employ it, this word denotes a holistic way of life. This holistic (or global) way of life centers on the mercy Jesus Christ preached in his parables and implemented in his life (curing the sick, welcoming the stranger, forgiving the sinner, admonishing the wealthy and powerful, lifting up the poor, and laying down his life for his friends).

We have already contended that neoliberalism has comprehensive pretensions, that it aims to marshal the whole of life toward markets or market logic. As Brown puts it, even when neoliberalism does not directly monetize realities, it reshapes these realities in market terms.[22] Neoliberalism's drive toward comprehensiveness places it starkly at odds with Catholicism. Catholicism's comprehensiveness claims all things for Christ. Neoliberalism claims all things for the market. Two types of comprehensive ethos are bound, at some time, to come to loggerheads. The way beyond the present impasse, we argue, opens with the works of mercy, deployed not only as discrete acts, but as what we call a politics of mercy.

This threefold process of critique intends to disclose the contingency of neoliberalism as a social formation, to judge or critically evaluate it from the perspective of Catholic social thought and the theology of mercy, and to offer a concrete vision for how we might begin to interpret and shape the world differently. Having made all of these efforts, we can start to imagine alternatives to the system whose adherents proclaim, "there is no alternative."

As theologians, we firmly believe that discourse is an important medium through which to spread the Gospel and to transform the world. This involves engaging in dialogue with various disciplines that help to bring neoliberalism to light (especially in our country where it often goes unnamed, being treated simply as "economics" or "business practice") and examining their findings in light of Catholic social thought. In doing so we stand in a long line of theologians like, again, Aquinas, who utilized discourses other than "specifically Catholic" ones, reconsidering and transforming them where necessary. Through distinctively theological questioning, using the standard of mercy, we believe we can put a finer point on "secular" critiques of neoliberal ideology, responsibilization, and social exclusion or expulsion.

Chapter Outlines

The book is divided into three parts, which include five chapters.

Chapter 1 explores how during the last three papacies, Catholic social teaching has become particularly sensitized to the danger of capitalist economism, a tendency to reduce the whole of life to economic matters. In so doing, Catholic social teaching has prepared the ground for a certain kind of critique of neoliberalism, namely, as a species of economism. A concern with economism enters in earnest (and by name) into Catholic social thought with John Paul's first social encyclical, and this concern grows in his subsequent social encyclicals. Benedict XVI links the error of economism to his criticisms of economic utopianism. He works to put the economy in its place as just one social space (with its attendant logic) among three distinct, never separate but unmixed social spaces and logics. He insists on the primacy of love, which pertains to the social space of civil society, over the economy and markets. Pope Francis continues the tradition of John Paul II and Benedict XVI by criticizing the contemporary dominant manifestation of economism, which he calls by various names, including "unfettered capitalism," "the faceless economy," and "the economy that kills." Having described the continuous papal critiques of the danger of capitalist economism, we end the chapter by discussing how neoliberalism has been made to seem friendly to Catholics by Michael Novak, George Weigel, Robert Sirico, and Rocco Buttiglione. We mark these authors' contributions to Catholic social thought as distortive. This comes most obviously to light in their inability to find authentic harmony between their ideas and the teachings of Benedict and Francis because of their selective readings of John Paul.

Chapter 2 moves the Catholic social thought conversation on neoliberalism forward by rendering the "economism" critique of contemporary capitalism more precise.[23] In fact, the chapter's verdict on neoliberalism will both corroborate the papal diagnosis and make it more damning. To see neoliberalism as economism would be to see it as naïve confidence in a market machine, assuming that it will work everywhere if allowed to operate properly. But neoliberalism, both in the principles of its major theorists and in the facts of its execution, is not so much confidence in an efficient machine as it is devotion to an inscrutable deity, which must be protected by legal and political institutions. As Quinn Slobodian puts it, at least with respect to one of neoliberalism's major schools of thought, it is appropriate to think of it as a "negative theology."[24] This negative theology entails total commitment to the "world economy," whatever the human or environmental costs. The neoliberal project was first conceived in the 1930s, out of a desire by theorists and businesspeople to stave off the threat to global capitalism posed by the *demos*, the mass of the world's population. It was first broadly enacted in the 1970s, in an effort to regain power for owners of capital and big business that was diminished during the post–World War II era, when Keynesian "mixed" economies reigned. Through varied yet overwhelmingly successful efforts to "encase" capital against the dangers of popular demands (whether political, economic, or cultural), neoliberalism gained a foothold that allowed its broad dissemination of market logic into previously noneconomic spheres. Gradually neoliberalism became common sense, a standard for judging what reality is. Neoliberalism redefined reality and reasonableness in market terms. As such, neoliberalism came to constitute a comprehensive ethos of sacrifice, including even everyday life itself, that now stands in fundamental conflict with the Catholic ethos of mercy.

Chapter 3 treats in greater detail the neoliberal ethos of sacrifice. It describes four social crises that are either generated or exacerbated by the neoliberal revolution: environmental destruction, slum proliferation, mass incarceration, and mass deportation. Using two analytical notions, "sacrifice zones" and "racial neoliberalism," it demonstrates some of the major costs involved in what neoliberals like to call "creative destruction." We begin by discussing the global cost of neoliberal creative destruction, or the damage wrought to the planet by the fossil-fuel economy, which has become supercharged under neoliberalism's encasement of the global economy against demands that could be made in favor of the health of the globe. Coordinate with the destruction of the climate and ecosystems— thus loss of habitat for numerous species of animals, plants, fungus, and so on—is the mass movement of people into urban slums. Slumdwellers are sacrificed to the needs of an increasingly urban world economy, and given neoliberal programs of cutting social welfare, they cannot make viable demands on the urban economy, either. Racial neoliberalism constitutes a mutation of racial capitalism, which utilizes race to justify and normalize differential value attributed to groups in society. Racial neoliberalism strategically deploys discourses and practices—such as color-blindness, securitization, and privatization—to exploit and profit from the punishment of communities of color. Mass incarceration and mass deportation represent two prominent means of managing social disorder and unwanted populations through the mechanisms of punishment and expulsion. We also reflect on how neoliberalism generates a culture of indifference to the sacrifices it makes, and we deepen our analysis of this idea from Pope Francis with his other idea of corruption, which we take as a key characteristic of neoliberal culture and which serves as a benchmark for the type of response that we will construct in chapters 4 and 5.

Chapter 4 describes a systematic theology of mercy. It contests the bedrock neoliberal commitment to impersonal reality (represented by the market) by laying out a Trinitarian theology focusing on the distinctive characters of the three persons of the Trinity. Each Trinitarian person exhibits a reality that is at its core mercy. Next, the chapter resists the neoliberal anthropology of human capital by describing what we call a neighbor anthropology and an innkeeper ecclesiology, that is a theological anthropology and ecclesiology conceptualized out of Jesus's parable of the Good Samaritan. Finally, against the neoliberal ethos of mercilessness and culture of indifference we direct the works of mercy, presented traditionally as charity, and reimagined as structural and political.

Chapter 5 responds to the neoliberal crises described in chapter 3 in light of the theology of mercy developed in chapter 4. In relation to each crisis, we offer a threefold response. First, we describe theological ideas from the church's tradition that provide theoretical-critical leverage over against the neoliberal vision for the world: the doctrine of creation, *imago dei*, the freedom of Christ, and the hospitality of Christ. Second, we examine a principle from Catholic social teaching or secular discourse (if the Catholic church has not developed an adequate response) that offers a moral horizon for discussing the crises and the long-term goal for social transformation. In relation to environmental destruction and slum proliferation we retrieve Catholic social teaching on the universal destination of goods, and in response to mass incarceration and mass deportation we argue for abolitionism. Finally, we describe selected corporal works of mercy as a response to neoliberal sacrifices. Against neoliberal destruction of the environment, we propose reflection and action on visiting the sick; for slum proliferation, feeding the hungry, giving drink to the thirsty, and clothing the naked; for mass incarceration, ransoming the captive; and for mass deportation, welcoming the stranger. We contend that these works must be made political by proposing not only direct action as a response to these crises, but also an interlocking set of actions that seek broader social transformation in the short-term, middle-term, and long-term (the universal destination of goods and abolitionism).

In our conclusion, we appeal for further reflection and action on the last work of mercy, bury the dead, since neoliberalism in its corruption of individual lives, social structures, and life on this planet in general faces Catholics with a test of their resurrection faith—whether they will decide to live it or to denounce it by aiding and abetting neoliberalism's way of death.

Send Lazarus

We titled this book *Send Lazarus*, evoking a statement by the "rich man" (sometimes called by the Latin word *Dives*) in Jesus's parable of the rich man and Lazarus (Lk 16:19–31). Lazarus is a poor man, covered in sores, who lies each day at the doorstep of a rich man who wears fine clothes and dines luxuriously every day. Lazarus dies and is taken to heaven with Abraham, where he is comforted. The rich man dies and passes to *hades*, where he is tormented. From his place of torment, he spies Lazarus and Abraham and calls out to the latter, pleading with him to "send Lazarus" to dip his finger in water and aid him in his thirst (Lk 16:24). Abraham explains that this is impossible, because a chasm now divides Lazarus, in his comfort, from the rich man in his torment. Again, the rich man begs Abraham to send Lazarus to the rich man's living brothers (presumably also wealthy) to warn them of their impending doom (Lk 16:28). Once more Abraham tells him this is impossible, now adding that they have the warnings of Moses and the prophets to turn around their lives—and that if his brothers do not listen to Moses and the prophets, their hearts will not be changed even should a man rise from the dead (Lk 16:29–31).

"Send Lazarus" expresses the rich man's callousness, his disobedience of the Law and the prophets, and, by implication of the parable, recorded by Luke decades after Jesus's resurrection, of Christ himself. The rich man's life provided him with ample resources and opportunity to show mercy to Lazarus, who suffered at his doorstep. The rich man did not show mercy. Even worse, his callousness continues in death, as he himself suffers, when he tries to order around Lazarus—and Abraham! His imperative, "send Lazarus," implies that Lazarus deserves no comfort; in fact, Lazarus's sole dignity resides in his capacity for supplying the rich man with comfort. The rich man desires no mercy for Lazarus, he desires only that Lazarus continue to be sacrificed, to enter into *hades*, so that the rich man can resume, or restore somewhat, the comfort he enjoyed in life.

This book's central contribution to theology and to discussions of neoliberalism is to reveal Catholicism and neoliberalism as rival systems that support either a politics of mercy or sacrifice. Neoliberalism devalues the human person and disdains creation by callously sacrificing them to an impersonal Market. Catholics must turn against this system by enacting a politics of mercy, modeled on God's creativity, Christ's saving love, and a Spirit-enlivened spirituality of structural transformation. We can hardly emphasize it enough: one who understands both neoliberalism and Catholicism is faced with a decision between them, between sacrifice and mercy, callousness and love, the rich man and Lazarus.

Part I: Catholic Social Thought and the Economy

1 Catholic Social Thought against Economism

In this chapter we represent the Catholic tradition in a tightly circumscribed way. We focus on the social encyclicals (and ancillary documents) of the three most recent popes. We focus on the popes because they, especially John Paul II and Benedict XVI, have played a particularly strong role as teachers within the Catholic Church's universal magisterium. Since over the past almost forty years the Catholic faithful have become accustomed to looking to the pope as the church's primary teaching voice, we will follow a similar tack, even with its potential ecclesiological pitfalls. The choice of the three most recent popes helps us to substantiate, if only in part, our thesis in this chapter: during the last three papacies, Catholic social teaching has become particularly critical of capitalist economism, a tendency to reduce the whole of life to economic matters; thus often without naming it, church tradition has turned against neoliberalism. This thesis cuts against a vocal constituency in the church (represented and critiqued in this chapter's final section) insisting that traditional Catholicism and contemporary capitalism cohere quite nicely and naturally. As we see it, this is far from the case, and finding in the popes that this is not the case is a serious step toward critiquing neoliberalism from a Catholic point of view.

Oftentimes Catholic social thought commentary is a reflection on what has been said regarding a set of guiding themes, such as subsidiarity, solidarity, human dignity, and so on. Although we do not leave these terms untouched, in this chapter we aim to do something different, precisely in light of the neoliberal revolution that we began explicating in the book's introduction.

First, we offer a brief overview of the tradition of Catholic social thought on the economy from the late nineteenth century to the papacy of John Paul II.[1] In response to capitalist and communist economic systems, popes from Leo XIII to Pius VI offered a set of theological reflections that set the parameters for the subsequent tradition by rejecting communism as well as unfettered capitalism.

Next, we trace how a concern with economism enters in earnest (and by name) into Catholic social thought with John Paul's first social encyclical and how the concern grows in his subsequent two social encyclicals. In particular, John Paul objects to a contemporary tendency of both the capitalist and communist systems to reduce human work to its economic valence only, then he criticizes the global economic notion of development, and he warns, in the wake of communism's collapse, of a relapse of early capitalism's error: prizing capital over labor, thus reducing all people to objects.

Then we consider Benedict XVI. We begin with his pre-pontifical activities as prefect of the Congregation for the Doctrine of the Faith, a Vatican post that necessitated close collaboration with John Paul II. We highlight a 1985 article on ethics and economics as a vital precursor to Benedict's only social encyclical, *Caritas in Veritate* (2009). In both documents, Benedict links the error of economism to his criticisms of impersonal approaches to the economy, and he works to put the economy in its place as just one social space among three distinct social spaces and logics. He insists on the primacy of love, which pertains to the social space of civil society over the economy and markets.

After that, we describe how Pope Francis continues the tradition of John Paul II and Benedict XVI by criticizing the contemporary dominant manifestation of economism, which he calls by various names, including "unfettered capitalism," "the faceless economy," and "the economy that kills." Furthermore, he denounces how ubiquitous economism has transformed contemporary global culture into a "throwaway culture" that sacrifices weak, vulnerable, and otherwise despised people and treats the whole earth with the same disdain. He lends a prophetic edge to John Paul II's appeals for human dignity and Benedict XVI's advocacy of charity, demanding justice, an end to idolatry, a new life that prizes mercy over markets and their "necessary" sacrifices, and the creation of communitarian economic practices consonant with Catholic social thought's teachings on the universal destination of goods.

With the popes' rejections of economism we will have a baseline for reflecting on neoliberalism. In closing, we conclude that the problem, at least in the United States, is that a dominant strand of discourse has made it sound as if Catholic social thought, foremost in John Paul II, is friendly to neoliberalism. We show how this impression is made by Michael Novak, George Weigel, Robert Sirico, and Rocco Buttiglione, some of whom appear to be sympathetic to a neoliberal economy, if not to a neoliberal culture. The chapter ends by calling into question these authors' interpretation of Catholic social thought. The problem with their approach comes most obviously to light in their inability to find authentic harmony between their ideas and the teachings of Benedict XVI and Francis.

All this effort will prime us for identifying neoliberalism as a virulent form of economism, achieving a utopian dream of spreading markets to all spheres of life, and in the process disseminating a culture of mercilessness. Despite the efforts of some Catholics to carve out a home for neoliberalism in Catholicism, we will learn in the coming chapters how this species of economism stands against anything recognizable as traditional, ecclesial Catholicism.

Modern Catholic Social Thought

Our main vehicle for presenting mercy, the heart of the Catholic message, is modern Catholic social thought, a venerable tradition that spans more than 125 years. Within the broader category of social thought, and in many respects driving this trajectory of Catholic discourse, is Catholic social teaching. This phrase designates official, magisterial teachings by popes, bishops, and other church leaders tasked with making pronouncements on faith and morals. Catholic social thought combines magisterial teachings with further theological, moral, and ethical reflection by clergy, religious, and laypeople, including lay theologians such as this book's authors. For our discussion, we group Catholic social teaching and Catholic social thought, hereafter abbreviated as CST. That said, since we focus on the three most recent popes in subsequent chapters, we will introduce CST by way of official, papal teaching on the economy.[2]

Rerum Novarum (1891), by Leo XIII, is generally viewed as the beginning of the modern tradition of CST.[3] Although the word capitalism never appears in this document ("capital" does), Leo offers extensive commentary on the dominant approaches to the economy during his time, which include what now we would call industrial capitalism and (Marxist) socialism. Leo cautions against economic systems that fail to protect workers' rights as well as supposed antidotes to such failures that inscribe other ones, that is, socialist class warfare and abolition of private property (e.g., *RN*, 3–6).[4] He sets forth initial formulations of teachings on the common good (*RN*, 8, 32, 34, 35, 38, 51), the proper roles of individuals, families, churches, and the state (*RN*, 12–14, 29–31, 32, 35, 36, 53), and mutual obligation (*RN*, 19, 55) that in later papal writings will coalesce into great principles of the universal destination of all goods, subsidiarity, and solidarity. All in all, he introduces what has become the dominant Catholic position on the economy: resolute rejection of Marxism and communism along with significant criticisms of free market approaches to the economy.

On the fortieth anniversary of the publication of *Rerum Novarum*, Pius XI extended the tradition with *Quadragesimo Anno* (1931), a sustained reflection on the economic situation during the Great Depression.[5] Pius offers a more explicit critical engagement with capitalism than did Leo. Pius argues that the owners of capital have transformed modern capitalism into a type of "despotic economic domination" (*QA*, 105). For Pius, an "unrestrained" form of competition had delivered virtually limitless power to economic elites and created a situation that permitted "the survival of those only who are strongest" (*QA*, 107). His assessment of capitalism is dire. By 1931, capitalism had effectively "committed suicide"; "economic dictatorship" had "replaced a free market" (*QA*, 88). Like Leo before him, Pius continues CST's fierce opposition to communism as a "cruel" and "monstrous" system (*QA*, 112). With two types of economic dictatorship identified and marked as unacceptable,[6] Pius offers a form of corporatism as a way beyond the stalemate between communism and economic liberalism (*QA*, 88). Perhaps Pius's signature achievement is his formulation of what will come to be called the principle of subsidiarity (or the subsidiary function of social bodies): "it is an injustice and at the same time a grave evil and disturbance of right order to assign to a greater and higher association what lesser and subordinate organizations can do" (*QA*, 79). As we will discuss at various points in this book, this principle is often perceived to apply to the size and scope of government only, but nothing Pius says here supports that perception.

The 1960s bring two major CST documents. John XXIII published *Mater et Magistra* (1961), whose chief contribution is its attention to the issue of global poverty.[7] In this document John redirects the concern with the exploitation of labor in *Rerum Novarum* to an international level, identifying the growing gap between rich and poor countries as the age's dominant "social question." *Mater et Magistra* continues to affirm the rights of private property (see *RN*, 4, 8, 15, 22, 38, 47). John calls, though, for greater government intervention in the economic sphere (*MM*, 54) and a renewed effort by political bodies to address economic inequality through more equitable distribution of property and wealth (*MM*, 113). John credits Leo XIII with formulating the principle of solidarity as a guiding ideal for social reconstruction, but this seems to be John's own declaration (*MM*, 23–26). In any event, John remains faithful in his principle of solidarity by contrasting it with both "unrestricted competition in the liberal sense, and the Marxist creed of class warfare," replacing these with "Christian brotherhood" (*MM*, 23). He applauds efforts of the state and other public agencies to address social problems, but reminds Christians of the ever-present duty of private charity (*MM*, 120).

Just six years later, Paul VI's *Populorum Progressio* (1967) sharpens John XXIII's reflections on global poverty by calling for a dramatic transformation of the global economic and political order to redress grave economic imbalances between nations.[8] In particular, Paul denounces colonialism (*PP*, 7) and neo-colonialism (*PP*, 52) as the root causes of global poverty. He urges the renegotiation of unfair trade agreements between developed and poorer nations (*PP*, 54–61) and for developed countries to redirect money from military expenditures into a fund to respond to the needs of impoverished peoples around the world (*PP*, 51). Furthermore, in somewhat of a development of CST (related to the Second Vatican Council's teaching on the matter), Paul places limits on private property, arguing that it is not an "absolute and unconditional right" (*PP*, 23). In concert with the early church fathers (he names St. Ambrose), Paul proclaims, "No one may appropriate surplus goods solely for his own private use when others lack the bare necessities of life" (*PP*, 23). Consequently, he articulates a threefold obligation especially incumbent upon wealthy nations in relation to poorer ones: mutual solidarity, social justice, and universal charity (*PP*, 44); so, too, does he appeal to the consciences of wealthy individuals (*PP*, 47). Testifying to growing global interconnectedness, Paul insists that "the future of world civilization" hinges on fulfilling these duties (*PP*, 44).

This quick summary of a few major signposts in the modern CST tradition yields at least three insights germane to this book. First, the Catholic

Church consistently opposes alternatives to capitalism that involve class warfare and the abolition of private property (Marxism, communism, and certain forms of socialism as discussed in *Rerum Novarum*). Second, nevertheless, the Church opposes unrestrained, unregulated capitalism, which can lead to a "survival of the fittest" ethos. Third, with increasing urgency CST demands broader distribution of private property and wealth, through economic reform, political initiatives, and private charity, which must collaborate to address economic imbalances (both domestically and internationally) and to build a more equitable world.

In the following sections, we offer a detailed exposition of the development of CST on the economy after Paul VI. John Paul II, Benedict XVI, and Francis share many commonalities, but the most significant for this book concerns the timing of their pontificates: their papacies coincide with the political ascendancy and entrenchment of neoliberalism across the globe, from the late 1970s to today.

John Paul II on Economism

John Paul II was a great writer of encyclicals, eventually publishing fourteen of them during his pontificate. Very soon after his election, he released his first encyclical, *Redemptor Hominis* (1979), which upheld the truth of Christ as the principle for reading and answering the problems of the late twentieth century.[9] His next encyclical, *Dives in Misericordia* (1980), continued along the same lines, reading the contemporary world situation in light of the specifically Christological and theological (pertaining to the Father) theme of mercy.[10] *Laborem Exercens*, John Paul's first social encyclical, appeared the following year (1981) and two others would follow over the next decade, *Sollicitudo Rei Socialis* (1987) and *Centesimus Annus* (1991).[11] John Paul's social teachings flow from his teachings regarding Christ as truth for humanity and the specification of this truth as mercy, or the Father's love made manifest.

In *Dives in Misericordia*, John Paul contends that against distortions of justice, the church proclaims God's mercy and seeks to put it into practice (*DM*, 12–14). John Paul II's social teachings consist in such proclamations and recommendations for practice, precisely by resisting contemporary impulses toward reducing all of human life to its economic valence alone. Early in the encyclical, when discussing God the Father, who is revealed as rich in mercy by Jesus Christ, John Paul turns to criticize a mindset rising in the world:

> The present-day mentality, more perhaps than that of people in the past, seems opposed to a God of mercy, and in fact tends to exclude from life and to remove from the human heart the very idea of mercy. The word and the concept of "mercy" seem to cause uneasiness in man, who, thanks to the enormous development of science and technology, never before known in history, has become the master of the earth and has subdued and dominated it. This dominion over the earth, sometimes understood in a one-sided and superficial way, seems to have no room for mercy. (*DM*, 2)

These words, penned at the dawn of the neoliberal era, prove ever more prophetic as the same era continues almost forty years later. Against a world priming itself to exclude mercy from reality, John Paul proclaims God's mercy and exhorts its practice. Early in his pontificate he frequently invokes Jesus's parable of the rich man and Lazarus to illustrate his exhortation to mercy. His homily from Yankee Stadium during his 1979 visit to the United States is a case in point:

> The parable of the rich man and Lazarus must always be present in our memory; it must form our conscience. Christ demands openness to our brothers and sisters in need—openness from the rich, the affluent, the economically advanced; openness to the poor, the underdeveloped and the disadvantaged. Christ demands an openness that is more than benign attention, more than token actions or half-hearted efforts that leave the poor as destitute as before or even more so.[12]

In brief, Christ demands mercy. John Paul encourages the crowd to translate this demand for mercy "into contemporary terms," "in terms of economics and politics."[13] His social teaching does precisely this, and in a powerful way by opposing what he calls "economism."

Here we show how John Paul introduces the concept "economism" in *Laborem Exercens*, as he criticizes the modern, industrial, capitalist organization of human work, which removes human subjectivity from work, reducing the human person to her economic aspect only. This is first and foremost a capitalist error (secondarily it becomes Marxism's error).[14] As a corrective, he posits the principle of labor's priority over capital, people over things. His second and third social encyclicals, *Sollicitudo*

Rei Socialis and *Centesimus Annus*, expand his critique of economism, de-
tecting its operation in the communist and capitalist "blocs" of the North
as they devastate the South (*SRS*), and admonishing capitalism's supporters after communism's fall to take care that their triumphalism not bring
them to repeat early capitalism's economistic errors (CA).

It has become commonplace to point out the connection between John
Paul's encyclical on work and his own life, especially as a young man, as
a quarry and factory worker. So, too, is it common knowledge that the Solidarity movement in Poland—an anticommunist trade union movement
founded on September 17, 1980, of which the Pope was an outspoken
supporter—served in part to inspire *Laborem Exercens*. Surely these bio-
graphical details are significant. John Paul II himself, though, insists that
the center of his concern for human work lies in theology and the life of
the church, which are founded on faith in God as Creator and Redeemer
(*LE*, 1–2). He invokes *Redemptor Hominis* at the outset, saying that he
wishes to study human work in light of the human person's redemption
in Christ, which "shows us all the wealth and at the same time all the toil
of human existence on earth" (*LE*, 2).

The basic contention of *Laborem Exercens* is that work stands at the center of the social question (*LE*, 2–3) because human dignity derives a good
measure of its dignity from work (*LE*, 1), since work constitutes a response
to God's original mandate to human persons "to subdue, to dominate, the
earth" and thereby to participate in God's creative activity (*LE*, 4, see also
Gen 1:28). This central thesis allows John Paul to construct a theological
account of human work that upholds human dignity, that resists reduction of human work to a merely economic or material activity (*LE*, 7), that
denounces labor conditions that make work into degrading toil as opposed
to dignified expression of creativity (*LE*, 9), and that, consequently, places
human work within a broader spiritual horizon, where human work aims
not only at "earthly progress" but also at "the development of the Kingdom of God" (*LE*, 27).

John Paul makes the encyclical's chief contribution to CST when he for-
mulates the "principle of the priority of labor over capital" (*LE*, 12). The
key to understanding this principle lies in understanding what John Paul
means by "labor" and "capital." Our initial discussion of Catholic social
thought should suggest that he does not mean two combatants in class
warfare. By "labor" he means any kind of human work, thus any kind of

worker, from a wage worker in manufacturing, to the person who cleans the factory floor, to the manager who oversees their duties, to the chief executive who conducts the company. And "capital," whereas for prior popes this term referred at least in part to a class of people who owned the means of economic production and aimed to reap profits from production (thus labor), is not really the referent here. Instead, with a subtle maneuver, John Paul defines capital as the physical means of production such as resources, tools, machines, factories, laboratories, and computers, symbolized in his lexicon by "the work bench" (LE, 12). It becomes rather obvious that John Paul has displaced the common usage of "labor" and "capital" in class analysis.[15] The "principle of the priority of labor over capital" means that the human person has primacy over the things with or on which the worker works.

This principle is a particular application of the wider principle of "the primacy of man over things" (LE, 12). No person can treat another person as a thing. Based on this principle, the "subjective" dimension, or creative quality of the image of God that impels all persons to work, must be continually respected. Neither individual persons nor society in general ought to be treated as "objective," or thing-like. For this reason, John Paul characterizes his argument as "personalist," centered on personal values that any economic system must respect. And this personalism is not first and foremost philosophical but deeply Christological,[16] as some of the encyclical's closing words illustrate: "In work, thanks to the light that penetrates us from the Resurrection of Christ, we always find a *glimmer* of new life, of the *new good*, as if it were an announcement of 'the new heavens and the new earth' in which man and the world participate precisely through the toil that goes with work. Through toil—and never without it" (LE, 27). The theological upshot is this: through labor, the expression of the human person's deep subjectivity, which is marked by the Incarnation, the world becomes less a "collection of things" (LE, 12) than expressions of divine life.

John Paul upholds the principle of labor's priority over capital as a counterpoint to what he calls "economism." The word occurs only seven times in the encyclical, but it is placed prominently. It first occurs in the section, "A Threat to the Right Order of Values," in which he introduces modern approaches to labor that the Christian "Gospel of work" must oppose. He names "materialism" and "economism" as two broad, intertwined modern trends (*LE*, 7). In his initial exposition, he defines economism in terms of the eighteenth- and nineteenth-century capitalist tendency to see human labor as "a sort of 'merchandise'" that employees sell to their employers (*LE*, 7). He states that this reduction of the human person to parity with things haunts contemporary capitalism as a constant danger, especially because contemporary economics tends to treat human labor impersonally, conceiving of people as a "work force" or merely as "instrument(s) of production" (*LE*, 7). Given his principle of labor's priority over capital, we can see that economism's chief error is its misrecognition (or nonrecognition) of human subjectivity. Economism errs by positing capital and labor as "two impersonal forces" (*LE*, 13). An understanding of human work that undermines personal subjectivity in favor of impersonal forces falls afoul of the Christian faith and solid philosophical reasoning. The antidote to the error of economism must come through "adequate changes both in theory and practice, changes *in line with* the definite *conviction of the primacy* of the person over things, and of human *labor over capital* as a whole collection of means of production" (*LE*, 13).

In *Laborem Exercens*, a critique of economism enters CST. "Economism" refers to the subsumption of human subjectivity made in God's image to an impersonal force called capital (a collection of "things," means of production, and money). John Paul's "personalist argument" holds that human work, when allowed its proper subjectivity, that is, without being subsumed to "capital," constitutes a "personal action" in which "the whole person, body and spirit," participates (*LE*, 15). As such, human work concerns the same subjectivity toward which "the word of the living God is directed" (*LE*, 15). Thus human work enters into God's work of creation, redemption, and sanctification, bears a heightened dignity that should not be degraded to the level of a capitalist object (see especially *LE*, 9). John Paul's first social encyclical provides us with a quintessential plank in the platform we will construct against neoliberalism: an economic system that prizes impersonality over the personal, things (capital) over people, objects over subjects.

Six years after he publishes *Laborem Exercens*, John Paul promulgates another social encyclical to commemorate Pope Paul VI's 1967 encyclical on human development, *Populorum Progressio*. John Paul's new offering, *Sollicitudo Rei Socialis*, develops his critique of economism into a criticism of how the development of peoples worldwide is conceived chiefly in economic terms. This critique entails John Paul reflecting more geographically and sociologically on disparities in wealth and opportunity between nations and different classes of people within nations.

While John Paul is often characterized as centrally focused on the East-West, communism-capitalism conflict (especially by the US commentators we treat later), *Sollicitudo Rei Socialis* helpfully complexifies the picture. This encyclical looks "at the world from the perspective of North-South, a shorthand expression for examining the global situation with the categories of rich and poor nations."[17] Thus it suggests that by 1987 "the human family had reached a crisis stage in the relationship between the minority rich and majority poor."[18] John Paul foregrounds the "gap" between the comparatively rich North and poor South, making this the lodestar for any treatment of East and West (*SRS*, 14). Surely, he treats the East-West conflict, and at length, but the point of this discussion is to present both East-communism and West-capitalism as competing economisms that are ravaging the South through new forms of imperialism (*SRS*, 20–24). Neither of the "blocs" is exonerated of this charge; both fall.[19] He poses the North-South dichotomy most pointedly when he contrasts (southern) underdevelopment and (northern) "superdevelopment" ("an excessive availability of every kind of material goods for the benefit of certain social groups"). The economic advantage of the (especially Western) North manifests itself in a virulent combination of consumerism and its natural partner: "throwing-away" and "waste." These phenomena arise from a separation of the dominant economic concept of "development" and any kind of "moral understanding" (*SRS*, 28).

The encyclical's main concern is to inquire as to whether the North's pathological foregrounding of *economic* development as its model for the development of the human person and whole peoples has led to the dire social situation of the 1980s (*SRS*, 15).[20] This situation's defining characteristic is "the reality of an innumerable multitude of people . . . who are suffering under the intolerable burden of poverty" (*SRS*, 13).[21] Not only poverty concerns John Paul but also "illiteracy, the difficulty or impossibility of obtaining higher education, the inability to share in the building of one's own nation, the various forms of exploitation and of economic, social, political, and even religious oppression of the individual and his or her rights, discrimination of every type, especially the exceptionally odious form based on difference of race" (*SRS*, 15). Later in the encyclical he

queries whether "today, perhaps more than in the past, the intrinsic con-
tradiction of a development limited only to its economic element is seen
more clearly. Such development easily subjects the human person and his
deepest needs to the demands of economic planning and selfish profit"
(*SRS*, 33). This question takes clear aim at both the East-communist bloc
("planning") and the West-capitalist bloc ("selfish profit"). Both blocs subsume person to economy, thus displaying the signature feature of economism. It cannot be emphasized strenuously enough that John Paul paints
both the East-communist and West-capitalist blocs with the same brush.
This pope, who arguably is the most anticommunist in history, judges
Western capitalism as similarly complicit in the ravaging of the Global
South as its Eastern communist counterpart.

Sollicitudo Rei Socialis culminates in a theological section that treats
two major themes: "structures of sin" and "solidarity" (*SRS*, 35–40). With
regard to the former, John Paul refers to his 1984 apostolic exhortation,
Reconciliatio et Paenitentia, where he develops the idea of "social sin."[22] In
that document, "social sin" has three possible meanings, which may all
be in play with regard to certain sins: (1) that each individual's sin affects
others; (2) sins against love of neighbor, which are always straightforwardly
social; and (3) ill relationships between human communities. John Paul
brings these meanings together to argue that social sins are, in fact, "the
result of the accumulation and concentration of many personal sins." *Sollicitudo Rei Socialis* deploys this teaching, changing the formulation from
"social sin" to "structures of sin" (*SRS*, 36). This category does not so much
establish that there is a social counterpart to personal sin, which is pat-
ent. Instead, it explains that any proper understanding of social situations
must include some consideration of sin. One must "give a name to the root
of the evils that affect us" (SRS 36). John Paul applies this name, "structures of sin," to the logic of blocs, which includes the structural compo-
nents of "imperialism" and "idolatry." Introducing the category of sin
points to a path beyond social problems, which can be summed up in one
word, "conversion" (*SRS*, 38). Authentic human development will come
only when people choose to turn away from sin, both personal and
structural.

The turn away from sin can be summed up with "solidarity" (*SRS*, 39).
In brief, solidarity means people "recogniz[ing] one another as persons"
(*SRS*, 39). Solidarity is a virtue. When seen in the light of Christian faith,

it retains its secular meaning of mutual recognition of persons but adds to it "the specifically Christian dimension of total gratuity, forgiveness, and reconciliation" (SRS, 40). Solidarity entails regarding the other person with a vision shaped by the Trinitarian God, where the other person "becomes the living image of God the Father, redeemed by the blood of Jesus Christ and placed under the permanent action of the Holy Spirit" (SRS, 40). True solidarity roots itself in the communion between the divine persons. It goes all the way down, thus issuing a deep challenge to any this-worldly logic that would exploit, oppress, or annihilate people, that would "produce the danger of war and excessive preoccupation with personal security," that would deprive "weaker nations" of their "autonomy [and] freedom of decision" (SRS, 39). Without serious, sustained conversion toward solidarity, rich nations and individuals become "like the 'rich man' who pretended not to know the beggar Lazarus lying at his gate" (SRS, 42, cf. 33). John Paul's discussion of solidarity, then, casts a particularly damning light on the North's competing economisms.

Let us add two further notes. First, we consider a summarizing quotation: "Development which is merely economic is incapable of setting man free, on the contrary, it will end by enslaving him further. . . . Human beings are totally free only when they are completely themselves, in the fullness of their rights and duties" (SRS, 46). These points are stated within the context of criticisms of liberation theology, but one must recognize implications for the East-West bloc logic. Both "blocs" must recalibrate their logics to allow for freedom, solidarity, and equality, without imperialism, warfare, and subjugation. Second, the encyclical concludes on the note of mercy, when John Paul places before the Blessed Virgin Mary, with her "eyes of mercy" the "international crisis" he has been describing (SRS, 49). His proclamation of mercy, which always contrasts with economism, continues.

1989 was a watershed year in world history and in the life of John Paul II. As a proud Pole, he joyfully witnessed the expulsion of communism from his native land. Within two years, he produced his third social encyclical, *Centesimus Annus*, which celebrated the centennial of *Rerum Novarum*'s publication and even more notably reflected upon the events of 1989 and what wisdom Catholic social teaching could offer in their wake (CA, 22–29). Palpably gleeful at communism's demise and cautiously optimistic that a new day was dawning, John Paul remains hesitant to accept capitalism as the exclusive way forward. He hesitates precisely because capitalism always threatens to revert to its early sins of exploitation, materialism, and, above all, economism. With *Centesimus Annus*, John Paul enshrines in CST approval of communism's collapse, thus the fall of one horrible variant of economism, alongside an understanding that capitalism must not be allowed free rein. Capitalism, or the "market economy," must be conditioned and restrained (as well as enriched and enlivened), by strong state regulation and a rich civil society.

John Paul knew well and from experience what kind of suffering occurred under communism, so it is hardly surprising to find him dancing on communism's grave in *Centesimus Annus*. While much could be written about this, we need only recount briefly the three main factors John Paul cites in making sense of communism's collapse. First, communism relied on failed Marxist social theory. Marxism thrives on social conflict, as opposed to peace (*CA*, 23), exploits injustice (*CA*, 26), fails to recognize the dignity of work (*CA*, 23, 26), and uses an outmoded and inadequate understanding of exploitation (*CA*, 41, see also 33). At the level of theory, communism could no longer speak to the world, so it lost all credibility. Second, communism espoused inefficient economics. Much of this came down, again, to flawed theory. Its central-planning economic model stood in "violation of the human rights to private initiative, to ownership of private property and to freedom in the economic sector" (*CA*, 24). Its definition of human person based on class only failed to account for human individuality and uniqueness, and thus conflicts arose between individual and collective interests (*CA*, 24–25). Such a confused economic system was bound to produce inefficiencies and deficiencies. Third, and most vexing for religious people, communism embraced an atheistic religiosity (*CA*, 24), a form of "secular religion" (*CA*, 25) that brought about antireligious totalitarianism (*CA*, 46). Given the human person's innate longing for God, a system predicated upon dismissing God from the picture could not last forever.

This would seem to leave just one economic system standing, as the world was divided between two alternatives (recall the "bloc logic" of *SRS*). Indeed, John Paul has many affirmations for communism's foe: capitalism, which he refers to alternately using "capitalism," the "business economy," "market economy," or "free economy" (see *CA*, 42). From the start, John Paul sets an evidently pro-capitalist tone by invoking "business leaders" as one constituency that had encouraged him to write this en-cyclical (CA, 1). A pro-business tone suffuses much of it, including what are perhaps its most innovative paragraphs (CA, 31–34). In these, John Paul takes an extraordinarily positive view of today's postcommunist eco-nomic condition. The interrelatedness of each person's work with that of others is becoming clearer and the world is becoming a "'community of work' which embraces ever widening circles" (CA, 31–32). "Initiative and entrepreneurial ability" is increasingly seen as decisive for economic pro-ductivity and provision for people's needs (CA, 32), so that the "decisive factor" in economies is no longer land, or capital, but "man himself," es-pecially his scientific knowledge (CA, 32). In brief, the economy is becom-ing more human, precisely as John Paul had hoped. If Marxism foundered on conflict, capitalism thrives on cooperation and collaboration. Likewise, capitalism's emphasis on work and initiative comports with prior CST on the right to private property, which communism unsuccessfully tried to abolish. By contrast with communist inefficiency, "it would appear that, on the level of individual nations and of international relations, the *free market* is the most efficient instrument for utilizing resources and effec-tively responding to needs" (CA, 34), precisely because it leaves room for respect of individual human dignity (not just classed, massified dignity). John Paul does not explicitly contrast capitalism with communism with regard to the latter's methodological atheism. Presumably capitalism, since it does not explicitly rule God out of the equation, allows God in.

John Paul is not uniformly positive, though. He issues cautions, and these relate to his anxiety over capitalism's potential for devolving into early-capitalist economism. About halfway through the encyclical, after having examined the issue of alienation in today's world economy, John Paul declares, "The collapse of the Communist system in so many coun-tries certainly removes an obstacle to facing these problems in an appro-priate and realistic way, but it is not enough to bring about their solution. Indeed, there is a risk that a radical capitalistic ideology could spread which refuses even to consider these problems, in the *a priori* belief that any attempt to solve them is doomed to failure, and which blindly entrusts their solution to the free development of market forces" (CA, 42). Later he again highlights the risk involved in the postcommunist situation: "The Western countries . . . run the risk of seeing this collapse as a one-sided victory of their own economic system, and thereby failing to make necessary corrections in that system" (*CA*, 56). There exists an impulse in capitalism to emphasize "the affluent society or the consumer society," which can claim a defeat of Marxism by surpassing it in materialism. But to do so would be to agree "with Marxism, in the sense that it totally reduces man to the sphere of economics and the satisfaction of material needs" (*CA*, 19). Consumerism, with its baneful human and ecological effects, must be avoided (*CA*, 36–37).

The types of problems John Paul had highlighted in *Sollicitudo Rei Socialis* should be evidence enough against a creeping capitalist economism. Rather than resting on their laurels, capitalist countries should "break down the barriers and monopolies which leave so many countries on the margins of development, and to provide all individuals and nations with the basic conditions which will enable them to share in development" (*CA*, 35). Despite his excitement at communism's fall, John Paul remains steadfast that the church can adopt no one model for economics. This is not just a political-economic position. It has theological warrant. Jesus's parable of the weeds and wheat should remind all that the ultimate judgment of history stands with God, not humans (Mt 13:24–30, 36–43; *CA*, 25). Nevertheless, Christians "in union with all people of good will" are tasked with "imbuing human realities with the Gospel" (*CA*, 25). This means that they must make provisional and prudential judgments about what forms of economic activity best approximate the Catholic vision for human flourishing.

John Paul offers his own summary statement with regard to all these points: "All of this can be summed up by repeating once more that economic freedom is only one element of human freedom. When it becomes autonomous, when man is seen more as a producer or consumer of goods than as a subject who produces and consumes in order to live, then economic freedom loses its necessary relationship to the human person and ends up by alienating and oppressing him" (*CA*, 39). Such autonomy, which we could rightly call economism, is what John Paul spends the remainder of the encyclical combatting, by urging that human social life be seen as threefold: economic, political, and moral-cultural. The way forward, after communism's collapse, is to put the economy in its place, through state regulation and, foremost, through building a robust culture or civil society.

John Paul characterizes the situation of individuals today as one of possible suffocation, between the state and the market. He writes, "At times it seems as though [the human person] exists only as a producer and consumer of goods, or as an object of State administration" (*CA*, 49). This leads to loss of a sense of purpose. The rightful task of human life lies in seeking truth and striving to live it, and to grow in understanding of the truth through intergenerational dialogue (see *CA*, 49). The human person ultimately serves neither state nor market. But both can be enlisted to foster the pursuit of authentic human purpose. We already saw John Paul's positive assessment of the market. It remains to be seen what John Paul has to say about the state. He contends,

> The State must contribute to the achievement of these goals [pursuit of truth, etc.] both directly and indirectly. Indirectly and according to the *principle of subsidiarity*, by creating favourable conditions for the free exercise of economic activity, which will lead to abundant opportunities for employment and sources of wealth. Directly and according to the *principle of solidarity*, by defending the weakest, by placing certain limits on the autonomy of the parties who determine working conditions, and by ensuring in every case the necessary minimum support for the unemployed worker. (*CA*, 15)

Clearly this is a vision for the state that sets it up as a bulwark against economism. John Paul describes it as such when he answers the question of whether capitalism is the economic model for the future, with communism now gone: "If by capitalism is meant a system in which freedom in the economic sector is not circumscribed within a strong juridical framework which places it at the service of human freedom in its totality, and which sees it as a particular aspect of that freedom, the core of which is ethical and religious, then the reply is certainly negative" (*CA*, 42). The task of the state is to keep the way clear for real human freedom, which at its heart pursues truth—not market value. Even further, the state must prevent an "'idolatry' of the market, an idolatry which ignores the existence of goods which by their nature are not and cannot be mere commodities" (*CA*, 40). This would include, obviously, human labor. There is always a danger that the state may assume too much control, too, as John Paul's fears regarding the social assistance state make plain (*CA*, 48). Thus, the state, like the economy, must be tempered by ethics and religion in order to serve authentic human freedom.

For this reason, John Paul's most powerful exhortations in *Centesimus Annus* center on the need to build a holistic culture. This is only appropriate because Catholicism means "according to the whole." John Paul sees the opportunity presented by the events of 1991 as one of capacious holism. He posits his vision with simplicity: "For an adequate formation of a culture, the involvement of the whole man is required, whereby he exercises his creativity, intelligence, and knowledge of the world and of people. Furthermore, he displays his capacity for self-control, personal sacrifice, solidarity and readiness to promote the common good" (CA, 51). Such holism takes root first in the human heart. And the church addresses this heart. The church contributes to building such a culture by testifying to two main truths that have massive social implications: divine creation of the world, in which humans must cooperate through work, and redemption in Jesus Christ, whereby all people are saved and made responsible for one another, hence the church's steadfast commitment to preaching love of neighbor (CA, 51). In this same spirit of holism, which pertains to civil society, much more than to economics or politics, John Paul ends the encyclical on a telling note. One hundred years after Rerum Novarum, the church continues Leo XIII's defense of the human person by denouncing "the fact that too many people live in the poverty of the developing countries amid conditions which are still 'a yoke little better than that of slavery itself'" (CA, 62). The church makes this denunciation knowing "that her call will not always win favor with everyone" (CA, 62). We must take note of these final words, placed before his closing doxology.[23] They turn the church's eyes of mercy toward those who need it most, while glancing askance at a global economic system that has, thus far, left them out.

In a speech in Latvia two years after the publication of Centesimus Annus, John Paul II observed: "The church, since Leo XIII's Rerum Novarum, has always distanced itself from capitalistic ideology, holding it responsible for grave social injustices . . . I myself, after the historical failure of communism, did not hesitate to raise serious doubts on the validity of capitalism."[24] And eight years after the publication of Centesimus Annus, in Ecclesia in America (1999), John Paul offered an even more forceful denunciation of the economistic tendencies present in capitalism, and explicitly named these tendencies neoliberal.[25] He declared:

> More and more, in many countries of America, a system known as "neoliberalism" prevails; based on a purely economic conception of man, this system considers profit and the law of the market as its

only parameters, to the detriment of the dignity of and the respect due to individuals and peoples. At times this system has become the ideological justification for certain attitudes and behavior in the social and political spheres leading to the neglect of the weaker members of society. Indeed, the poor are becoming ever more numerous, victims of specific policies and structures which are often unjust. (*EA*, 56)

From his first social encyclical, *Laborem Exercens*, through his third, *Centesimus Annus*, John Paul develops a consistent critique of economism, a tendency to reduce the pluriform wholeness of human life to the comparative narrowness of its economic dimension. From this critique, made quite explicit in *Ecclesia in America*, we can see that John Paul's teachings provide critical resources for resisting neoliberalism, today's economism.

Benedict XVI: Against an Impersonal Economy

Joseph Ratzinger, who as prefect of the Congregation for the Doctrine of the Faith was a close associate of John Paul II's before his own accession to the papacy in 2005 as Pope Benedict XVI, provides further resources for resisting today's economism. We argue that his contribution faithfully carries forward John Paul's legacy, but it would be misleading to say that he carries it forward with the same terms and in equal fashion. Benedict is a masterful theologian with a distinctive voice that strikes noticeably different tones than John Paul's. While John Paul's voice is inflected by study of phenomenological ethics (hence his focus on subjectivity), Benedict's is accented by the theology of the Church Fathers, foremost Augustine, and theological critiques of modernity, especially the philosophical modernity of G. W. F. Hegel, German idealism, and Marx (hence, as we will see, a pronounced emphasis on "history"). Our concern, though, is to show amid these distinctions the continuity between these popes. When Ratzinger was consecrated a bishop in 1977, he chose as his episcopal motto, placed on his coat of arms, "Co-Workers of the Truth," a reference to 3 John 8. Ratzinger reports that he did so because, for John, "these words signify the participation of all the faithful in the service of the Gospel and, by consequence, the 'catholic' dimension of the Faith."[26] The "truth" referred to in 3 John 8 is not some abstract truth, Ratzinger notes, but the work of hospitality. Violations of hospitality are "a rejection of catholicity and a repudiation of the truth." In this brief phrase, Ratzinger explains, "we encounter . . . the interweaving of truth and love." The interweaving of truth and love—Christ's love made manifest in love of neighbor—constitutes the center of Benedict XVI's social teaching, summed up in the title of his social encyclical, *Caritas in Veritate* (2009), charity (divine love) in truth. The interweaving of charity and truth, and the coworking of the truth as hospitality (a long-practiced Benedictine virtue), structures Benedict's rejections of two major forms of what, using tools gathered from John Paul, we can identify as economism.

What follows discusses Benedict's diagnosis of Marxist economism, which takes at least two different forms: determinism and the excision of morality from economic matters; and utopian economism, or secularized eschatology.[27] Then it examines his less explicit, yet no less serious indictment of capitalist economism. Like its Marxist counterpart, this economism sidelines morality, replaces the personal God with the invisible hand of the market, and collapses civil society and the political realm into the economic. Benedict worries about the possibility of such a capitalism during the 1980s, and, as pope, laments its actualization in the form of capitalism that precipitated the 2008 financial crisis. As a response to these economisms, Benedict insists on Christian truth: its eschatology against Marxism and its commitment to love as the foundation of civil, political, and economic life against totalizing capitalism.[28] In this way, he continues John Paul's tradition.

While "economism" is never expressly named as a concern of Benedict's, "Marxism" most certainly is. At various points in his corpus Benedict offers a multifaceted critique of Marxism as a deterministic ideology that subordinates morality to economic laws.[29] Marxism fashions itself as a scientific approach to politics that identifies the fundamental structure of society and history. This fundamental structure is economic. Marxism depicts history as a series of antagonistic struggles between economic classes that march dialectically toward history's fulfillment in a classless society. Here Benedict interprets Marxism as a species of Hegelianism. Like Hegel's philosophical system, which pretends to be a comprehensive "science," attained after many eras of spirit's historical development, Marxism adopts a progressive view of history that, while dialectical, is fundamentally deterministic, since it comprehends history's end even as it proceeds.[30] For Marxists, history "has its laws and its course which can be resisted but not ultimately thwarted. Evolution has replaced God here.

'God' now means development, progress."[31] Clearly such a replacement of God is unacceptable for Catholic theology.

Marxism's deterministic view of history proves constitutive of its approach to economics.[32] Although Marxism envisions a future decisively shaped by freedom from exploitation, this freedom can emerge only as a necessary resolution of class antagonisms. According to Benedict, such a view of history and freedom as determined by necessity dismisses sin by reducing it to an economic problem solved through necessary economic means: private property's abolition, state seizure of the means of production, and elimination of profit-seeking endeavors.[33] Benedict observes of Marx:

> He forgot that man always remains man. He forgot man and he forgot man's freedom. He forgot that freedom always remains also freedom for evil. He thought that once the economy had been put right, everything would automatically be put right. His real error is materialism: man, in fact, is not merely the product of economic conditions, and it is not possible to redeem him purely from the outside by creating a favorable economic environment. (SS, 21)[34]

Marx's materialism is part and parcel with his historical determinism; both obscure human freedom, precluding any authentic discussion of it. If one is to attend to economic problems, one must contend with the human heart's capacity for willing evil, which is not an economic question. Thus, for Benedict, the most basic flaw of Marxism is its economism, its definition of the human person in exclusively economic terms. It effected "the devastation of souls . . . the destruction of moral consciousness . . . the dissolution of the primal certainties of man about God, about himself, and about the universe."[35] Marxism's supposed historical comprehension fails because of its sharply limited inquiry into history. Its message of freedom fails because it takes into account such a small sliver of freedom. At best it offers an impersonal, amoral view of certain historical structures, never a clear view of the historical dynamics underpinning them. In addition to his criticism of Marxism as a form of impersonal, amoral economism, Benedict also interprets Marxism as *utopian* economism. In *Eschatology: Death and Eternal Life* (1971) Benedict warns of the danger of the widespread secularization of Christian eschatology in modernity.[36] Multiple strands of secularized eschatology emerge in the modern era, but Marxism represents the most worrisome form because it offers an "all-embracing interpretation of reality" and, as an "anti-theistic" messianism, it parodies Christianity by eliminating the vertical dimension of Christian hope.[37] Benedict returns to this charge against Marxism in his second papal encyclical, *Spe Salvi* (2007): "The critique of Heaven is transformed into the critique of earth, the critique of theology into the critique of politics. Progress towards the better, towards the definitively good world, no longer comes simply from science but from politics—from a scientifically conceived politics that recognizes the structure of history and society and thus points out the road towards revolution, towards all-encompassing change" (SS 20). Benedict illustrates Marxism's thorough reduction of transcendent realities to history. The essay "To Change or Preserve" (2002) further specifies Marxism as a secularized species of apocalypticism, with its "refusal to accept the dominant powers of the world and its hope for healing through the overthrow of those powers."[38] As with most other forms of apocalypticism, this secular variety looks to an agent of reconciliation to resolve the current crisis. With Marxism, the agent of reconciliation is no longer God, but rather the proletariat. With God absent, moral considerations can be dismissed, and they are. All that matters is the hope for a final, this-worldly utopia. This hope turns sacrificial: it appears rational to sacrifice present lives in the hopes of achieving it. Benedict's complex genealogy of Marxism as utopian economism discovers this basic, theological, even liturgical error: "people of the present are sacrificed to the *moloch* of the future—a future whose effective realization is at best doubtful" (*DC*, 31). Marxism is, in effect, idolatrous.[39]

Marxism's attractiveness as an ersatz religion, aided perhaps by the sacrificial character we have just noted, most vexes Benedict. Marxism takes on a quasi-religious form for nonbelievers who view its aims as salvific. Many religious believers fall prey to Marxist politics precisely because it provides them with a concrete politics to work toward the realization of the kingdom of God on earth. Somewhat ironically, the antireligious animus of Marx and his followers lends this religious air. Benedict observes, "The very attack on God and the historical religions fosters a religious pathos which attracts the often-deracinated religious energies of numerous contemporary men and women to itself, as a magnet draws ore. This pathos also affects theology, which detects in it the opportunity fill the eschatological message with a tangible, realistic content."[40] Here Benedict appears anxious about the insidious ways in which Marxism has been "internalized" in perhaps the most unlikely of places: Catholic theology.[41] The most potent illustration of this anxiety appears in the 1984 CDF document "Instruction on Certain Aspects of the 'Theology of Liberation,'" whose seventh part criticizes the use of Marxist analysis in some Latin American liberation theologies.[42] Given the problems Benedict identifies with Marxism—its impersonality, amorality, or utopianism—he has little patience for its presence in Catholic liberation and political theologies. So, too, does he remain concerned throughout his life about espousal of Marxism-inspired forms of life, especially among religious people. While in *Values in a Time of Upheaval*, a post-1989 text, Benedict acknowledges that Marxism suffered a devastating blow with the fall of the Berlin Wall and the collapse of Soviet-style communism, he warns that the threat of Marxism has yet to be extinguished: "it still leads a ghostly existence deep in the souls of many people, and it has the potential to emerge again and again in new forms."[43] Benedict stands convinced, as is evidenced by his repeated return to critical reflection on Marxism after the fall of communism, including in his social teaching as pope, that Marxism has the capacity to reemerge in mutated forms in response to new economic and political crises in our world.[44]

We did not dwell at length on John Paul II's condemnations of communism. The most space we spent on this topic was his accounting in *Centesimus Annus* for communism's collapse. We suggested often enough, though, that for John Paul, Marxism falls under the ban of his critique of economism. With Benedict we have encountered further description of Marxism's flaws, and, most interestingly given these flaws, its attractiveness to religious people. Reading this description of Marxism in association with John Paul's critique of economism, we come to the following insight: Catholic theology must raise alarm bells when an economic system that because of its impersonality, amorality, and utopianism stands rather obviously against Catholic faith and life nevertheless attracts Catholics to it. As we will see starting with this chapter's final part on the Catholic neoconservatives, precisely this appears to have happened with neoliberalism.

With this major insight in hand, we move from Marxism, the economic-political system that most fully occupies Benedict's attention, to capitalism, an economic system about which he says less. But what he does say is critical. Benedict deliberately and seriously engages capitalism in two important texts. "Church and Economy" (1985) ties capitalism to Marxism as a deterministic and amoral system. *Caritas in Veritate* (2009), Benedict's social encyclical, reflects on a Catholic approach to the economy in the wake of the 2008 financial crisis. In both cases we find criticisms of capitalism resonant with John Paul's critique of economism, and with Benedict's critique of the pseudo-religious allure of Marxist economics.

In "Church and Economy," Benedict notes that at first glance the Marxist approach to the economy appears to represent the antithesis of capitalism, in its commitment to the abolition of private property, the eradication of competition, and the regulation of economic activity by a central planner. He insists, however, that despite their real differences, they share an underlying similarity: both excise morality from economic activity as a result of their commitment to historical determinism.

Free market theorists generally follow Adam Smith's lead and claim that "the market is incompatible with ethics because voluntary 'moral' actions contradict market rules and drive the moralizing entrepreneur out of the game."[45] The phrase "business ethics" rings hollow within this tradition because efficiency and profit, not ethical norms, serve as the only reliable metrics of success. Furthermore, it is claimed that free competition between individuals, irrespective of their individual morality, produces the greatest good in society. Advocates of the free market maintain that the free play of market forces "best guarantees progress and even distributive justice," independent of any moral or political intervention. Benedict detects here a kind of determinism, analogous to the historical determinism he criticizes in Marxism. Capitalism's deterministic core lies in the assumption that "the free play of market forces can operate in one direction only, given the constitution of man and the world, namely, toward the self-regulation of supply and demand, and toward economic efficiency and progress."[46] As with Marxism, the "free market" promises freedom, but cannot deliver it. Instead, it delivers seemingly "free" people over to market laws. Additionally, free market advocates' enthusiasm for these "market laws" is colored by the "astounding presupposition" that "the natural laws of the market are in essence good . . . and necessarily work for the good, whatever may be true of the morality of individuals."[47] One can detect echoes of Benedict's objection to Marxism's inability to recognize that freedom is also freedom for evil.

Benedict's case against the free market at this point is twofold. First, capitalists accept the premise that allowing the market to unfold on its own, free of human intervention, will lead automatically to greater efficiency and progress; this premise entails a misleading notion of freedom. Second, he attacks the view that the laws of the market are somehow moral or good independent of the individual morality of those engaged in economic activity; therefore he objects to capitalism's prizing of the impersonal over the person. In response to these two objections, Benedict insists that a market conceiving of itself as independent from morality will be fundamentally unstable. And since the market left to its own devices is incapable of producing morality or moral agents, it must look to resources outside of itself to direct market activity toward moral ends (and thereby to remain stable).[48] This is a consistent theme in Benedict's writing, and serves as his central critique of economism in its Marxist and capitalist forms. Benedict recommends that, in order to cultivate a morality capable of supporting properly ordered economic activity, economics look to moral resources found in religious traditions. He states:

> It is becoming an increasingly obvious fact of economic history that the development of economic systems which concentrate on the common good depends on a determinate ethical system, which in turn can be born and sustained *only* by strong religious convictions. Conversely, it has also become obvious that the decline of such discipline can actually cause the laws of the market to collapse. An economic policy that is ordered not only to the good of the group—indeed, not only to the common good of a determinate state—but to the common good of the family of man demands a maximum of ethical discipline and thus a maximum of religious strength.[49]

This argument will reemerge in a theological register in *Caritas in Veritate* when Benedict insists once again on a moral foundation for economic activity, and presents the theological proclamation of the church, that God is love, as that foundation.

"Church and Economy" offers a fascinating analysis of moral and metaphysical errors of both Marxism and capitalism. Often viewed as opposing economic systems, these systems are driven by a shared aversion to morality born of deterministic assumptions. As we transition to a discussion of *Caritas in Veritate*, it can hardly be emphasized enough that twenty-four years earlier, Benedict expressed serious reservations about capitalism. Presciently, he cautioned that "we can no longer regard so naively the liberal-capitalistic system" as somehow "the salvation of the world."[50] Benedict's caution will be intensified into an admonition in the wake of the 2008 financial crisis. *Caritas in Veritate* criticizes the "grave deviations and failures" (*CV*, 40) of capitalism through which "the pernicious effects of sin are evident" (*CV*, 34). Largely, *Caritas in Veritate* repeats the basic criticisms of capitalism in "Church and the Economy." But distinctive to *Caritas in Veritate* is its setting of these criticisms within a broader theological framework. In turn, this occasions acute reflections on the proper relationship between the economy, politics, and civil society. In *Caritas in Veritate*, Benedict offers a profoundly Christological and metaphysical framework for approaching economic issues. He begins, "Charity in truth, to which Jesus Christ bore witness by his earthly life and especially by his death and resurrection, is the principal driving force behind the authentic development of every person and of all humanity" (*CV*, 1). Jesus Christ, as the "face" of charity in truth (*CV*, 1), has revealed that "God is love" and that "everything has its origin in God's love, everything is shaped by it, everything is directed toward it" (*CV*, 2). Through redemption in Christ, human beings, "as object of God's love . . . become subjects of charity" and "instruments of grace" (*CV*, 5). This truth, which Benedict describes as the logic of the gift—that God is love, that this love is revealed to creation in Jesus Christ, and that human persons are called to embody this love in creation—becomes the basis for Benedict's distinctive approach to economic and political concerns.

With this theological framework in place, let us reflect on the two main elements of the encyclical: truth and charity. First, Benedict argues that it is especially important to foreground the centrality of truth in CST in a cultural climate characterized by "a widespread tendency to relativize truth" (*CV*, 4). In the face of this relativism, Benedict calls on Christians to *live* truth: "practicing charity in truth helps people to understand that adhering to the values of Christianity is not merely useful but essential for building a good society and for true integral human development" (*CV*, 4). Elsewhere, Benedict has identified a "dictatorship of relativism" and vigorously defended Catholic doctrine and moral teachings against those who deny the very possibility of objective truth.[51] In relation to economic concerns, Benedict insists that the truth of God's love revealed in Jesus Christ represents the key to cultivating a just social order. Placing himself in the line of papal teachings on human development, stretching from Paul VI's *Populorum Progressio* through John Paul II's *Sollicitudo Rei Socialis*, Benedict posits charity in truth as the guiding principle for development. This principle expresses the fact that development is not "a purely human product . . . not based simply on human choice but is an intrinsic part of a plan that is prior to us and constitutes for all of us a duty to be freely accepted. That which is prior to us and constitutes us—subsistent Love and Truth—shows us what goodness is and in what our true happiness consists" (*CV*, 52). True development comes from a divine gift, a personal gift, not through human calculation or, even worse, through the necessary operation of impersonal economic laws.

Second, the connection he draws between truth and charity yields a distinctive theory of charity. The relationship between charity and truth guards against the confusion of charity "with a pool of good sentiments," which may be "helpful for social cohesion, but [would be] of little relevance" (*CV*, 4). Further, he contends that charity, fortified by the truth of the Gospel, can permeate every feature of society. We underscore this point; the claim that charity, galvanized by truth, is primed to suffuse society drives the encyclical's unique contribution, a charity-centered theory of social spaces. Charity is not external to economics and politics, nor does it function only in a privatized and individualized manner. Rather, charity is a moral force with real social import at all levels of existence, whether personal, civil, economic, or political. Charity is "the principle not only of micro-relationships (with friends, with family members or within small groups) but also of macro-relationships (social, economic, and political ones)" (*CV*, 2). Out of this principle, Benedict weaves his account of the relationship between the three major social spaces: civil society, the economy, and the political realm. This account proves complex, in that each sphere is governed by its own logic. But holding the whole together is charity, whose truth underlies all three spaces.

Benedict's critique of capitalism in *Caritas in Veritate* rests on his discussion of the three main social spaces and their attendant social logics: the market (commercial logic), the political realm (the logic of justice), and civil society (the logic of the gift). In his discussion of these three spaces Benedict expands John Paul's discussion of them in *Centesimus Annus* where he insists that the state must prevent market idolatry and culture must provide a bulwark against economistic limitation of human creative subjectivity, and offers a radical interpretation of the moral and social justice imperatives that must govern market activities (*CV*, 38).

Benedict describes the economy as a legitimate, distinct social space with its own proper logic, commercial logic (*CV*, 36). When properly ordered, the market is a social institution that supports the exchange of goods and services that allows basic societal needs to be met (*CV*, 35). This social institution's logic is ordered properly when it observes commutative justice, or fair exchange, between consenting parties. While the economy and markets have their own legitimacy, proper character, logic, and form of justice, these alone are not sufficient for producing an environment that can support the right order, which must be defined by a "climate of mutual trust" (*CV*, 35). Running the economy on commercial logic alone leads to distorted social relations and "grave imbalances" in society (*CV*, 36). The economy operating strictly on its own devices cannot perform even its own tasks: "Without internal forms of solidarity and mutual trust, the market cannot completely fulfil its proper economic function" (*CV*, 35). Solidarity and mutuality come from the other two social spaces. "Today," Benedict teaches, "we can say that economic life must be understood as a multi-layered phenomenon: in every one of these layers, to varying degrees and in ways specifically suited to each, the aspect of fraternal reciprocity must be present" (*CV*, 38).

The logic of the gift, which pertains to the social space of civil society, represents an integral dimension of economic activity, not as a supplement but rather as an internal, guiding norm. Benedict observes: "in *commercial relationships* the *principle of gratuitousness* and the logic of gift as an expression of fraternity can and must *find their place within normal economic activity*. This is a human demand at the present time, but it is also demanded by economic logic. It is a demand both of charity and of truth" (*CV*, 36). A properly functioning economy must allow space for fraternity in civil society and assume this fraternity and solidarity as an inner moment of its own operation.

The same goes for the political order. It plays a critical role in developing a just social order. The "political path" of charity is "no less excellent and effective than the kind of charity which encounters the neighbor directly" (CV, 7). To the economic space's model of justice, commutative justice, the political adds distributive justice (CV, 36, 39). Since the economy has become globalized, the political space's demand for distributive justice should be global, too. Benedict proposes a "world political authority," consistent here with the demands of John XXIII in *Mater et Magistra* and Paul VI in *Populorum Progressio*, to regulate and monitor the global economy (CV, 67).

Benedict's insistence upon the need to interrelate these three social spheres remains continuous with John Paul's in *Centesimus Annus*, but he pushes this point even further. He not only emphasizes that the economic sphere must be shaped by moral impulses (the logic of the gift) and regulated by distributive justice (the logic of justice). Even more remarkably, he also argues that these commitments need to be internalized within economic activity, for "every economic decision has a moral consequence" and *"justice must be applied to every phase of economic activity"* (CV, 37). Because economic activity is now globalized and no longer circumscribed by the boundaries of nation-states it is difficult for governments to perform their distributive function. It is no longer tenable to assume that the wealth generated in the private sector can be effectively redistributed by national political authorities alone. As a consequence, "the canons of justice must be respected from the outset, as the economic process unfolds, and not just afterwards or incidentally" (CV, 37). The only way to ensure this is to reimagine economics from the inside out, with the logics of gift and distributive justice reconfiguring commercial logic from within. This demands the creation of new forms of economic activity that freely choose to pursue ends other than that of "pure profit" (CV, 37). Benedict remarks,

> Alongside profit-oriented private enterprise and the various types of public enterprise, there must be room for commercial entities based on mutualist principles and pursuing social ends to take root and express themselves. It is from their reciprocal encounter in the marketplace that one may expect hybrid forms of commercial behavior to emerge, and hence an attentiveness to ways of civilizing the economy. Charity in truth, in this case, requires that shape and structure be given to those types of economic initiative which, without rejecting profit, aim at a higher goal than the mere logic of the exchange of equivalents, of profit as an end in itself. (CV, 38)

In the wake of the worst capitalist economic disaster since the Great Depression, Benedict boldly looks toward an economic future defined not by
economism, not by the economic alone, but by the civilized interrelation
of the three social spaces.

At its core, *Caritas in Veritate* calls for the reorganization of market economics on a new foundation, a stratum deeper than this world: God's
love and truth revealed in Christ. This foundation would support commercial activity—not denigrating business, not ridding the world of private
property, not abolishing markets, or anything else like this. But the foundation rules out commercial activity's preeminence, in the sense of dominance over the other spaces. Economism is unacceptable. The new
foundation demands that commercial activity be restructured from within
by moral precepts and the demands of justice, both commutative and distributive, in each step. Benedict summarizes his distinctive take on the
interrelation between the market, the political, and civil society in *Caritas in Veritate* in this way:

> *Economic life* undoubtedly requires *contracts*, in order to regulate rela-
> tions of exchange between goods of equivalent value. But it also needs
> *just laws* and *forms of redistribution* governed by politics, and what is
> more, it needs works redolent of the *spirit of gift*. The economy in the
> global era seems to privilege the former logic, that of contractual
> exchange, but directly or indirectly it also demonstrates its need for
> the other two: political logic, and the logic of the unconditional gift.
> (*CV*, 37)

Benedict does not endorse any concrete economic-political paradigm as
an alternative to the current form of capitalism. But his emphasis on the
importance of "economic democracy" (*CV*, 38) and his call for an international body to oversee capitalism signals a significant break with capitalism as we know it. In this respect, Benedict's earlier comment that "in
many respects, democratic socialism was and is close to Catholic social
doctrine and has in any case made a remarkable contribution to the formation of a social consciousness" points to the distance between Benedict's social vision and that of proponents of American-style "democratic
capitalism."[52] Even here, though, Benedict cautions that the "binary model
of market-plus-state" (*CV*, 39) is inadequate and so he calls for a radical

reorientation of the economy, the political realm, and civil society on the basis of a deeper commitment to charity in truth.

Benedict's vision for the relationship between morality, politics, and the economy is stridently anti-economistic and anti-neoliberal. For now, we can state two relevant points. First, political life (as defined by the logic of justice) and civil society (as defined by the logic of the gift) should serve as a check on market action in all spheres of life. As we will see in chapter 2, the ambition of neoliberalism is to disseminate market logic into these realms. Second, and even more radically, Benedict argues that economic activity itself must have a moral element and must pursue justice as a matter of course in all of its activity. This twofold argument about the requirements of an economy from the perspective of CST represents a powerful rebuke of the basic premises of neoliberal thinking.

Constructively, Benedict opposes all forms of economism that fail to make the human person and morality central, and by this standard evaluates Marxism and capitalism as deficient. Benedict stands directly opposite Marxism and capitalism at a fundamental level. While both Marxism and capitalism follow immanent norms, Benedict is convinced that transcendent norms alone can secure the forms of morality needed to sustain proper economic functioning. In a 2007 speech at Aparecida, Benedict indicts Marxism and capitalism for the same error. Both are "systems that marginalize God."[53] Neither asks *the* fundamental question, so they get their fundamentals wrong. Neither asks, "What is this 'reality'? What is real? Are only material goods, social, economic and political problems 'reality'?" He continues,

> This was precisely the great error of the dominant tendencies of the last century, a most destructive error, as we can see from the results of both Marxist and capitalist systems. They falsify the notion of reality by detaching it from the foundational and decisive reality which is God. Anyone who excludes God from his horizons falsifies the notion of "reality" and, in consequence, can only end up in blind alleys or with recipes for destruction.

Although Benedict XVI, following John Paul II and his many predecessors in CST, does not provide every detail of a counter-recipe against Marxist and capitalist recipes for destruction, with his continuation of John

Paul's critique of economism and his theory of three social spaces, he provides a few ingredients for imagining a world beyond neoliberalism.

Francis: No to a Faceless Economy

However much his supporters and his critics treat Francis's papacy as sharply divergent from that of his predecessors, this erroneous narrative proves particularly false with regard to the ongoing and continuous development of a critique of economism in Catholic social teaching. Granted, as was the case with respect to the transition between John Paul and Benedict, new emphases emerge, illuminating different facets of economism and its errors. Francis effects two major developments in the tradition stretching from John Paul through Benedict into his own papacy. He amplifies an already-present theme in CST, idolatry, training this theme on economism as his preferred object of critique. And he makes a vital clarification with regard to capitalist economism, by offering a frontal confrontation with neoliberalism as capitalism's dominant contemporary form. It is true that Francis has not yet as pope criticized neoliberalism by name, but he did as archbishop of Buenos Aires,[54] and he has kept his papal criticisms of the economy consistent with what earlier he had found blameworthy in neoliberalism. This particular development in CST, quite obviously, is pivotal for our book. The substance of his criticisms makes it clear that his target is neoliberalism, which he views as a deeply compromised economic-political form as well as the primary carrier of idolatry in the modern world.[55]

As we did with John Paul and Benedict, before we exposit Francis's own interventions with respect to economism, we will set these within a theological context. Francis has never been a professional philosopher or theologian, as were his predecessors, but his rich background offers many possible in-roads for theological commentary. For our purposes in this chapter, we deem a section titled "From the Heart of the Gospel" from his 2013 apostolic exhortation on evangelization best for theologically situating his critique of neoliberal economism (*EG*, 34–39).

Francis observes that in our culture of instant communication, the context for individual moral teachings of the church is often lost or ignored, thus distorting these teachings and people's perception of church teachings generally. Certainly, this has happened in the case of Francis's teachings on the economy, in which he has been vilified by the political Right for being a "Marxist" and celebrated by the Left for the same perceived reason. Neither side is correct. Against such a tendency (though acknowledging compassionately that most people should not be expected to understand the full context of the church's moral teaching with perspicacity), Francis maintains that evangelization must "concentrate on the essentials" (*EG*, 35), those relatively few "revealed truths" that "are most important for giving direct expression to the heart of the Gospel" (*EG*, 36). Seeking reliable guides to navigate this "hierarchy of truths" with regard to the church's moral teachings, Francis turns to Paul and to Thomas Aquinas. Citing Paul's Letter to the Galatians, Francis states, "What counts above all else is 'faith working through love' (Gal 5:6)" (*EG*, 37). These two theological virtues—and certainly the third, hope—that make manifest the "interior grace of the Holy Spirit" comprise the heart of Catholic moral teaching. Then he adduces several texts from Thomas, the upshot of which is this: "as far as external works are concerned, mercy is the greatest of all the virtues" (*EG*, 37). We must quote here the text Francis includes in a footnote to this section, as the statements from Thomas it includes resonate deeply with our argument: "We do not worship God through external sacrifices and gifts for God's own sake, but for ours and our neighbors'; indeed God does not need our sacrifices, but wants them to be offered to him for the sake of our devotion and our neighbors' welfare." Hence mercy, by which we supply the needs of others, is a sacrifice more acceptable to him, since it leads more nearly to the welfare of our neighbors, in accordance with Hebrews [13:16]: "Do not forget to do good and to share, for such sacrifices are pleasing to God."[56] In order to understand Francis's condemnations of neoliberalism, one must view them through the prism of mercy.

This part shows how Francis specifies the central truth of mercy in our time, carrying forward John Paul and Benedict's critiques of economism and setting them into prophetic relief. He unmasks today's economism as merciless, by putting the global economy under the microscope of idolatry critique and adding trenchancy to John Paul and Benedict's concerns with capitalist economism's impersonality. Francis criticizes the global economic order as a "faceless economy," an "economy of exclusion," and an "economy that kills," and links it to three major social crises: environmental destruction, global poverty, and migration. We discuss all these points and conclude by briefly considering Francis's call for a radical retrieval of the church's teaching on mercy and the universal destination of all goods.

The last two popes share a concern to identify and critique secular formations that undermine and threaten the Christian faith. As we have shown, Benedict XVI offers eschatology as a doctrinal frame through which to diagnose and contest parodies of Christianity, with a specific focus on Marxism as a false eschatology. For his part, Francis turns to idolatry critique in order to diagnose and critique secular formations that rival the Christian faith.[57] Shortly after he was elected pope in May 2013, Francis offered the following description of the cultural situation:

> Poverty is becoming more and more evident. People have to struggle to live and, frequently, to live in an undignified way. One cause of this situation, in my opinion, is in our relationship with money, and our acceptance of its power over ourselves and our society. Consequently the financial crisis which we are experiencing makes us forget that its ultimate origin is to be found in a profound human crisis. In the denial of the primacy of human beings! We have created new idols. The worship of the golden calf of old (cf. Ex 32:15–34) has found a new and heartless image in the cult of money and the dictatorship of an economy which is faceless and lacking any truly humane goal.[58]

Here, as often, Francis lends living flesh to John Paul's sometimes abstract formulations. John Paul diagnoses economism as confounding people with things, rendering economic and social life as a whole impersonal, and thus should be viewed as objectionable by Christian standards. Francis offers new language for expressing this same critique: the contemporary economy, which has escalated into a dictatorship, is faceless, heartless, without a human goal. This new economism is a "cult of money"—idolatry. With Francis's distinctive voice, which flows in equal parts from his personality and the urgency of the present world situation (which did not seem so dire in, for example, 1991), papal resistance to capitalist economism hits a new pitch.

Francis maintains this same tone in a section of *Evangelii Gaudium*, his apostolic exhortation on evangelization in today's world, which became widely discussed in the news immediately upon its publication. The section's title is "no to the new idolatry of money" (*EG*, 55–56). This section was one of four in which Francis described cultural challenges to evangelization presented by today's dominant global economy, the other three being "no to an economy of exclusion" (*EG*, 53–54), "no to a financial system that rules rather than serves" (*EG*, 57–58), and "no to the inequality which spawns violence" (*EG*, 59–60). By foregrounding these economic challenges to evangelization, Francis suggests that today's global economy drowns out the words of the Gospel, inhibiting moral, religious, and political life. "Idolatry" is the perfect descriptor. Idols shape cultures; they shape what we are attentive to, what we see and fail to see. When the market is "deified" (*EG*, 56), much in reality becomes invisible, including the true and living God. As Francis sees it, ethics and God are rejected today because were they affirmed, the importance of money and power would be relativized (*EG*, 57). In today's world, a situation somehow worse than early capitalist exploitation arises. Today's world still has lower and under classes, but also something new, a growing non-class of people, the excluded, who "are no longer society's underside or its fringes or its disenfranchised—they are no longer even a part of it. The excluded are not the 'exploited' but the outcast, the 'leftovers'" (*EG*, 53).

Francis contends that the idolatry of money, which is his figure for contemporary neoliberalism—a financialized version of capitalist economism whose signature is heightened social exclusion—generates a "culture of indifference," a "throw-away culture," and a "culture of prosperity [that] deadens us" (*EG*, 53–54). By dedicating themselves through "blind and naive trust in the goodness of those wielding economic power and in the sacralized workings of the prevailing economic system" to an impersonal market (*EG*, 54), people become complacent in lifestyles predicated upon selfishness and, even worse, sacrifice of human lives and God's wider creation. For Francis, neoliberalism has created a social environment in which the loss of a few points in the stock market is viewed as a tragedy that garners significant news commentary, but the death of a homeless person from exposure fails to register as an event worthy of attention (*EG*, 53). Money—particularly financialized, speculative capital—endlessly occupies our attention in neoliberal culture, which Francis characterizes as "a seedbed for collective selfishness," for "when people become self-centered and self-enclosed, their greed increases" (*LS*, 204). What we miss is others' misfortune, their suffering faces, which should prove more determinative than the intensity of our self-regard.

Francis contends that a neoliberal culture is a "throw-away culture" where realities not directly related to money, profits, and capital enhancement are discarded, for they have no intrinsic value. Francis remarks upon this culture's pervasiveness: "[It] tends to become a common mentality that infects everyone. Human life, the person, are no longer seen as a primary value to be respected and safeguarded, especially if they are poor or disabled. . . . This culture of waste has also made us insensitive to wasting and throwing out excess foodstuffs, which is especially condemnable when, in every part of the world, unfortunately, many people and families suffer hunger and malnutrition."[59] The idolatry of money, which promises high value, in reality devalues. And as we will discuss in chapter 2, whatever this idolatry devalues, it eventually sacrifices, with virtually any negative connotation of that word firmly in play.

In the May 16, 2013 statement, which also appears in a slightly amended form in *Evangelii Gaudium*, Francis points to "the dictatorship of an economy which is faceless and lacking any truly humane goal." Let us say more about this peculiar phrase, "the dictatorship of faceless economy." Benedict XVI employed the term "dictatorship" to describe relativism as the dominant cultural form in modern society. Francis invokes the same term to signal his own diagnosis: that our culture's overarching ethos is dominated by a faceless economy. This change in phraseology should not distract us from the continuity between the two most recent popes. Francis has something in mind akin to Benedict's understanding of capitalism as an impersonal and amoral economy. Francis describes it as a "deified market" that "devour(s) everything which stands in the way of increased profits, whatever is fragile, like the environment, is defenseless" (*EG*, 56).[60] As an autonomous and impersonal force, the market pursues efficiency and profit above all else and resists any attempt to introduce moral considerations into its calculations.[61] Therefore, Francis expresses concern that we have created a situation in which the market rules human beings and imposes its own inhumane laws on all social relations. He observes that advocates of autonomous markets "reject the right of states, charged with vigilance for the common good, to exercise any form of control. A new tyranny is thus born, invisible and often virtual, which unilaterally and relentlessly imposes its own laws and rules" (*EG*, 56).[62] Here Francis, like Benedict before him, explicitly rejects the invisible hand of the market and maintains that a just economy requires moral deliberation and political guidance. The following statement from Francis could have been penned by Benedict, or even John Paul: "we can no longer trust in the unseen forces and the invisible hand of the market. Growth in justice requires more than economic growth, while presupposing such growth: it requires decisions, programs, mechanisms, and processes specifically geared to a better distribution of income, the creation of sources of employment and an integral promotion of the poor which goes beyond a simple welfare mentality" (EG, 204). The upshot is that the economy must be personal—an overarching thesis of the three most recent popes.

Let us highlight two central features of the global, neoliberalized economic system to get a better sense of Francis's concerns: trickle-down economics and the emergence of a new colonialism between the Global North and the Global South.

First, Francis strikes at the heart of neoliberal ideology when he rejects the theory of trickle-down economics.[63] Advocates of neoliberalism such as Ronald Reagan and Margaret Thatcher utilized trickle-down theories to defend their attempt to reorganize society on the basis of neoliberal principles. The argument was that so long as the economy was growing there was no need to worry about the redistribution of wealth, since the economy would take care of wealth distribution on its own. In effect, excess wealth would inevitably trickle down to the poor. In *Laudato Si'* Francis dubs this "a magical conception of the market" (LS, 100) that presumes that an increase in profits will somehow solve inequality. In *Evangelii Gaudium* he maintains that while "some people continue to defend trickle down theories" this represents an "opinion, which has never been confirmed by the facts" and which "expresses a crude and naïve trust in the goodness of those wielding economic power and in the sacralized workings of the prevailing economic system" (EG, 54). Very much in line with Benedict XVI's criticisms of capitalism and the invisible hand of the market, Francis contends that proponents of trickle-down economics falsely assume that the workings of the free market system produce the greatest good for the greatest number of people. But he argues that it is simply false to assume that "economic growth, encouraged by a free market, will inevitably succeed in bringing about greater justice and inclusiveness in the world."[64]

Second, consistent with the analyses of Paul VI in *Populorum Progressio* (PP, 7, 52), John Paul II in *Sollicitudo Rei Socialis* (SRS, 21–22), and Benedict

XVI in *Caritas in Veritate* (*CV*, 33), Francis criticizes the emergence of a new form of colonialism which pits the North-Atlantic world against the Global South. Francis observes: "The new colonialism takes on different faces. At times it appears as the anonymous influence of mammon: corporations, loan agencies, certain 'free trade' treaties, and the imposition of measures of 'austerity' which always tighten the belt of workers and the poor."[65] The fundamental architecture of neoliberal policy is tied inextricably to the processes of neocolonization and the dispossession of the poor: financialization, structural adjustment policies, and free trade. Francis specifically denounces the tendency under global capitalism to reduce "poor countries to mere providers of raw material and cheap labor" for the benefit of affluent countries in the Global North. This new colonialism constructs a "periphery" and a "center" in which the South is sacrificed environmentally and in terms of the well-being of its population to benefit to the Global North.

Francis rejects neoliberal capitalism for both its ideological commitments and its effects. The following comments sum up his view:

> Just as the commandment "Thou shalt not kill" sets a clear limit in order to safeguard the value of human life, today we also have to say "thou shalt not" to an economy of exclusion and inequality. Such an economy kills. How can it be that it is not a news item when an elderly homeless person dies of exposure, but it is news when the stock market loses two points? This is a case of exclusion. Can we continue to stand by when food is thrown away while people are starving? This is a case of inequality. Today everything comes under the laws of competition and the survival of the fittest, where the powerful feed upon the powerless. As a consequence, masses of people find themselves excluded and marginalized: without work, without possibilities, without any means of escape. (*EG*, 53)

It is not simply that people have little hope in the future. People are quite literally put to death by the faceless logic of a system that permits ruthless market laws to decide the fate of vulnerable lives. Here Francis returns to the theme of sacrifice. When human beings deliver their freedom over to the market "it is no longer man who commands, but money, money, cash commands. And God our Father gave us the task of protecting the earth—not for money, but for ourselves: for men and women. We have this task! Nevertheless, men and women are sacrificed to the idols of profit and consumption."[66] Francis draws a link between neoliberalism as an economy of exclusion and sacrifice and the social crises of environmental destruction, proliferation of slums, and mass migration (see chapters 3 and 5).

As with John Paul II and Benedict XVI, Francis does not offer a fullfledged alternative to the economic paradigm he criticizes, instead insisting that central principles of CST be taken under consideration when deliberating over economic matters. In view of his criticisms of the "faceless" economy, it is unsurprising that he supports the following: "those charged with promoting economic development have the responsibility of ensuring that it always has a human face. Economic development must have a human face. We say no to an economy without such a face!"[67] Constructively, Francis advocates for a "truly communitarian economy," in which "the economy should not be a mechanism for accumulating goods, but rather the proper administration of our common home. This entails a commitment to care for that home and to the fitting distribution of its goods among all." Francis specifically points to the need to create economic and political structures that guarantee the three "Ls" ("Ts" in Spanish) of land, labor, lodging (*tierra, trabajo, techo*) to all human beings. This demands economic activity directed not toward wealth accumulation, the dominant imperative under the prevailing model, but protection of the rights of the poor and distribution of the goods so that the poor's basic necessities—their "sacred rights"—are met.[68]

As we showed in the previous section, Benedict approaches the issue of distribution in terms of voluntary charitable acts and the state's distributive function. Francis approaches distribution by retrieving the traditional Catholic notion of the universal destination of goods. There are diverse scriptural warrants for this teaching: God's injunction to the first humans to fill and govern the earth (Gen 1:28); the Jubilee tradition (Lv 25; Dt 15); the parable of the rich man and Lazarus (Lk 16:19–31); and the Lukan depiction of the church's earliest days, defined by communitarian living sustained by the Holy Spirit (Acts 2:43–47; 4:32–37). John Paul II references Genesis 1:28 in *Centesimus Annus* (*CA*, 31) and Francis invokes both Luke 16 and Acts 2 to defend the universal destination of goods. Furthermore, the patristic tradition is referred to by the popes in their elaboration of this teaching: Paul VI, following in the wake of Vatican II's defense of this principle in *Gaudium et Spes*, invoked St. Ambrose (*PP*, 23) and Francis has repeatedly referred to St. John of Chrysostom in his speeches and writings (most prominently in *EG*, 57).

Francis regards the early chapters of Acts as a model of authentic Christian witness and mandate for contemporary Christian life: "'They sold their possessions and goods and distributed them to all, as any had need'" (Acts 2:45). In these words, we see clearly expressed the lively concern of the first Christians. The evangelist Luke, who more than any other speaks of mercy, does not exaggerate when he describes the practice of sharing in the early community. On the contrary, his words are addressed to believers in every generation, and thus also to us, in order to sustain our own witness and to encourage our care for those most in need."[69] Benedict XVI reflected on this same passage in *Deus Caritas Est*, noting that the early church held "all things in common" so that "among them, there is no longer any distinction between rich and poor" (*DC*, 20). As the church grew, this radical vision became unsustainable, but the principle that generated this practice remained relevant: that Christians are called to share goods in order to eliminate social situations in which extreme poverty threatens bare life (*DC*, 20).

For Benedict and Francis, the approach to the Christian community depicted in Acts serves as an important precedent for reflecting on the responsibilities of the Christian community in the modern world. For Francis in particular, the call to share one's goods is not simply a private choice but rather a solemn obligation to distribute the gifts of creation, which are gifts from God. This "shared inheritance" charges Christians with subordinating private property to the needs of the commons (*LS*, 93). Francis put this pithily in a 2015 address in Bolivia:

Working for a just distribution of the fruits of the earth and human labour is not mere philanthropy. It is a moral obligation. For Christians, the responsibility is even greater: it is a commandment. It is about giving to the poor and to peoples what is theirs by right. The universal destination of goods is not a figure of speech found in the Church's social teaching. It is a reality prior to private property. Property, especially when it affects natural resources, must always serve the needs of peoples. And those needs are not restricted to consumption.[70]

This understanding of the relationship between natural resources and the goods of the earth undermines a central tenet of neoliberal doctrine insofar as it rejects an individualist understanding of property.[71] Property is not to be enjoyed only by the privileged few, but as a *social* good that should be equitably distributed so that the sacred rights of all may be secured. Francis's analysis is literally unthinkable for neoliberals, who dismiss redistribution as redolent of Marxist class warfare. But as Pius VI, John Paul II, Benedict XVI, and Francis all insist, the idea of the universal destination of all goods stands at CST's heart, serving as the foundational principle for imagining more egalitarian—thus more holy—economic and political forms. We will return to this important element of CST when we explore responses to environmental destruction and the proliferation of slums.

We began our discussion of the popes with John Paul II's interpretation of the significance of the parable of the rich man and Lazarus, wherein he encouraged his audience to reflect on the meaning of mercy for "economics and politics."[72] We now close our discussion of the popes with Francis's reflections on the same parable.

On May 18, 2016, Francis gave a brief address at his weekly general audience titled "Poverty and Mercy," in which he upheld the parable as a timely warning concerning wealth. Its timeliness results from its relevance to any era: "Lazarus is a good example of the silent cry of the poor throughout the ages and the contradictions of a world in which immense wealth and resources are in the hands of the few."[73] But God condemns the rich man not primarily for his wealth. More at issue is his inability to feel mercy for a hungry, wounded human being who lies at his doorstep in the hopes of receiving even a few crumbs from his table. Lack of mercy, not the possession of material goods, condemns the rich man. According to Francis, "as long as Lazarus was outside his house, the rich man had the opportunity for salvation, to thrust open the door, to help Lazarus, but now that they are both dead, the situation has become irreparable. God is never called upon directly, but the parable clearly warns: God's mercy toward us is linked to our mercy toward our neighbour; when this is lacking, also that of not finding room in our closed heart, He cannot enter." This scene suggests that the "mystery of our salvation" is revealed when "Christ links poverty with mercy." Those who show mercy to the poor open themselves to God's mercy (Mt 25:40); those who fail to respond to the poor's needs close their hearts to God's mercy (Mt 25:45).

Francis had already treated this parable in *Evangelii Gaudium*, where he elucidated the link between mercy toward the poor and the universal destination of goods. St. John Chrysostom's homily, "On Lazarus and the Rich Man," illustrates the connection: "I encourage financial experts and political leaders to ponder the words of one of the sages of antiquity (St. John Chrysostom): 'Not to share one's wealth with the poor is to steal from them and to take away their livelihood. It is not our own goods which we hold, but theirs'" (*EG*, 57).[74] For Francis a communitarian economy subordinates private property to the common good because it recognizes that the goods of creation were intended by God to meet the basic needs of all of humanity. Failing to share one's wealth with the poor is theft, an act of self-closure against the poor and God's mercy. Francis regards this closure starkly: "If I do not thrust open the door of my heart to the poor, that door remains closed. Even to God."[75]

Papal Continuity

As we have shown, there is a remarkable continuity in the teaching of the three popes of the era that marked neoliberalism's rise to dominance. All three popes, in distinctive yet consonant voices, oppose what John Paul II calls "economism," or varieties of political-economic thinking and practice that subsume noneconomic areas of life to the economy. John Paul objects to economism, both capitalist and communist, with respect to work and development, and warns consistently, from the 1981 *Laborem Exercens* through the 1991 *Centesimus Annus* and beyond, of capitalism's tendency to repeat its early sin of viewing human subjectivity and development solely on the order of things or objects. Benedict condemns Marxism and capitalism alike for their economistic presuppositions; both assume that reality is fundamentally economic, following impersonal laws (whether of class conflict or market exchange), and both, especially Marxism although capitalism scarcely less, exhibit a utopian tendency to preview the future through the lens of an ersatz economic "kingdom." Francis is unique among the last three popes in his frontal confrontation with neoliberalism as today's dominant economism (communism is no longer a concern for him, as it largely collapsed in 1989). He denounces the economic idolatry of our time, a cult of impersonality (the "faceless economy") that breeds ever nastier forms of social exclusion and ever greater violations of the universal destination of goods. Through these three popes' teachings runs a thread of continuity: a rejection of economism that grew increasingly necessary as a new form of economism took hold worldwide.

This continuity between the popes arises not from antipathy to economics or markets (people need to exchange goods and services to live), nor from a bias harbored in the Vatican against modernity (arguably neoliberalism is a form of postmodernism, itself set against central tenets of modernity), but from their commitment to catholicity. Economisms, whether communist or neoliberal, diminish the whole of life to one aspect only, focusing social life on this single sliver. John Paul, Benedict, and Francis demand that social thought and practice be ordered according to the whole, *kata-holon*, catholically, so the whole of life may be kept open to redemption, reconfiguration, reconciliation, and resurrection through Jesus Christ and the Holy Spirit, and in the love of neighbor that coordinates with the right worship of God.

We make our argument for the continuity of outlook between these three popes in the face of what, in United States Catholicism, has become an influential interpretation of these three popes' economic teachings: the so-called neoconservative reading of discontinuity presented by Michael Novak, George Weigel, Rocco Buttiglione, Robert Sirico, and others.[76] Here we focus less on what qualifies these authors as neoconservatives, and more on how they serve as allies of neoliberalism.[77] Two of them (Novak and Sirico) write for neoliberal think tanks (American Enterprise Institute and Acton Institute; Novak was also one of only five hundred worldwide members of perhaps *the* central neoliberal organization, the Mont Pèlerin Society); another (Weigel) works for a procorporate think tank (Economics and Public Policy Center) that, although not as recognizably neoliberal, aligns itself closely enough for this ascription; and Novak and Buttiglione expressly support the economic teachings of the leading neoliberal thinker Friedrich A. Hayek. This group has exhibited an uneven response to papal teachings on the economy. In brief, they see John Paul II's *Centesimus Annus* as the epitome of CST, from which Benedict XVI and Francis have deviated and fallen.

Overall, our view is that the neoconservatives have mischaracterized and misappropriated the resources of Catholic social teaching. They have mischaracterized them because they have privileged a partial reading of John Paul II's writings (especially *Centesimus Annus*) over Benedict XVI's and Francis's, even positing a discontinuity between them. They misappropriated these resources by utilizing them to give ideological cover to neoliberal economistic policies, strategies, and structures. To be sure, this group of authors would not expressly support economism. But the results of their collective labors have been to lend support to today's dominant economism.

At the beginning of John Paul's pontificate, Michael Novak wrote forcefully against papal teaching on the economy, especially on capitalism, in general and John Paul's incipient teaching in particular.[78] But over the course of the 1980s, Novak and Weigel believed they recognized their own concerns emerging as John Paul's, especially with his affirmation of the "right of economic initiative" in *Sollicitudo Rei Socialis* (*SRS*, 15).[79] Weigel avers, in "*Sollicitudo Rei Socialis*, we may indeed see the beginnings of a move toward the moral legitimation, indeed celebration, of some forms of entrepreneurship on the part of the Roman magisterium."[80] A full opening occurs in Catholic social teaching with *Centesimus Annus*'s account of the "cause of the wealth of nations," which from Novak's perspective "embodies insights . . . usually attributed to the Austrian school of economics, in particular to Friedrich Hayek."[81] John Paul's affirmation of the "business economy" or "free economy" draws resounding praise from Novak and Weigel from their laudatory op-eds just after the encyclical's publication to their continued adulation over the document up through the 2010s.[82] While these authors express gratification at John Paul's religious and moral reflection on human freedom, the economic motive is clearly paramount, as Novak's reference to Hayek reveals.[83] This group's responses to CST, then, evolved from criticisms at the beginning of the 1980s to enthusiastic affirmation of John Paul's particular social teaching in *Centesimus Annus* by 1991 and for decades to come.

The pendulum, however, would swing the other way. With Benedict XVI and Francis, CST's purported embrace of the free market would end; it would slip back into the night of "traditional" thinking.[84] The reception history of *Caritas in Veritate* is a case in point. In advance of *Caritas in Veritate*'s publication, Novak sets his criteria for judging it. If the encyclical railed against "unregulated markets" and "capitalist greed" and did not recommend liberating the poor through wealth creation, it had to be judged a leftist distortion of authentic CST.[85] The pope would do well to follow the wisdom of his predecessor's *Centesimus Annus*. Upon the encyclical's public release, Novak produces a column for *First Things* with seemingly complimentary commentary on Benedict's theological, specifically Trinitarian, depth and his rich appropriation of St. Augustine.[86] But the title, "The Pope of Caritapolis," paired with the final three paragraphs, reveal Novak's critical judgment. Novak intimates that Benedict, who should know better, has not fortified his encyclical with proper awareness of sin, and its hold over this world. Benedict's theoretical orientation leads him away from practical solutions into ineffectual sermonizing about "*caritas*, virtue, justice, and good intentions." Even worse, Benedict evidences "nostalgia for the European welfare-state." Novak concludes that Benedict should have followed paragraph 48 of *Centesimus Annus*.[87]

In perhaps what is an even more frontal confrontation with *Caritas in Veritate*, Weigel suggests that John Paul II "routed" the Pontifical Council for Justice and Peace with *Centesimus Annus*, refusing their input to come up with his own commemoration of *Rerum Novarum*. The Pontifical Council for Justice and Peace's special pleading for an encyclical worthy of their social justice agenda was rejected for the rest of John Paul's pontificate, and the first part of Benedict's. Undeterred, they prevailed upon the pope to write a compromise document, some in his voice, some in theirs. This is *Caritas in Veritate*, a "duck-billed platypus" of an encyclical, a messy "hybrid" that resulted from Benedict's desire "to maintain peace in his curial household." Weigel casts Benedict as a "truly gentle soul" who let his convictions slip to appease the Pontifical Council for Justice and Peace. By the article's end, Weigel encourages readers to ignore the encyclical's *social* teachings in favor of its teachings about "the nature of the human person." In brief, Novak and Weigel treat *Caritas in Veritate* as less than serious about political and economic matters and as discontinuous with John Paul's achievement.

The discontinuity worsens with Francis. If Benedict is depicted as an impractical theologian, Francis, the Argentine, is derided as myopic and backward, without experiential knowledge of "real capitalism." George Weigel stipulates, "What the pope knows from Argentina and elsewhere in Latin America is not 'capitalism' in the sense of markets regulated by law and culture; what you find in Latin America is, primarily, either a very ugly form of so-called 'crony-capitalism' or mercantilism that pretends to be populism."[88] Novak, responding to *Evangelii Gaudium*, declares that, after "reading it through the eyes of a professor-bishop-pope who grew up in Argentina," he came to have a certain "sympathy" with its arguments—but only inasmuch as these arguments hit upon Latin American "capitalism."[89] US capitalism remains unscathed. Timothy Cardinal Dolan's *Wall Street Journal* op-ed elaborates on this line of argumentation: "What many people around the world experience as 'capitalism' isn't recognizable to Americans. For many in developing or newly industrialized countries, what passes as capitalism is an exploitative racket for the benefit of the few powerful and wealthy. Americans must remember that the holy father is speaking to this world-wide audience."[90] In effect, US capitalism is let off the hook; the third-world pope's target lies elsewhere. Having done this work to obviate any real-world application of the pope's criticisms of capitalism, the neoconservatives then extend this criticism to *Laudato Si'* as another Caritapolis-style reflection on the nature of the human person, in no way a serious contribution to empirically-based papal economic teaching.[91] Perhaps most telling of all, though, is Buttiglione's reading suggestion for Pope Francis. In a 2014 interview, he stated that if he could recommend one book to Pope Francis, it would be Hayek's *The Counter-Revolution of Science: Studies on the Abuse of Reason*.[92] Effectively, Buttiglione is upholding Hayek, arguably the most influential theorist of neoliberalism, as a needed corrective to the direction Catholic social teaching has taken with Francis.

As is likely clear from our presentation, we reject the neoconservative reading of discontinuity in papal teaching, on both textual and theological grounds. Textually, our reading of continuity between the popes on the central issue of economism can account for a wider variety of quotations from their social teachings. Where the authors examined above view *Centesimus Annus* as the definitive statement of CST and see subsequent reflection as discontinuous with its achievement, we view *Centesimus Annus* as continuous with John Paul's earlier writings, those of his predecessors, and those of his successors. Surely John Paul has a distinctive voice, albeit not a discrete one, separated from all others. This brings us back to our theological criticism of the neoconservatives. With regard to catholicity and tradition, the themes that began this chapter, it is a nonstarter to separate one papal writing off from others. *Centesimus Annus*'s holism and deference to tradition precludes this, or it should. We do not claim to know for certain whether there is, between the neoconservatives and us, an intellectual disagreement over how best to interpret these documents or if there are other motives at play in their reading of the tradition.[93] But what the facts bear out is this: as the neoconservatives observed developments in a capitalist economy that they themselves, with their genuine appreciation for culture, human dignity, the family, subsidiarity, and many other values, should have found destructive and unacceptable, their commitment to capitalism appears to have trumped their other convictions. We want to emphasize here that our argument is not that the neoconservatives are proponents of economism. Rather, it is that they have lent "Catholic" intellectual cover to an economism that the church must oppose: neoliberalism.

Part II: Neoliberalism

2 Neoliberal Capitalism

Catholic social teaching over the past three decades has opposed economism, yet only lately, for legitimate historical reasons, has come frontally to address the globally dominant form of economism during this same period: neoliberalism. Communism was, for the first decade of John Paul's pontificate, a really existing economism, but it fell in 1989. As John Paul's tenure continued, even through the famed *Centesimus Annus*, neoliberalism (another candidate for economistic ascription) grew apace, exploding in its reach by the time of the 2008 economic collapse to which Benedict XVI responded in *Caritas in Veritate* in 2009. The confrontation with neoliberalism, although that label was seldom used, has intensified with Pope Francis, and, as we examined in chapter 1, he has provided stark diagnoses with regard to its general failings: its market idolatry, its "facelessness" or impersonality, its propensity to exclude, and, put most pointedly, its mercilessness. While we agree with Francis's assessment—and see it as confirming John Paul's worst fears about a triumphalist capitalism after 1989—we see the need for greater specificity with regard to it.

John Sniegocki must be commended for starting the conversation that we extend in this chapter.[1] He critiqued the neoliberal political economy from the standpoint of Catholic social teaching, showing how signature features of neoliberal globalization stand at odds with CST principles. We will do the same here but augment his diagnosis by identifying neoliberalism as a utopian (even a theological) project, a new form of political common sense, and, even more, as an ethos of mercilessness inhabited by numerous people across the globe. Neoliberalism is, in effect, more than just an objectionable type of political economy. It is a new form of economism aimed at producing a new reality whose sole aim is to serve markets. This chapter shows, in brief, how neoliberalism came into existence, how it rose to dominance, and how its distinctive principles have affected human persons' self-understanding and day-to-day living.

Neoliberalism as Political Economy

The major thesis that we defend here is that neoliberalism is a political economy of class warfare, and that this results from its roots as an episte-mological and social experiment. In order to make that claim we have to examine a few aspects of the theoretical and historical roots of neoliber-alism. We focus specifically on its utopian and theological character as it has been discussed by recent historians. Then we trace a narrative of neo-liberalism's global ascendancy since the 1970s with the theme of class warfare firmly in view.

Neoliberalism as Utopian

Friedrich Hayek, one of the founders of neoliberalism, bemoaned in a 1949 article that socialists had utopian visions that appealed to young people, while economic liberals did not. He wrote:

> We must make the building of a free society once more an intellectual adventure, a deed of courage. What we lack is a liberal Utopia, a pro-gram which seems neither a mere defense of things as they are nor a diluted kind of socialism, but a truly liberal radicalism which does not spare the susceptibilities of the mighty (including the trade unions), which is not too severely practical, and which does not confine itself to what appears today as politically possible. We need intellectual lead-ers who are willing to work for an ideal, however small may be the prospects of its early realization.[2]

He goes on to write that economic liberals must push not just for "rea-sonable freedom of trade" or "relaxation of controls" but have the utopian courage to fight for the full realization of these ideals. This is precisely what happened since neoliberalism's global ascendancy since the 1970s. The economic reality we have in much of the world today is, we suspect, a utopia beyond Hayek's wildest imaginings, especially since the dawn of financialization (the dominance of an economy driven overwhelmingly by finance as opposed to production, industry, and labor).

This utopia had its beginnings prior to Hayek's 1949 article, and its as-cendancy in the 1970s is embedded in a long and involved intellectual and political-economic history.[3] Daniel Stedman Jones differentiates three historical phases of neoliberalism's maturation. First, in the 1920s through

1950, Austrian and German economists and like-minded people in business and government "worked to define a market-based society, which they believed was the best way to organize an economy and guarantee individual liberty."[4] Second, from 1950 to the late 1970s, "neoliberalism generated intellectual coherence and matured politically" in Europe and the United States, despite the fact that it enjoyed little concrete political success, given the dominance of its intellectual and political rival, Keynesianism.[5] Third, from 1980 to today, the world saw the "advance of an agenda of market liberalization and fiscal discipline into development and trade policy." In effect, the neoliberal ideas, policies, and strategies germinated in the first phase and ripened in the second are harvested in the third.[6]

Quinn Slobodian's recent book, *Globalists: The End of Empire and the Birth of Neoliberalism* (2018), focuses on neoliberalism's first phase, which laid the groundwork and set the trajectory for the utopian project that Hayek advocated in 1949. Slobodian argues that such a utopia became attractive in the 1920s through the 1940s because this was the age of the end of empires.[7] The global capitalist economic order, which hitherto was upheld and enforced by empires, faced possible collapse, or at the very least a serious decline in health. The early neoliberals, who were economists in academia but also in chambers of commerce and elsewhere in the business world, proposed a new form of globalism. Slobodian makes a key clarification with regard to what this globalism would look like. Often accounts of neoliberalism treat it as a movement to "liberate markets" so that markets may "self-regulate."[8] This reinforces the commonly held impression that neoliberals historically, or neoliberalized politicians today, are interested in freeing markets from government control or in shrinking government. Slobodian retorts, "Against the intention of the authors of neoliberal theory, this metaphor [of liberation] essentializes the object of critique: the market becomes a thing capable of being liberated by agents, instead of being, as neoliberals themselves believed, a set of relationships that rely on an institutional framework."[9] Neoliberals did not seek to liberate markets, but to "encase" them.[10] By this Slobodian means that neoliberals sought the development of institutions, whether state or private, national or international, built to ensure that "the world economy would survive threats to its holistic integrity."[11] These threats, in the age after empire, would come first and foremost from the *demos* (the people) and their demands for "social justice and redistributive equality."[12] For the neo-liberals, the defining social reality in the age after empire should not be people, but it should be the "world economy." All institutions should be constructed "to sustain and protect the sacrosanct space of the world economy."[13]

With the word *sacrosanct*, Slobodian intimates that neoliberalism is not simply or straightforwardly an economic project. Instead, in a manner of speaking, neoliberalism has a "theological" valence. This theology begins in epistemology. The fundamental neoliberal claim, which structures all else, is that human knowledge is imperfect, especially with regard to the global economy, and that, consequently, the global economy must be en-cased against intrusion by those who pretend to have definitive economic knowledge (read: socialist planners).[14] This epistemological claim takes on theological proportions: "neoliberalism would be not about seeing the world economy but about declaring its invisibility; not measuring it but casting it as sublime and beyond capture; not surveying its workings but theorizing it as a spontaneous order eluding comprehension."[15] These pro-portions lead Slobodian to call neoliberalism a "negative theology."[16] Neoliberals would avoid speaking of the world economy, ascribing any clear qualities to it. Instead, they would set about encasing and enshrin-ing it, guarding its ineffability.

The correlate to neoliberals' negative project of respecting the world economy with silence was a "proactive project."[17] Slobodian's account of this neoliberal venture in reformulating law and the state suggests a "sac-rificial" reading of neoliberal institution building. This is perhaps most potently visible in neoliberal efforts to reformulate the system of global trade. Neoliberals made concerted efforts over the decades from the 1940s through the 1990s to depersonalize trade. Slobodian tells how neoliber-als like Michael Heilperin and Philip Cortney worked in the immediate aftermath of World War II to defeat the formation of the International Trade Organization, whose aim would have been to facilitate greater eco-nomic parity between the Global North and the Global South.[18] The grounds for their opposition was that the personal needs of the Global South had to be placed second (or third, or not at all) to the health of the world economy, which by its very nature was impersonal. Thus they pro-posed, in the face of the burgeoning discourse of human rights, the new idea of the "human rights of capital," which Cortney posed more pointedly as "the right of free capital movement."[19] People's needs, desires, and aspirations for political democracy should be sharply limited, while impersonal capital should be protected by law, its free range across national borders fostered through binding trade agreements, and thereby its health guaranteed.

It should be noted, especially as we combine our treatment of CST with Slobodian's history of neoliberalism, that with the assertion of the human rights of capital over against the rights of actual humans, some clever neoliberal sleight of hand is at play with regard to "private property." For neoliberals, "private property" is often not defined straightforwardly as personal possessions needed for life (such as housing, tools, modes of transportation, and so on), but precisely as money or finance capital and foreign investment in real estate or businesses. We offer an illustration: what Heilperin, Cortney, Hayek, Wilhelm Röpke, and other neoliberals feared in the postwar period was the "precariousness of private property," meaning "investor rights."[20] They contended that foreign investment should be given primacy over citizens' rights in order, once again, to protect the integrity of the world economy. Neoliberals honestly thought, it seems, that such privileging of capital's "human" rights over the rights of actual humans would, eventually, benefit humans overall. But in light of CST, especially the popes' strenuous defense of economic personalism, the neoliberal recipe for economic health, with its definition of "private property" and its willingness to sacrifice persons' rights to an abstract market, is certainly suspect.

Neoliberalism is almost ubiquitously tarred with the label "market fundamentalism," but our brief account so far (and what we will say later about the cunning of neoliberalism) should indicate that it is far more sophisticated than that label would imply. Neoliberalism is economism, even an economistic theology, with a complex epistemology, a variegated strategy for redefining global social relationships, and an extraordinary capacity for garnering support across the socio-economic spectrum. There is, though, a blunt edge to much of what theorists call "neoliberalization," the attempt to realize neoliberal utopian theology in the world. Slobodian explains that from neoliberalism's origins in the Austrian Chamber of Commerce, which, on the advice of Ludwig von Mises, attacked organized labor when the market's needs seemed to demand it (1920s), to the International Chamber of Commerce's extension of legal protections and the

global capital class (1940s), to the institutionalization of neoliberal epistemology and enforcement of capital's rights in the World Trade Organization (1995), neoliberalization involved class warfare waged from above.[21]
In acknowledging this, Slobodian joins his voice to that of David Harvey,
whose account of neoliberalism we consider next.

Neoliberalism as Class Warfare

If Slobodian centers his book on neoliberalism's first phase, Harvey's influential *A Brief History of Neoliberalism* focuses on the third. Harvey corroborates Slobodian's contention that neoliberalism's social program
included class warfare; in fact, Harvey contends that neoliberalization is
a project of class warfare.[22] Harvey takes seriously Hayek's description of
neoliberalism as a utopian project designed to remake global capitalism.
Harvey argues that we can "interpret neoliberalization either as a *utopian*
project to realize a theoretical design for the reorganization of international capitalism or as a *political* project to re-establish the conditions for
capital accumulation and to restore the power of economic elites."[23] He
maintains that the *political* project of restoring wealth and power has dominated in practice, while the *utopian* project of reorganizing capitalism
has worked "as a system of justification or legitimation."[24] When the theoretical principles of the utopian project have conflicted with concrete
policies that would restore class power, the utopian principles have been
abandoned. Thus, at its core, neoliberalism is a political-economic project motivated by class warfare, even as it is legitimated as a utopian project designed to enhance human flourishing "by liberating individual
entrepreneurial freedoms and skills within an institutional framework
characterized by strong private property rights, free markets, and free
trade."[25]

   For Harvey, neoliberalism represents a new formation of capitalism or
a new stage of economic liberalism that attacks any structures that limit
the power of capital. Neoliberalism came to prominence as a project to
turn back the Keynesian tide—a regulatory state, progressive taxation,
labor controls, and the redistribution of wealth by a welfare state—and
restore power for the capital class. And while neoliberalism developed in
distinctive ways in response to political and economic pressures in different parts of the world, each of these manifestations held one feature in

common: they constituted a response to the capital accumulation crisis of the 1970s which threatened the economic and political power of the ruling class. In response to this crisis, economic and political elites orchestrated a multifaceted assault on domestic and international structures that restricted the power of capital and obstructed accumulation strategies. Harvey observes: "The ruling class wasn't omniscient but they recognized that there were a number of fronts on which they had to struggle: the ideological front, the political front, and above all they had struggle to curb the power of labor by whatever means possible. Out of this merged a political project which I would call neoliberalism."[26] The result of these efforts was dramatic: the rapid ascendancy of neoliberalism, which gained state power throughout the Global North in the 1980s and achieved hegemony in the Global South in the 1990s through a variety of means, but most importantly, the efforts of international economic bodies—the International Monetary Fund, the World Bank, and the World Trade Organization.[27]

In the Global North—particularly in England and the United States— the fundamental strategy for dissemination was ideological. Neoliberals recognized that because it would be impossible to convince the general public to consent to a political-economic project whose aim was to restore class power, it would be necessary to cultivate consent by appealing to deeply held convictions and values "of regional or national traditions."[28] Neoliberals chose well when they seized on individual freedom as the ideal to sell neoliberal reforms to a popular base. Freedom not only represents a core value of Western civilization, but also has served as an ideological bulwark against twentieth-century totalitarian regimes: fascism, socialism, and communism. While individual freedom served as the ideological rallying cry, neoliberals labored to draw the link between individual freedom and private property rights, free markets, and free trade. And because the regulatory and distributive power of the state was cast as a threat to these institutional arrangements, neoliberalism emerged "as the exclusive guarantor of freedom."[29]

Harvey highlights the role that the ideological struggle played in the ascendancy of neoliberalism, noting that Hayek recognized that the battle of ideas would be critical, and it would take some time to defeat all forms of political-economic organization opposed to the neoliberal vision of economic freedom (communism, socialism, Keynesianism).[30] Neoliberals used corporations, the media, and institutions of civil society (schools, churches, and professional associations) to wage this battle. The Business Roundtable was created (1972) and, alongside the Chamber of Commerce of the United States, served as the lobbying arm of the neoliberal movement. Additionally, because neoliberals viewed universities as inhospitable terrain for the cultivation and dissemination of their ideas, they funded a series of think tanks that could serve as neoliberal laboratories: the American Enterprise Institute (founded in 1938), the Heritage Foundation (1973), and the Manhattan Institute (1977). These think tanks were given the task of producing "serious technical and empirical studies and political-philosophical arguments broadly in support of neoliberal policies."[31]

All of these efforts—lobbies, think tanks, and media—contributed to neoliberalism's ideological success, but Harvey maintains that the political victories of Thatcher and Reagan proved decisive. He contends, "Once the state apparatus made the neo-liberal turn it could use its powers of persuasion, co-optation, bribery, and threat to maintain the climate of consent necessary to perpetuate its power. This was Thatcher's and Reagan's particular forte."[32] Reagan and Thatcher utilized political power to discipline and transform the population by offering reforms that emerged out of the same playbook: attack and dismantle unions (coal mining with Thatcher and air traffic control with Reagan), reduce taxes, privatize and deregulate industries, and cut welfare provisions. These policies had a two-fold effect. First, they served the interest of their corporate donors and supporters and created enormous wealth for the capital class. Second, these policies shaped the population and began to remake social relations and reform expectations about the function of government. In this, Reagan and Thatcher made decisive progress toward the neoliberal goal of producing new subjects, because, as Thatcher famously quipped, "'Economics was the method . . . but the object is to change the soul.'"[33] Later in this chapter, we will examine the topic of neoliberal subject formation in conversation with the work of Wendy Brown and Philip Mirowski.

The cultivation of democratic consent to these policies tells only a part of the story, even if it represents the dominant piece of it in the Global North. The creation and manipulation of crises—natural disasters, coups, wars, and financial crises—were often the central means by which neoliberal policies were imposed on society.[34] In the United States and Europe financial crises have led to austerity measures which further facilitated the neoliberal reorganization of society. It was in the Global South, however, that the creation, management, and manipulation of crises represented the primary method of neoliberalization. Chile in 1973 and Iraq in 2003 represent bookends of the process through which military intervention served as a precursor to neoliberalization. In Chile in the 1970s the imposition of neoliberalism "was swift, brutal, and sure: a military coup backed by the traditional upper class (as well as by the US government), followed by the fierce repression of all solidarities created within the labour and urban social movements which had so threatened their power." Iraq was similar; after the "Shock and Awe" campaign in 2003 the United States went about the business of establishing a "capitalist dream" in the Middle East.[35] Paul Bremer, the head of the Coalition Provisional Authority in Iraq, dictated orders to reorganize the economy of Iraq which included privatization of public enterprises, the elimination of trade barriers, the disciplining of the labor market, a regressive "flat tax," the full repatriation of foreign profits, and full ownership of Iraqi business by foreign firms.[36] This represented a veritable wish list for neoliberals insofar as these orders secured economic "freedoms" for Iraqis "that reflect[ed] the interests of private property owners, businesses, multinational corporations, and financial capital."[37]

As evidenced by Chile and Iraq, military force represented one means of establishing neoliberalism globally. The more common practice, however, was to employ the power of the International Monetary Fund (IMF) and the World Bank to impose neoliberal policies on countries in the Global South.[38] This tactic was created in response to the economic crisis in Mexico when it defaulted on its debt in the early 1980s. The Reagan administration pushed the US Treasury and the IMF to roll over the debt but did so on the condition that Mexico would undertake neoliberal reforms. This policy served to protect New York bankers from Mexico's debt default and to disseminate neoliberal policies in the so-called developing world. These "structural adjustment policies," which were created in response to the crisis in Mexico, would soon become the standard practice of the IMF and World Bank (which by the mid-1980s had purged itself of any "Keynesian influence"). In return for debt rescheduling, structural adjustment policies required indebted countries to cut welfare, disband unions, and privatize public industries.[39] Thus, while debt represents a very different type of crisis than military intervention, it nevertheless served as a central means by which the United States imposed neoliberal policy on the Global South.

This brief narrative gives a sense of how neoliberalism spread globally over the past forty years. Once installed, the neoliberal approach to political economy followed a fairly standard set of policies: privatization, deregulation, the reduction or elimination of social spending (welfare, healthcare, education, pensions), liberalization of trade, tax cuts, and the eradication of unions and other organized forms of solidarity.[40] For Harvey, the end result of these policies, across geographical and sociopolitical diversity, has been to restore class power for global elites.

We return here to the tension between the utopian and political dimensions of the neoliberal project. According to Harvey, the utopian interpretation posits that the freedom of the market—of businesses, corporations, and individual entrepreneurial initiative—is critical to wealth creation, which eventually increases the living standards and well-being of everyone. As Harvey puts it, "Under the assumption that 'a rising tide lifts all boats,' or of 'trickle down,' neoliberal theory holds the elimination of poverty (both domestically and worldwide) can best be secured through free markets and free trade." But while neoliberalism presents itself as an utopian political-economic project that institutes policies that will benefit everyone, "the main substantive achievement of neoliberalization . . . has been to redistribute, rather than to generate, wealth and income."[41] Harvey contends that the utopian justification of neoliberalism is nothing more than an ideological facade and claims that, on the basis of its material effects, neoliberalism should be recognized as a class warfare project and not a poverty alleviation program, or a set of reforms oriented toward enhancing human life. Harvey defines the foundational principle of neoliberalism as follows:

> There shall be no serious challenge to the absolute power of money to rule absolutely. And that power is to be exercised with one objective. Those possessed of money power shall not only be privileged to accumulate wealth endlessly at will, but they shall have the right to inherit the earth, taking either direct or indirect dominion not only of the land and all the resources and productive capacities that reside therein, but also assume absolute command, directly or indirectly, over the labor and creative potentialities of all those others it needs. The rest of humanity shall be deemed disposable.[42]

The restructuring of society to support the generation of wealth for economic elites is described by Harvey as a process of "accumulation by dispossession."[43] Harvey argues that neoliberalization has often entailed new forms of colonialism that have concentrated wealth in the hands of the elite through policies and actions that dispossess the public of its wealth, natural resources, and land. This line of argumentation resonates well with Paul VI, John Paul II, Benedict XVI, and Francis's denunciations of neocolonialism and the process by which the "center" is enriched at the cost of the "periphery."[44]

According to Harvey, neoliberalism engages in four types of accumulation by dispossession: (1) the privatization of public goods, which range from utilities (water, electricity, transportation) and welfare provisions (education, pension, and healthcare) to public institutions (prisons and schools); (2) financialization through deregulation; (3) the management and manipulation of debt crises, the result of which has been the "deliberative redistribution of wealth from poor countries to the rich"; and (4) state redistribution through revisions in the tax code and subsidies and tax breaks for corporations.[45] By its very design neoliberalism exacerbates inequalities between the rich and the poor. But Harvey describes several other worrisome consequences of neoliberal hegemony, which range from commodification and widespread environmental degradation to the disposability of labor and erosion of democratic modes of social organization.[46]

For Harvey, the situation could not be clearer: neoliberalism represents an intensified capitalist assault on the values of equality and justice, the commons and democracy, and the environment. In response to this situation, he offers a Marxist inspired critique of neoliberalism that posits that the discourses on freedom and liberty represent a benevolent ideological mask that hides the class warfare that actually animates neoliberal policies.[47] Accordingly, the fundamental task of resistance is to unmask the ideological apparatus that legitimates neoliberalism and reveal the truth of economic-political order as class struggle. Toward the end of A Brief History of Neoliberalism, Harvey declares, "The first lesson we must learn, therefore, is that if it looks like class struggle and acts like class war then we have to name it unashamedly for what it is. The mass of the population has either to resign itself to the historical and geographical trajectory defined by overwhelming and ever-increasing upper-class power, or respond to it in class terms."[48] As we will show shortly, this false-consciousness approach differs from the Foucauldian inspired approach adopted by Brown and, to a certain extent, Mirowski, but it logically follows from the class analytic that drives Harvey's account of neoliberalism.[49]

Harvey's Marxist critique of neoliberalism is important because it foregrounds the neoliberal transformation of political economy and focuses on inequality as its primary accomplishment. From a Catholic perspective, we take seriously the concerns of John Paul II and Benedict XVI regarding Marxist antidotes to inequality, particularly insofar as those antidotes adopt a materialist perspective and offer violent class struggle as the remedy. But we have already noted that ideas similar to Harvey's are present in CST. Furthermore, in a manner very much in line with Harvey, Francis famously denounced inequality as "the root of social evil" and has railed against new and old forms of colonialism and the "violence, poverty, forced migrations and all the evils which go hand in hand with these."[50] If we combine Harvey's analysis with that of Slobodian, whose work we used as a preface to Harvey's contribution, the convergence appears even more clearly. While Harvey does not share our theological objection, it seems that he would share our concern with neoliberalism as a system of sacrifice centered on inequality, where the needs and desires of the *demos* are destroyed in favor of the market's (and thus the wealthy's) needs and desires.

Neoliberalism as Common Sense

In *Undoing the Demos* (2015), Wendy Brown approaches neoliberalism from the perspective of Michel Foucault's analyses in *The Birth of Biopolitics* (1978–79), which distinguishes her approach from Harvey's Marxist-inflected analysis.[51] Brown differs from Harvey in her view that neoliberalism is not a development of economic liberalism. She comes closer to arguing that neoliberalism transforms political liberalism, although her case is hardly so simple.[52] While Harvey's account provides a clear (if perhaps too straightforward) picture of who the agents of the neoliberal revolution were, namely, the capital class and their political allies, Brown does not name specific agents of neoliberalism's rise. She offers a description of what she sees happening in the 1970s up through the 2010s, with few normative claims about class or wealth. She provides a potent counterpart to Harvey's reading of neoliberalism that can help us to understand it and how Catholic theology and life can oppose it. She does so first and foremost by describing neoliberalism as a "political rationality," or the gatekeeper of existence, the final arbiter of truth and falsity, the judge of reality.

Brown reaches for the language of "ontology" when explaining what "political rationality" means.[53] Since it operates at such a deep level, a political rationality facilitates formation of subjects.[54] Here we get the sense of the ubiquity of a political rationality (it is not limited to the political sphere alone), and its persistence even when particular governmental manifestations seem to deviate from it. This is an important insight for our study of neoliberalism, as its specific forms can vary widely while still belonging to a field of conditions properly named "neoliberalism." But most determinative for our purposes is Brown's contention that, for liberalism but still more for neoliberalism, a political rationality functions as a "reality principle remaking institutions and human beings everywhere it settles, nestles, and gains affirmation," and that "brings new subjects, conduct, relations, and worlds into being."[55] As Brown puts it, "neoliberalism has come to be our way of life."[56] Posed even more pointedly, given what we have just learned about "political rationality," neoliberalism teaches us—often using our own, produced voice—what life is. The upshot of all this is chilling: that neoliberalism, as a political rationality, can only be resisted by calling reality itself into question.

With the following quotation from Brown, we can get a sense of neoliberal political rationality's "ontological" thoroughness, the way it underpins the whole of social life, along with the pivotal clarification that, although neoliberal political rationality is a market rationality, this is not the same as saying that neoliberalism orders the whole in literal monetary terms. Brown states, "Neoliberal rationality disseminates the model of the market to all domains and activities—even where money is not at issue—and configures human beings exhaustively as market actors, always, only, and everywhere as homo oeconomicus."[57] She continues, "Widespread economization of heretofore noneconomic domains, activities, and subjects, but not necessarily marketization or monetization of them, then, is the distinctive signature of neoliberal rationality."[58] Neoliberalism produces a reality wholly economized, including human subjects who are economic actors in virtually every respect.

Let us consider Brown's narrative, which differs markedly (without contradicting) from Harvey's. Brown provides more detail regarding the dissemination of neoliberalism, how it takes hold as a political rationality subtending various disciplines, discourses, and practices—from law and education to dating and parenting.[59] We will focus on her account of neoliberalism's redesigning of the state and the human subject.

The State

We have already discussed neoliberalism's hold on the state with Harvey's analysis of neoliberal political economy. Brown detects something more pervasive and lethal at work in neoliberalism's transformation of the state. It is not just that a political elite has captured power and instituted policies that benefit the capital class. More deeply, at the level of political rationality, neoliberalism has eroded the basic lexicon, commitments, and norms of democracy. She agrees with Slobodian's thesis that neoliberalism aims for a global order that disregards the needs and desires of the *demos*. Neoliberalism, as a reality principle, replaces the democratic commitment to equality and justice with the market commitment to "economic growth, competitive positioning and capital enhancement."[60] In effect, neoliberalism redesigns the state as thoroughgoing market order: no longer, properly speaking, an institution charged with upholding the common good but rather a firm implementing a diffuse set of practices aimed at (re)producing market reality and disciplining market subjects.

We remarked in this book's introduction that neoliberalism began as a "conservative" trajectory of academic discourse, politics, and business practice, but has, especially since the 1990s, become the common sense of all manner of politicians, both Democrats and Republicans in the United States, the Labour and Conservative parties in the United Kingdom, and so on. Two examples from Brown will elaborate this crucial point, which establishes that neoliberalism does, indeed, operate as a political rationality, a gatekeeper for reality.

In *Undoing the Demos*, Brown turns to Barack Obama's presidency to demonstrate the powerful hold that neoliberalism has on political common sense. At the very beginning of Obama's second term, he delivered two major policy speeches, his second Inaugural Address and the State of the Union.[61] Both focused on those "left out of the American dream by virtue of class, race, sexuality, gender, disability, or immigration status."[62] While his first term was characterized by a series of compromises with Republicans and centrist Democrats, these speeches appeared to announce a return to his progressive roots. Obama called for the protection of Medicare, immigration reform, progressive tax reform, the development of clean energy, and the elimination of sexual discrimination and domestic violence.[63] These policies were something of a wish list for progressives and represented the type of agenda many on the Left expected from Obama when he was elected in 2008. But just beneath the surface of Obama's renewed progressive rhetoric Brown detects a tension. Obama justified these policies not on the basis of their moral rectitude or because they comported with the egalitarian aspirations of American democracy. Rather, he pitched these policies to the American public on the basis of their capacity to make the United States economically competitive. For Obama: "clean energy would keep us competitive—'as long as countries like China keep going all-in on clean energy, so must we' . . . immigration reform will 'harness the talents and ingenuity of striving, hopeful immigrants' and attract 'the highly skilled entrepreneurs and engineers that will help create jobs and grow our economy' . . . economic growth would also result 'when our wives, mothers and daughters can live their lives free from discrimination . . . and . . . fear of domestic violence.'"[64] At the level of Obama's rhetoric, the fight for equality and justice is not an end in itself but rather a means to achieve the neoliberal end of economic growth and competitiveness.

Brown adduces this episode because it summarizes the core truth of neoliberalism as it relates to the state: "economic growth has become the end and legitimation of government."[65] The state now functions like a firm and shares with it similar priorities: competitive positioning and a healthy credit rating; "other ends—from sustainable production practices to worker justice—are pursued insofar as they contribute to this end."[66] For example, it is now common practice for firms and corporations to view it as an effective business decision, a prudent marketing exercise, to engage in fair trade and green business practices. This is done not because of their concern for the rights of global workers, or because of the threat of climate change. Instead, they see in this type of activity an opportunity to appeal to a niche market and increase profit and shareholder value. In this respect, Obama's speeches depart only minimally from the strategies of contemporary business firms. Both the state and the firm are committed to justice and sustainability, but not as "end[s] in themselves."[67] These commitments are valued to the extent that they create economic growth and stock/credit rating health. Or, in the case of Obama, while these goods appear to express his authentic political commitments, he recognized that the most effective way to advocate for them is to couch them in economic language. Brown concludes that Obama's speeches indicate the degree to which political discourse has become so marinated in neoliberal reason that the "goals of the world's oldest democracy led by a justice-minded president in the twenty-first century" have been reduced to "attracting investors and developing an adequately remunerated skilled workforce."[68]

If Obama's speeches disclose the manner in which progressive ideals are often couched in the neoliberal values of economic growth and competitive advantage, the presidency of Donald Trump depicts a scene of the near wholesale co-optation of democracy and the state by neoliberalism. The election of a businessman with no political experience and little knowledge of the Constitution, democratic norms and procedures, or judicial principles reveals the extent to which neoliberalism has been successful at capturing the political sense of citizens and recasting the function of the state in economic terms.[69]

The economization of the state during the first year of Trump's presidency can be demonstrated by a few examples. First, Trump's constant refrain that previous politicians have made "bad deals"—NAFTA, the Paris Climate Accord, the Iran Nuclear Deal, and so on—and that as a business person he is uniquely qualified to replace these deals with better deals, betrays the extent to which he and many Americans view democracy as little more than business conduct. This approach to democracy as dealmaking and negotiation even extends to his tendency to punish critics as those on the losing side of a deal. Business conduct mandates that there are winners and losers. As a "good CEO, [Trump] will reward supporters and punish detractors or competitors, whether these are cities or states, groups or individuals, nations or international organizations."[70]

Second, Trump's presidency reveals the degree to which neoliberalism has successfully cast the political realm as both an unhelpful and unnecessary intrusion into the market. An approach to politics rooted in a commitment to equality, fairness, and social justice is, at best, viewed as hostile to competition and market logic and, at worst, as leading to "tyrannical social justice programs and totalitarianism."[71] The situation is quite clear: politics is viewed by neoliberals as a hindrance or obstacle to market rule. In this sense, Trump's call to "drain the swamp" was not a demand to restrain Wall Street or restrict the influence of monied interests on politics, but rather a call to purge Washington of politicians, to "get politics and politicians out of politics." Politics, now recast in market terms, is best left to business people, who need not be bothered by democratic procedures and norms in their pursuit of profits and economic growth. Brown suggests that this represents an antipolitical posture and not an anti-state posture. It demonstrates an opposition to the kind of politics in which the state regulates commerce, provides labor protections, and redistributes wealth. We must emphasize this once more: neoliberalism is often presented as a rejection of the state *tout court* because the state's intervention disturbs the sovereign logic of the market; but this presentation is inaccurate. Neoliberalism has no problem affirming and approving of a state that intervenes on behalf of markets.[72] In fact, as we learned from Slobodian, it is precisely the state's role under neoliberalism to encase the global economy and ensure its healthy, free operation. In this regard, Trump is a quintessentially neoliberal instrument, perfectly happy to employ the power of the state to eliminate those things that present a barrier to a friendly business climate: "regulations, procedures, checks and balances, separation of powers, internal opposition or disloyalty, demands for transparency, an independent press."[73]

The election of Trump points to the economization of politics through which the fundamental commitments of democracy (freedom, equality, popular sovereignty, etc.) have been transposed into market terms (economic freedom, inequality, market sovereignty, etc.). But in addition to this assault on the fundamentals of democracy, the Trump administration has implemented what amounts to an undiluted neoliberal policy package: elimination of labor protections, deregulation, cuts to public funding for education, healthcare, and the arts, removal of the United States from climate treaties, and enormous tax cuts for the affluent.[74] In this sense, Trump, as a businessman, embodies neoliberalized politics, just as his policies serve to deepen and solidify the neoliberalization of society that led to his presidency.

The examples of Obama and Trump demonstrate that the neoliberalization of the state is a bipartisan affair. The foundational neoliberal commitment to economic health represents the normative basis for consensus in American politics. Democrats and Republicans inflect their neoliberalism differently, with Democrats offering what Nancy Fraser describes as a "progressive" form that blends cultural emancipation (feminism, multiculturalist, and LGBTQ rights) with a commitment to financialization and neoliberal economic policies, and Republicans increasingly offering ethnoracial and punitive forms of neoliberal policy.[75] Despite these differences—which are important and significant—they converge in their view of the state as a firm that is responsive to the market above all else. This reality lies beneath the oft-voiced sentiment that while there exist two political parties in the United States, both pledge their most basic allegiance to Wall Street. Relatedly, neoliberalism transforms the scope of the state's responsibilities from a political to an economic register so that, as Brown notes, the state's strategic function is viewed as facilitating economic growth and attracting investors. Traditional concerns about equality, justice, and the well-being of citizens are now demoted, viewed as marginal to the primary responsibility of government, and useful only as instruments that can be deployed to sell neoliberal economic policies to the public.[76] Political reality, then, is economized or related to economization. But perhaps even more serious than the neoliberal recreation of the state is its transformation of the human person. In fact, with this transformation of the human person (or subject), the hold the neoliberal state has on citizens becomes ever stronger.

Human Capital

Among his most significant findings in *The Birth of Biopolitics*, Foucault discovers that by 1978 American neoliberalism has gone furthest in forming a human subject befitting market political rationality. This subject is called "human capital."[77] The descriptor "human capital" was developed most influentially by University of Chicago economist Theodore Schultz and his student Gary Becker, who also became a University of Chicago economist.[78] A recent article in the *Economist* touted the concept of "human capital" as one of "six big ideas" in economics worthy of special attention.[79] Currently, "human capital" is a term used across the business world to refer to the skill sets that employees bring to their firms. It is not, as a Khan Academy primer puts it, supposed to be confused with "people."[80]

In reality, though, precisely this elision has been made. Foucault saw its beginnings in 1978. We examine it, in concert with Brown, to discern how neoliberalism has, in disastrous fashion, used the concept of "human capital" to reshape what it means to be human in today's world.

In order to understand what "human capital" means, one must understand how this notion effects a revolutionary shift from classical-liberal to neoliberal economics. Foucault explains that while classical-liberal economists from Adam Smith forward studied mechanisms of production and exchange and data of consumption, neoliberal economists changed the frame of reference to "the nature and consequences of . . . substitutable choices, that is to say, . . . the way in which scarce means are allocated to competing ends."[81] If the *primum ens* of neoliberalism is the market, individuals making choices within the market are a close second. These individuals are not really actors, or "partners in the process of exchange," as was the case with classical-liberal economics. Instead, for Schultz and Becker, these individuals are instantiations of "capital-ability," of capability for "producing an earnings stream."[82] This "ability" or "capacity," developed and held together by a series of market choices, is human capital. The human subject is defined less as an autonomous agent who trucks and barters, and more as a bundle of potentiality for serving and being rewarded or rejected by the market. Human capital becomes "an entrepreneur of himself"—with "entrepreneurship" understood as reacting to market rules.[83]

Following yet revising Foucault, Michel Feher argues that human capital does not so much center on earnings streams or return on investment as on self-evaluation and self-appreciation.[84] This revision is significant because it paints an even darker picture than Foucault's. Whereas for Foucault it seems that individuals still have some control over their human capital, Feher clarifies that "neoliberal subjects do not exactly own their human capital; they invest in it."[85] The subject, figured as human capital, stands at a distance from its own abilities—or even identity. Feher continues, "Rather than a *possessive* relationship, as that of the free laborer with his or her labor power, the relationship between the neoliberal subject and his or her human capital should be called *speculative*, in every sense of the word."[86] Neoliberal political rationality holds that market truth must constantly be produced, with the reformulated state's help; so, too, must market subjects be vigilantly and continuously produced. There is no substantial self, so the subject must be speculated into existence.[87] Sarah Burnside describes the recent phenomenon of the "personal brand," and in the process shows just how the empty neoliberal subject is speculated into a particular, odd kind of existence.[88] From popular media to college career advising, people are repeatedly advised both "to adapt completely to the needs of the marketplace" and to remain "unique and authentic," that is to say, to be a "brand" while also being "humanized." Although employers try to sell employees on the idea that branding is "liberating . . . it could also be seen as limiting: whatever the branded self is, it doesn't look much like a human being possessed of rights which must be respected by employers." What is left of the human person, which Burnside sardonically calls YOU™, is a produced subject characterized by investability rather than dignity. In this way, the reduction of the human person to human capital, a portfolio of investments, fits exceedingly well with a global economy increasingly dominated by trade in speculative values of financial instruments.[89]

Brown elaborates on Foucault and Feher's analyses in the context of the global economy's financial turn, where anything from housing to crops to human life itself (e.g., in the form of insurance) has been transformed into financial instruments available for purchase on the open market.[90] This rise in finance's import has momentously altered the meaning of "human capital," taking the notion far from Smithean "truck and barter" anthropology. No longer an enterprising peddler trying to sell his wares, the "human capital" variant of homo oeconomicus sets his sights on "attracting investors."[91] Or, as Brown said in a 2016 public lecture in Cape Town, there has been a marked shift since the 1990s from a shopkeeper's mentality defined by entrepreneurialism, profits, immediate return on investment to a shareholder mentality distinguished by concerns with branding, credit rating (including ratings such as stars on Uber), and future value.[92] Likewise, pursuit of individual interest (enlightened or not) becomes eclipsed as a question under financialization: "teamwork, responsibilization, and stakeholder consensus" replace it.[93] This means that "human capital" has no value of its own, but must be cogged together with other human capital; nevertheless, hiccups or outright failures devolve to each bit of capital individually; and human capital can be promoted or dismissed depending on others' whims. The former agent of interest now undergoes management and governance. At an even more expansive (macroeconomic) level, individual interest is overshadowed by overall economic growth; human capital finds itself "integrated," again without appreciable individual value.[94] Consequently, human capital simultaneously experiences what Brown calls "massification" (fitting within the macroeconomic long view) and "isolation" (each bit can be summarily sloughed off should economic growth demand it, or should investor attraction abate).[95]

Such "isolation" is the result of "responsibilization," which Brown explains like this: "Responsibilized individuals are required to provide for themselves in the context of powers and contingencies radically limiting their ability to do so."[96] Each person is made to feel responsible for enacting the neoliberal order, supporting the economy at all costs, even at the cost of one's own livelihood or life. Human capital is "expendable and unprotected," and "at persistent risk of failure, redundancy and abandonment through no doing of its own, regardless of how savvy and responsible it is."[97] This is why many theorists have described life under neoliberalism as "precarious" for most people.[98] Under this order, most people (wage laborers, service industry employees, independent contractors, participants in the misnamed "sharing economy" or euphemized "gig economy") are one step away from disaster. The proneness of human capital to disaster leads Brown to utilize "religious" language, and indicate that any bit of human capital can be "sacrificed when necessary."[99] Human capital in our contemporary, financialized setting, "alters the principle of 'inclusion of all'" in the economy, which Foucault hopefully regarded as a positive sign under neoliberalism, even with its faults. The tide has turned for the worse: "Everyone is still rendered as human capital, but the protections [Foucault] imagined extended to all have vanished."[100]

While Brown approaches "human capital" from pure political theory, where religion and God are not active questions, we should note that the very definition of this financialized *anthropos*, which Brown finds illicit on secular grounds, also proves entirely objectionable to CST. Inequality, not the equality of all persons created in God's image and likeness (Gen 1:27), is the "medium and relation of competing capitals. When we are figured as human capital in all that we do and in every venue, equality ceases to be our presumed natural relation with one another."[101] In chapter 1 we showed that John Paul II foregrounds the creation of the human person in the image of God as the foundation for human dignity and the impulse for human creativity. We will take up this theme again in chapter 5. There exists a stark contrast between construing the human person as human capital, without intrinsic value, and the human person as *imago dei*, with inestimably high intrinsic value. Human capital can be sacrificed, expelled, thrown out of the economy to live in a slum, be locked in a prison, be deported, or die in a gutter. Any of this is unacceptable for the human person—any and every human person—as God's dignified image. But under a human capital anthropology, particularly within the context of financialization, it is tolerable. Furthermore, under the human capital anthropology, "labor" disappears as a category for analyzing human relations and activities.[102] Accepting such an anthropology would render John Paul II's gorgeous meditation on human labor in *Laborem Exercens* completely nonsensical. Obviously, CST cannot accept such a conclusion, and we must reject the premise. Furthermore, a human capital anthropology erodes the foundation for the common good.[103] The closest that bits of human capital can come to sincere cooperation is organizational "teamwork" on projects that are tracked onto an impersonal horizon of economic growth. Consequently, the notion of "common good," too, appears nonsensical, and the "universal destination of all goods" becomes a parody— all goods can be sacrificed to the abstract universal of the market.

Ethos of Mercilessness

We have now encountered two markedly different, though not necessarily conflicting, accounts of the existence, motivations, spread, and import of neoliberalism: Harvey on class warfare and Brown on political rationality.[104] Harvey heavily emphasizes public policy dimensions of neoliberalism, such as privatization, deregulation, welfare cuts, tax cuts, and disciplining of labor. Brown accepts dimensions of this reading but supplements it with an analysis of neoliberalism as a reality principle that disposes every economic, political, and personal decision on the model of markets. Harvey's Marxist interpretation of neoliberalism discusses "freedom" as the ideological figure that masks the material effects of the neoliberal capitalist order; the mass of people are sold "greater freedom," while the upper class enjoys all the spoils of the masses' sharply constricted liberty. Brown's genealogy rejects this "false consciousness" view, tracing instead how neoliberalism reconfigures the bounds of reality and, in keeping with and support of this reconfiguration, redesigns the state and the human person.[105]

Let us think about these two readings of neoliberalism heuristically, rather than adopting them in all their details. Harvey offers a macroscopic view of neoliberalism. As a geographer, he concerns himself with local manifestations of a wide-ranging international phenomenon, that is to say, the process of neoliberali*zation* that constitutes neoliberali*sm.*[106] In the case of his history of neoliberalism, this approach lends itself to a meta-level view: an all-out global assault by the capital class against all others. Brown's consideration of the neoliberal redesign of the state and the human person operates almost at a mesoscopic level. Her main concern lies in discovering how neoliberalism loosens the ties that bind the democratic citizenry in public pursuit of the common good through marketization of federal, state, and local government, law, and education. She takes neither a bird's eye nor worm's eye view; instead she shows how neoliberalism becomes par for the political course.

Since we are making the case in this chapter that neoliberalism falls under CST's ban of "economism," which we have come to define as the subsumption of all of life to economic or market logic, it would make sense to elucidate one more level: the microscopic, the granular, worm's eye level of everyday life. We ask, how does neoliberalism really take hold in people's lives so that it can have staying power? Philip Mirowski answers that neoliberalism has found ways, particularly through mass media, to extend market logic into our living rooms. Under neoliberalism, we have become habituated into a market logic that designates winners and losers, the included and excluded, those who please the market and who do not. This is not just a class project at the level of political economy, not just a reformation of government, but a conscious, carefully executed cultural project. We will find in the following pages that there could hardly be a type of formation more contrary to Christian formation, a formation centered on Christ who says "the last shall be first" (Mk 10:31; Mt 19:30, 20:16; Lk 13:30), who himself is the "stone that the builders rejected" (Mk 12:10; Mt 21:42; Lk 20:17; Acts 4:11; Ps 118:22; Is 28:16), and who seeks the lost sheep (Lk 15:4–6; Mt 18:12).

Human Capital Anthropology in Everyday Life

Mirowski agrees with Brown that "human capital" plays a central role in neoliberalism and neoliberalization. He goes even further to show how a human capital anthropology becomes disseminated through various modes of discipline into everyday life.[107]

We consider here two aspects of human capital's education that change everyday life. First, human capital is educated into a life of risk, which for all but the wealthiest means a precarious life, a life always in danger of running afoul of the market. Second, human capital is educated into a life of mercilessness, meaning that each bit of human capital is trained in quotidian ways to blame other human capitals for their problems and to practice, or at the very least to endorse, the expulsion of those whose precarity conflicts with the market's whims, all so one can feel strong oneself, even in one's own precarity. The overall effect of this everyday education of human capital is that people become conscious and willing subjects of sacrifice to the market. Risk means giving all you have to the market. Mercilessness means accepting and even cheering the market's judgments.

Let us delve more deeply into these points. Mirowski intricately argues that to embrace market risk is to mark oneself as entrepreneurial, displaying one's ostensible striving after self-interest. But we know from Brown that financialized human capital is no Smithean "truck-and-barter" entrepreneur, so this entrepreneurialism must be complex. "Risk," in an advanced neoliberal situation, does not mean bending the rules of cost-benefit analysis, hopefully pursuing the possible benefits. Instead, distinctively neoliberal "risk" denotes "bald impetuous abandon in the face of an intrinsically unknowable future."[108] Risk is not "the fine balancing of probabilities," but "wanton ecstasy: the utter subjection of the self to the market by offering oneself up to powers greater than we can ever fully comprehend."[109] It is self-sacrifice in the bad religion sense, an "irrational leap of faith."[110] Such a view of risk coheres amply with neoliberal market ontology, or, to use Slobodian's term, negative theology. The utterly inscrutable market needs its human devotees, who double as its fodder. This may all seem relatively high-minded and abstract, until one considers the flesh-and-blood realities of debt, for most people today an inescapable feature of their life.

Maurizio Lazzarato has gone furthest in describing debt (for housing, cars, student loans, payday loans, and, of course, credit cards, which stoke consumption when wages are too meager to honor capital sufficiently) as the basis of social life in a neoliberal world.[111] If Wendy Brown rightly argues that we have all been figured as human capital, and in an age of finan-cialization all seek to enhance our human capital, Lazzarato explains why: we aim to increase our social capital so we may be extended social credit. The alternative to this would be social exclusion. Thus we are formed as subjects who seek credit and, consequently, go into debt—and not debt of the sort that may be paid, but perpetual or infinite debt.[112] Pervasive debt financing constructs a castle on air; the economy and personal lives fall every decade or so under neoliberalism (e.g., market crashes in the United States in 1987, 1999, and 2008), with rescue operations going only to the strongest and largest "portfolios," never the weakest and smallest. Mirowski explains the upshot of neoliberal risk-addiction: "This is how neoliberalism works: first it moves heaven and earth to induce you to manage your port-folio and assume more risk; then it demonizes the victim when the entire structure comes crashing down as it inevitably must."[113] Surely this is what happened after the 2008 financial crisis. When the brief chastisement of banks was over, what lasted was victim-blaming of all the people who "took bad loans." This pernicious edge to neoliberal training in risk leads quite naturally into the next and, for this book, more important aspect of everyday neoliberalism: everyday mercilessness.

Everyday Mercilessness

What happens when human capital anthropology becomes more than a model for the economics, more than a pillar of market ontology, more than people's political self-understanding or even notional common sense? What really transpires when human capital anthropology comes to struc-ture our lives at the most basic level? What results when human capital becomes what Raymond Williams calls a "structure of feeling," a living, affective, cultural process?[114]

Were one to ask a neoliberal, such as Milton Friedman, the answer is clear: human capital anthropology, driven as it is by competition, yields great benefits, from creative products that meet consumer needs to a gen-eralized diffusion of power that funds democracy. And lest one get squea-mish about competition, Friedman can assure that *economic* competition is nonrivalrous, precisely because "the essence of a competitive market is its impersonal character" (impersonality is, for neoliberals, an asset).[115] For a variety of reasons this is difficult to take seriously, but paramount among these is neoliberal blindness, from its Hayekian and Friedmanian infancy to its Clintonian-Obaman maturity, to social difference.[116] Presumably human capital anthropology bears the gift of freeing all individuals from social determination of any sort; all have the opportunity to become human capital should they be sufficiently open to the opaque directives of the inscrutable market. But this rosy view of human capital and its capacity to elide all ostensive differences into flexible market posturing belies the empirically undeniable persistence of difference, and it ignores how neoliberalism, with its human capital anthropology, actually operates—particularly at the visceral level. Just as much as freeing people to invest in themselves, neoliberalism effectively habituates into human capital a gut-level disdain for individuals and groups perceived as *failed* human capital. Competition, unsurprisingly, is not always so friendly.

Brown already clued us in to a possible downside of human capital. It demands (often in positive ways) personal responsibility and creativity but also renders responsibilized individuals' lives precarious by siloing people off from one another, as each pursues her own self-investment strategy. Simply put, the more this anthropology takes root, life turns more dangerous. Brown answers, in part, our questions. But Mirowski is even more pointed when he describes everyday neoliberalism as "everyday sadism." Because of some unsavory and extreme connotations of this phrase, we prefer to revise it into "everyday mercilessness." The point, though, is plain. Once human capital becomes a structure of feeling, often punitive feelings fill this structure.

Mirowski develops his ideas on the everyday mercilessness of human capital in conversation with political economist and critic of neoliberalism Martijn Konings, who pinpoints a particular twofold character to neoliberal cultural cohesion (such as it is). It proceeds dialectically between "affirmatively therapeutic" and "sadistic" sensibilities.[117] These sensibilities show up most obviously in mass media (see below), but for the moment let us stick with human capital's shaping of subjectivity. Konings ties the duality of the therapeutic and the sadistic to what he calls a "dynamics of narcissism." The necessary self-regard of neoliberal subjects (constant monitoring of the "portfolio" that one is) breeds self-centeredness, even self-enclosedness, which teeters on shifting ground and thus involves a wrenching mood of anxiety.[118] Consequently, "the dynamics of narcissism," Konings writes, "must involve an active *externalization* of our insecurity, the opportunity to see others falter, and to disapprove of their lives."[119] No better way to right my rocking ship than to witness others navigating rougher waves. Human capital has an edge to it, an "underbelly" that wallows in what Mirowski calls a "theater of cruelty."[120] Investor human capital is also, all-too-often, punitive.

Varied pieces of evidence coalesce into Mirowski's depiction of the everyday mercilessness of the theater of cruelty. One may surmise that debt provides some examples. Mirowski notes the contemporaneity of neoliberalism's maturation and the return of what used to be called "salary purchase," or in current parlance, "payday loans."[121] The fact that such loans are made to poor people living paycheck to paycheck and that they involve exorbitant interest rates and service fees, along with intentionally unclear or virtually unexpressed terms and conditions, makes them obvious exemplars of cruel and unusual behavior toward those on the market's "bad" side. Whatever neoliberals' denial that "predatory lending" can even exist, it patently does, and payday loans constitute one of its forms.[122] Furthermore, whether debt derives from payday loans, mortgages, credit cards, or student loans, debtors have become targets for imprisonment and "creative" modes of debt peonage.[123] Student loans are, in many ways, the most vicious of loans, in that once one takes them on, they are virtually inescapable should one find oneself unable to pay. Debtors cannot escape even through death, but only by "proving hopelessness" in multiple court hearings.[124] A social climate defined by neoliberalism's competitive investor logic has allowed these structures and relations to develop. The climate's refrain is "your debt is not my problem," a saying that came to define the Tea Party movement, which perhaps began as a grassroots movement but was quickly "astroturfed," as Mirowski puts it, by neoliberal organizations such as the Koch-funded FreedomWorks, effectively blaming debtors—not neoliberal finance—for neoliberalism's 2008 collapse.[125]

There is, though, a better realm than finance, and a slightly less obvious one, for observing neoliberalism's everyday mercilessness. In a growing literature, especially in cultural studies, reality TV has come to be seen as the prime example of neoliberalism's dissemination of the human capital anthropology and its penchant toward cruelty.[126] Reality TV is, in the main, competitive. Whether contestants scramble to prove their survival, singing, cooking, fashion designing, dancing, or romantic skills, every week they compete to avoid being voted off the show. In numerous cases, most notably *The Apprentice* and *Shark Tank*, entrepreneurship, or at the very least some type of business savvy, is the main medium. But we know from our study of Brown that neoliberalism entails more (and something qualitatively other) than competition and entrepreneurship. Reality shows from *American Idol* to *Project Runway* to *Master Chef* to *The Batchelor(ette)* and thousands of lower budget YouTube channels necessarily reduce their participants to up-and-coming brands, voracious and often desperate for "investors," whether this means the "buy-in" of celebrity judges (whose purpose is just as much to abuse contestants as to invest in them), "votes" from viewers, or actual product purchases (song downloads, clothing, cookbooks, magazines, etc.).

The desperation of these branded individuals is most germane to Mirowski's analysis, which resonates somewhat, albeit with finer granularity, with Harvey's account of neoliberalism. The desperation stems from the fact that many reality television contestants are, certainly by comparison with their celebrity mentors and evaluators and the shows' creators, producers, and chief beneficiaries, relatively or actually poor. We have already mentioned that reality TV contestants face, at one point or another in the show, maltreatment—embarrassment, shaming, and forced confession of their trials, usually accompanied with tears—at the hands of the more powerful. This proves particularly the case for contestants being "voted off." The viewer can feel the thrill of vicarious vilification, of bullying a failed brand from behind a protective screen. Mirowski persuasively contends that, consequently, reality TV is not a diversion, not rubbernecking at others' missteps; instead, it is a "a technology for recasting economy and society."[127] And again we must keep in mind that reality TV contestants tend to come from impoverished backgrounds, small towns, or, at the very least, difficult situations, be they personal, financial, or whatever else. We must combine this awareness with recognition that, for neoliberals, there are no social classes, and we all enter the market "game" on an even playing field. This potent combination yields the following state of affairs: "Since . . . the poor no longer exist as a class, it is easier to hate them as individuals. They are the detritus of the market. Those wretched souls subsist at our munificence, it is hinted; therefore it is the indigent who owe us, it is implied; hence we qualify as the righteous and willing audience at the theater of cruelty."[128] Watching Gordon Ramsay or Donald Trump berate a lowly bit of defective human capital is not merely entertainment; it is reeducation. Mirowski adds, "It is not so much that explicit portrayals of violence or aggression need to be paraded . . . as it is that pageants of the ostracized appear to accept the dictates of the market as final, and also in the audience coming to appreciate that it is legitimate for themselves and others to take advantage of those who fail."[129] Reality TV shows are training grounds for a life of mercilessness, whether through active participation or resigned indifference.

Neoliberal training via reality TV does not operate on the level of the intellect, of ideas, or even of morals, but at a visceral register. People come to feel under their skin that the world would be a better place if market castaways would accept their market fate and be gone.[130] The desperate situations of which reality TV shows avail themselves, and which they produce and reformulate, manifest with frightening directness the precaritization of life for growing numbers of people under neoliberalism. Furthermore, they emblematize the de-Christianizing effects of neoliberalism. Reality TV flatly assumes market idolatry: the market for singers, fashion designers, chefs, and so on is the final arbiter for contestants' worth, and the market must be honored as such. And this idolatry embeds a punitive ethos: because the market arbitrates so forcefully, social exclusion rather than inclusion is normative and desirable; mercy and love be damned.

Of our three main diagnosticians of neoliberalism, Harvey, Brown, and Mirowski, the last is perhaps bleakest, since he traces neoliberalism's influence all the way down to the grittiness of everyday life. Neoliberalism's "stealth revolution," as the subtitle to Brown's book, *Undoing the Demos*, calls it, looks most thorough and pernicious through Mirowski's eyes. He writes, summing up his account of everyday neoliberalism, "In these thousand and one little encounters spread over a lifetime, the average person begins to absorb a set of images, casual scenarios, and precepts that begin to add up to something approaching a worldview," with this final word being intended in the strongest possible sense, as a comprehensive pattern for life.[131] Neoliberalism, it would seem, has taken over just about everything, highjacking all of life and moving beyond bare economism into a narcissistic and punitive life of mercilessness, against which resistance would appear futile.

3   Sacrifice, Race, and Indifference

In this chapter we explain what a world subjected to the neoliberal ethos looks like. Normally neoliberalism is presented exclusively in terms of its benefits: lifting people out of extreme poverty, bringing comfort to a large swath of people, and spreading democracy and freedom worldwide. But the truth of neoliberalism emerges more clearly if we scrutinize it in terms of the crises it precipitates and exacerbates.

As we discussed in chapter 1, Francis argues that an "economy of exclusion" now dominates our world and has generated a broader ethos of marginalization that supports a "culture of exclusion." For him, "it's no longer simply about exploitation and oppression . . . those excluded are no longer society's underside or its fringes or its disenfranchised—they are no longer even a part of it. The excluded are not the 'exploited' but the outcast, the 'leftovers'" (EG, 53). Francis maintains that exclusion is the dominant form of structural sin in our world, manifest in the practices of nation-states, religions, and racial and ethnic groups. However diverse the manifestations of this culture of exclusion, the underlying cause is inequality: "The need to resolve the structural causes of poverty cannot be delayed . . . as long as the problems of the poor are not radically resolved by rejecting the absolute autonomy of markets and financial speculation and by attacking the structural causes of inequality, no solution will be found for the world's problems, or, for that matter, to any problems. Inequality is the root of all social evils" (EG, 202). The tyranny of a faceless economy, contoured by extreme inequality, generates not only poverty, but also terrorism, the migrant crisis, and the intensification of xenophobic forms of political populism.[1]

In Expulsions: Brutality and Complexity in the Global Economy, Saskia Sassen offers a similar diagnosis concerning the violent consequences of the dominant economic order.[2] But where Francis describes our societal disorder as the dominance of a faceless economy that supports a culture of exclusion, Sassen uses the term *expulsion* to describe the pathologies generated by a neoliberal order. People are routinely, forcibly, and often violently barred from participating in the central economic, political, and cultural orders of society. Expulsion varies enormously across different geographical locales and distinctive cultural contexts, but in each situation entire groups of people are deemed surplus and expelled from society's core and past its outskirts. These are the "countless displaced people warehoused in formal and informal refugee camps, the minoritized groups in rich countries who are warehoused in prisons, and the able-bodied unemployed men and women warehoused in ghettos and slums."[3] Further, this expulsion is not limited to surplus human populations, but extends to the biosphere itself. According to Sassen, today we are witnessing the widespread expulsion of life from the biosphere, a human generated destruction of land and water that has already brought about massive species extinction.[4]

Francis and Sassen contend that the transformation of the global economy has in some cases exacerbated existing forms of oppression and, in other cases, created new forms of exclusion and expulsion. These practices implement a logic of sacrifice, specified as elimination of the abjectly poor through starvation or slum warehousing, violent extinction of millions of species, and punitive racism that stigmatizes and controls populations judged expendable and exploitable. In what follows we analyze this neoliberal sacrificial logic as it relates to, sustains, and intensifies neocolonial and racist forms of exclusion. Environmental destruction, the proliferation of slums, mass incarceration, and mass deportation represent distinct yet fundamentally interconnected manifestations of this logic. We analyze these four crises together precisely because, together, they depict neoliberalism's multilayered global assault on vulnerable populations, creation, and life itself.

Recognizing these crises as interlinked exposes the true gravity of our current situation—and reveals possibilities for alternatives. As Pope Francis avers repeatedly in *Laudato Si*, everything is connected (*LS*, 16, 42, 70, 91, 117, 138, 240). This is true of both the crises we face and the alternatives that we sketch in chapter 5. A new social order will not emerge without seeing neoliberalism as the connective tissue between varied crises that threaten life here and now.

Environmental destruction, the proliferation of slums, mass incarceration, and mass deportation exemplify the sacrificial ethos of neoliberalism in particularly painful ways. Easily one could object that environmental problems, slums, prisons, and migration predated neoliberalism and therefore could hardly function as illustrations of distinctively neoliberal threats to humanity and the wider creation. But we argue that neoliberalism finds "creative" ways to redesign social problems, thus rendering them peculiarly neoliberal. In short, it subjects them to thoroughly economized logic and often aims to profit from them. We use the analytic categories of *sacrifice zones*, which elucidates environmental destruction and slum proliferation, and *racial neoliberalism*, which illuminates mass incarceration and mass deportation. Having done this analytic work, we reexamine the governing ethos of neoliberalism, this time under Pope Francis's rubric of the *culture of indifference*, in order to account for why, in the face of massive crises, most people do not care or feel unequipped to address them.

Sacrifice Zones, Earth, and Slums

Here we commence our consideration of neoliberal crises by introducing the analytic category of sacrifice zones, which we then use as a heuristic for understanding how the neoliberal ethos of sacrifice is performed with respect to the planet and slum populations.

Sacrifice Zones

David Harvey defines neoliberalism as "a theory of political economic practices proposing that human well-being can best be advanced by the maximization of entrepreneurial freedoms within an institutional framework characterized by private property rights, individual liberty, unencumbered markets, and free trade."[5] This definition appears in a paper titled "Neoliberalism as Creative Destruction." Harvey evokes the famous phrase of Austrian economist Joseph Schumpeter, who coined "creative destruction" in 1942.[6] Originally, this term, which linked entrepreneurial creativity to economic instability, was intended critically, but by the year 2000 it was adopted by neoliberal economists such as Alan Greenspan and Lawrence Summers as expressing the condition for capitalism's flourishing.[7] We may viably call neoliberalism a utopian deployment of creative destruction. Creativity, which today we unreflectively call "innovation," comes virtually always with mass destruction, environmental and human. For this reason, Naomi Klein has recently drawn a connection between neoliberal ideology and practice and the notion of "sacrifice zones."[8] This idea was first developed in the 1950s by the United States government to denote areas used for uranium mining. Steve Lerner reports, "The label *sacrifice zones* comes from 'National Sacrifice Zones,' an Orwellian term coined by government officials to designate areas dangerously contaminated as a result of the mining and processing of uranium into nuclear weapons."[9] Today it sums up the neoliberal attitude toward the environmental and human costs of doing business. And it refers to zones polluted and poisoned by economic projects of extraction as well as those abandoned through economic and governmental disinvestment.

Klein's commentary on sacrifice zones complements her consideration of what she calls "extractivism."[10] A major critic of extractivism, Ecuadoran economist and former minister of energy and mines, Alberto Acosta, defines extractivism against the background of the five-hundred-year history of conquest and colonization of the Americas, Africa, and Asia which served and, even after the end of what is usually recognized as colonialism, serves as a primary mode of capital accumulation.[11] The term itself signifies "activities that remove large quantities of natural resources that are not processed (or processed only to a limited degree), especially for export," including mining of minerals, drilling for oil, farming, forestry, fishing, and other such activities.[12] This definition, with its emphasis on export-driven economics, highlights the colonial character of extractivism, which consists not simply in resource extraction but in what Acosta calls "a mechanism of colonial and neocolonial plunder and appropriation" that has driven the "industrial development and prosperity of the global North."[13] For her part, Klein defines extractivism as a "nonreciprocal, dominance-based relationship with the earth, one purely of taking. It is the opposite of stewardship, which involves taking but also taking care that regeneration and future life continue."[14] The same type of relationship that characterizes conquest and colonization on a social plane also applies in capitalism's methods of wealth accumulation—the bare conditions of life, let alone the possibility for dignified life, are ignored in pursuit of the sorts of development and progress that neoliberals laud. For this reason, Klein links extractivism, especially in its neoliberal forms, with sacrifice zones, "places that, to their extractors, somehow don't count and therefore can be poisoned, drained, or otherwise destroyed, for the supposed greater good of economic progress."[15] To the god of the market, through the religion of economic growth (*la religión del crecimiento económico*),[16] anywhere or anyone can be sacrificed—starting with (formerly) colonized and "raced" people—so long as the market is encased against demands for equality and distributive justice.

Here we explicate two prominent contemporary examples of sacrifice zones, or the destructiveness that attends neoliberal, market "creativity": environmental destruction and slums. Obviously, environmental degradation and poor housing, food, water, and sanitation predated the onset of the neoliberal revolution. We do not accuse neoliberal economics or business practices of being solely responsible for all destroyed biospheres and squalid living quarters in today's world. That said, we outline in the following sections how neoliberalism bears large responsibility for the global environmental and slum proliferation crises we now face, for exacerbating these crises, and for exploiting these crises for epistemic, political, and economic gain. There are identifiable aspects of today's environmental destruction and slum proliferation around the world that prove distinctively neoliberal, that bear the *vestigia* of its peculiar mercilessness.

We begin with environmental destruction, as this constitutes the most massive illustration of neoliberal sacrifice: its willingness to destroy the entire planet at the behest of market rationality, by sickening it and bringing widespread death (e.g., mass extinction of species), all the while profiting from this and proposing "market solutions" to the crisis. We then relate the global environmental crisis to a global crisis bearing upon the basic conditions for human life and flourishing: the worldwide proliferation of urban slums. While neoliberal ideology holds that slums are temporary waystations toward urban prosperity, we diagnose them as, increasingly, areas of permanent social exclusion or expulsion. Slumdwellers are the "waste" of the neoliberal economy, revealing the obverse of the neoliberal ideology of freedom: they are "free" to be judged by market logic, and entirely "free" from the protection of the state or any other social safety net.

The Earth as a Neoliberal Sacrifice Zone

In 2000 Paul Crutzen and Eugene Stoermer published a landmark essay arguing that a new age characterized by human-caused climate catastrophe should be added to the geological timescale: the Anthropocene. The effects of this catastrophe range from climate change and widespread species extinction to environmental displacement and extreme weather events that disproportionately harm the global poor.[17] The contribution of Crutzen and Stoermer is significant because it highlights the fact that humans have dramatically altered geological time and the biosphere. But where "Anthropocene" improves upon the relatively neutral language of "climate change," as well as the potentially misleading language of "global warming," it ultimately fails to describe adequately the specific cause of the multifaceted crisis to which it points. The truth of the matter is that a relatively small percentage of the global population has caused this crisis: not humanity in general—those who inhabited the earth roughly six million years ago to the seventeenth century are excluded from any culpability—but the most affluent people during the capitalist period. This comparatively tiny population has generated widespread biospheric destruction. Since the industrial revolution approximately 25 percent of the global population is responsible for 75 percent of cumulative CO_2 emissions. The term *Anthropocene* does not highlight that the capitalist growth imperatives that represent the primary mechanism of environmental destruction. Accordingly, it is more accurate and useful to characterize our situation as *capitalocene* and to name the cause of environmental destruction as capitalogenic rather than anthropogenic.[18]

Furthermore, it is not simply the growth imperatives of capitalism but also specifically *neoliberal* strategies for managing crises that has delayed any substantive response to capitalogenic environmental destruction. Philip Mirowski provides a broad overview of these strategies in *Never Let a Serious Crisis Go to Waste*. According to neoliberals, climate change poses a threat inasmuch as it may cause the greater public to demand socialism, a planned economy, which could, the hope would be, avert climate catastrophe by limiting carbon emissions through restraint of the market. Such a response to climate change is, in principle, unacceptable to neoliberals. They will, in fact, "concede that it may appear that the existing market system sometimes fails; but the answer to these hiccups is to impose more markets."[19] Their justification comes down to the neoliberal "negative theology" discussed in chapter 2. For neoliberals, the market is the ultimate information processor; to every quandary or crisis, the market has answers, and no human mind can grasp them. The answer to climate change, then, is not to cave in to the demands of a fearful *demos*, but to buy time for the market to figure out the best of all possible responses. The sacrificial system can and should continue, or better continue to evolve, in the face of climate change, lest demands for climate justice make matters even worse.

Mirowski suggests that the neoliberal state serves a threefold function in relation to crises of this sort: (1) to calm the public and dissuade them from implementing regulatory controls on the market; (2) to provide positive arguments that convince the public that the most effective response to any societal problem is more markets; (3) and to support and facilitate the discovery of market solutions to crises.[20] Mirowski contends that this approach is the primary reason for the enormous success of the neoliberal paradigm—it has refused the simplicity of a single "fix" and instead offered a complex, layered approach that can appeal to different constituencies and push them toward the capitulation of nature and society to the market. The neoliberal response to climate change evidences how neoliberals can integrate even seemingly contradictory political strategies over different periods of time to achieve a desired result.

The short-term strategy adopted by neoliberalism with regard to climate change is denialism, denying to whoever will listen that climate change is not occurring. This short-term strategy is easy to implement and distracts people from what really needs to be done to address climate change. We should be clear that neoliberals in general do not actually believe that anthropogenic (or even capitalogenic) climate change does not exist. Instead, given their belief in the market as an information processor beyond human knowledge, neoliberals believe that the truth or reality of climate change is beside the point. Mirowski explains, "The neoliberal think tanks behind the denial of climate change don't seriously believe they are going to win the war of ideas within academic science in the long run."[21] Instead, they hold that the "first response to a political challenge should always be epistemological, in the sense that the marketplace of ideas has to be seeded with doubt and confusion."[22] With this accomplished, the market can sort out what is functionally true (that is, "true" enough to keep the world economy going) and functionally false (that is, which threatens to interrupt economic growth or answer to the needs and concerns of the *demos*). In the United States neoliberal climate-change denialism has been given a broad base of support through its alliance with Evangelical Christians—

and even some Catholics—who already distrust scientists because of their rejection of creationism. This combustible mix of market epistemology and religious suspicion has already bought over a decade for more time-intensive market-based approaches to climate change to be conceived, incubated, and tried.

Neoliberals also developed a mid-term strategy. Neoliberal think tanks and affiliated political actors concocted a market-based strategy for addressing climate change. The common name for this strategy is "cap and trade." In brief, it consists in a "pragmatic" response to climate change that involves, supposedly, reducing greenhouse gas emissions by creating a market for tradable pollution permits. According to Mirowski, where denialism appeals to Christian fundamentalists and politicians with attenuated relationships with truth, cap and trade is targeted at government officials, NGOs, and educated segments in society, who may accept the judgments of scientists but also hold faith that markets can autocorrect.[23] Mirowski expresses serious doubts that cap and trade actually does anything to mitigate carbon levels in the atmosphere. He interprets it instead as a diversion that throws those who wish to use state power to limit carbon emissions into "endless technicalities of the institution and maintenance of novel markets for carbon permits."[24] Effectively, no substantive or meaningful restrictions are placed on corporations, and the neoliberal economy continues to emit vast amounts of carbon into the atmosphere, without regard to future effects, in the pursuit of profitability now. The real achievement of cap and trade has been to provide neoliberals with legitimation. They can defensibly claim that they are working to provide solutions to the climate crisis.

If cap and trade is a diversionary tactic designed to distract in the middle term (over the course of several years), neoliberals have an even grander design for the longer term (a matter of decades). Mirowski identifies "geoengineering" as the neoliberal long-term strategy to addressing climate change with markets. Geoengineering comes in many forms, but the most prominent examples of it are carbon sequestration and direct weather modification. With the former, carbon would be removed from the environment using various technologies. With the latter, the attempt would be made to modify weather patterns by "cloud seeding," or spraying chemicals like sulphur dioxide into clouds to reflect the sun's rays away from the Earth. Mirowski describes the overall program of geoengineering as a utopian scheme of "sheer lunacy." It assumes the possibility of climate manipulation without unintended consequences by, as Klein puts it, answering pollution with more pollution.[25] Furthermore, geoengineering pretends to offer "solutions" to a global problem simply by treating symptoms without actually confronting the deeper structural causes. Despite these limitations it has played and will continue to play a central role in the neoliberal response to the climate crisis, precisely because it offers its proponents the prospect of market success. Just one successful sun-reflecting technique could bring a market windfall.[26] Along with cap and trade, geoengineering serves further to entrench the view that market solutions represent the only plausible remedies to large-scale social problems.[27]

Mirowski's concern is to describe the complex, multilayered strategy that neoliberalism has deployed to delay immediate (socialist) responses to a crisis, to argue for market-based responses, and to limit the field of vision to market-based responses alone.[28] In *Birth of a New Earth* (2017) and *Natural Catastrophe: Climate Change and Neoliberal Governance* (2016), Adrian Parr and Brian Elliott add to Mirowski's analysis by exploring neoliberal approaches to "neoliberal environmentalism" and "green governmentality," which are adopted by seemingly "leftist" politicians and their supporters.[29] By "neoliberal environmentalism," Parr and Elliott mean a political response to climate catastrophe characterized by a turn to sustainable and green economic growth. Where denialism has captured the conservative electorate in the United States, sustainable and green growth have become the privileged models touted by the Center and the Center-Left. If denialism serves as an accurate representation of the Trump administration's approach to the environment, the Obama administration's approach was characterized by a commitment to a green growth platform.[30] In this regard, Trump and Obama, who, respectively, represent the political Right and Left in the United States, serve as two sides of the neoliberal coin with respect to the environmental crisis. Parr and Elliott view the right-leaning neoliberal strategy of denialism as odious, as does Mirowski, but view the neoliberal strategy on the Left as deeply compromised as well. Even though a "green" strategy appears to take seriously the threat of environmental catastrophe, it ends in the same place, because it fails to face the scope of the crises and to engage in the dramatic action necessary to avert disaster.

Parr and Elliott's concerns dovetail with those of Pope Francis (and, notably, many economists),[31] in that they question whether more consumption and more growth—even if it is green—is the most effective way forward, with regard to the environment but also with regard to people's lives. Francis lays out the problem in *Laudato Si'*, when he points out that we tend to "accept the idea of infinite or unlimited growth, which proves so attractive to economists, financiers and experts in technology," but we fail to see that this idea "is based on the lie that there is an infinite supply of the earth's goods, and this leads to the planet being squeezed dry beyond every limit" (*LS*, 106).[32] Francis calls for a renewed commitment to voluntary asceticism that limits consumption and for the enforcement of regulations that curtail growth, all the while redistributing the benefits of economic growth more equitably. Naomi Klein comes to the same conclusion as Pope Francis, namely, that it is impossible to leave the primary driver of environmental destruction untouched when reflecting on how best to respond to the crisis to mitigate its most grave consequences. Klein observes: "The bottom line is that an ecological crisis that has its roots in the overconsumption of natural resources must be addressed not just by improving the efficiency of our economies but by reducing the amount of material stuff we produce and consume."[33]

Together, Mirowski, Parr, Elliot, Klein, and Francis help us reach the conclusion that a response more radical than "more markets" is needed to confront the sacrifice of creation sanctioned by the neoliberal order. With the word *radical*, we have in mind the term's etymological sense; we need to return to the "roots" (*radices*). Neoliberalism must be rooted out— solutions aimed merely at symptoms will fail. Thus we must specify the roots of our current crisis as capitalogenic, not simply anthropogenic. Only by doing this can we propose proper alternatives. The neoliberal strategy of proposing market solutions (even if they are "green") to a market-generated problem should be resisted, because, in reality, neoliberal responses serve only to obfuscate the problem and to prevent serious action that responds structurally and substantively to a crisis that is so deeply entangled with other crises of pressing concern—global poverty, racism, indigenous rights, and gender equality to name just a few.

Slums as Neoliberal Sacrifice Zones

Today, one-third of the world's urban population inhabits slums.[34] There exist more than 200,000 slums on earth and around 1.3 billion people

(14 percent of the global population) worldwide currently live in slums, a figure that could double by 2050 (30 percent of the global population). These numbers set alongside inequality statistics—26 human beings possess as much total wealth as the bottom 50 percent of the global population (3.8 billion people)—serve as shocking reminders of the extreme inequality that defines our neoliberal world.

Mike Davis created a sensation with his 2006 *Planet of Slums*, which argued that the price of mass urbanization, a much-vaunted effect of globalized capitalism, has been proliferation of slums.[35] Davis's sixth chapter, "Slum Ecology," avers that slums are "poverty's niche in the ecology of the city, and very poor people have little choice but to live with disaster."[36] As Javier Auyero puts it when reflecting upon the populations of the *villas miseria* in Buenos Aires, "poor people's lives do not unfold on the head of a pin; theirs is an often polluted environment that has dire consequences for their present health and their future capabilities."[37] The ecology of the slum emblematizes the type of environmental destruction that proceeds apace worldwide: just as "the market" seems more than willing to sacrifice ecosystems, the atmosphere, and so forth to the Moloch of economic growth, so, too, will people end up on the same altar. The United Nations definition for a slum makes this plain, as it includes among its criteria inadequate access to safe water, to sanitation and infrastructure (including lack of toilets or even of latrines), to proper living space (overcrowding characterizes slums), and to secure residential status.[38] Slum life involves deprivation of many sorts of the bare conditions for life and flourishing.

Neil Brenner and Nik Theodore argue in a now widely influential 2002 geographical study that cities have proven to be "strategically crucial arenas in which neoliberal forms of creative destruction" unfolded.[39] Brenner and Theodore schematize the neoliberal restructuring of urban life, which has, in turn, reconstituted all of life globally. Their schema has three phases, extending from the 1970s up through the early 2000s: "proto-neoliberalism" (1970s), "roll-back neoliberalism" (1980s), and "roll-out neoliberalism" (1990s, early 2000s).[40] Proto-neoliberalism was characterized by a struggle between preservationist (largely Keynesian) and modernizing (incipiently neoliberal) policies that saw the gradual erosion of social safety net provision. Roll-back neoliberalism ramped up the modernizing tendencies of proto-neoliberalism, achieving drastic cutbacks in

municipal spending (austerity) and championing cost-cutting entrepreneurialism (privatization), thereby clearing a space for the creation of a
neoliberal, market-driven state. Roll-out neoliberalism focused on creative
destruction of the urban environment, mobilizing the city as "purified
arena for capitalist growth."[41] Brenner and Theodore recognize that these
overall projects were realized heterogeneously in distinctive urban en-
vironments across the globe; nevertheless, they see the progression of
proto- to roll-back to roll-out neoliberalism playing out across the globe
over the past several decades.

Important for our specific topic of slums are the ramifications of these
larger projects for the urban poor. Jan Nijman contends that neoliberalism relates to slums in three discernable ways: (1) "the shift from reliance
on government intervention to reliance on the free market," (2) "the shift
of responsibility from government to civil society," and (3) "the rescaling
of government from central to local levels."[42] The "creative" aspects of neoliberal creative destruction that Brenner and Theodore identify as occurring in the roll-out phase of neoliberalism relate to all three. "Creative"
proliferations of low-wage and contingent labor markets and a strengthening impulse to expand informal economies (thus shrinking tax bases)
ensure the permanence of poverty and the difficulty of moving out of slum
housing, all the while neoliberal reformers insist that these labor market
innovations will empower the poor.[43] Since roll-back neoliberalism tended
to bring the destruction of public housing projects, emergency shelters
have come to serve as "warehouses" for the homeless, and low-income
people are offered rent vouchers instead of housing; this marketization has
driven up housing costs even in slums. The retreat of the state has birthed
proliferation of nongovernmental organizations that, despite their stated
missions to do good and their obvious successes in many arenas, have led
to further regression of state provision of basic services and have greased
the wheels for the thorough marketization of civil society as regards slum
life and attempted rehabilitation of slum conditions.[44] This marketization
often benefits economic elites rather than slumdwellers. At the nexus of
civil society and local government, really existing neoliberalism in the roll-
out phase establishes "new institutional relays through which elite business interests can directly influence major local development decisions,"
so resources tend to funnel more toward skyscrapers than slums, gated
communities for the wealthy rather than low-income areas.[45] In an era of

rapid urbanization this means asking ever more from municipalities—to sustain countries' global aspirations, represented by cutting-edge economic zones—with ever fewer available resources, thus leaving less and less possible help for slumdwellers.[46]

Given all this, we must ask pointedly how slums function in today's global economy. Two trajectories in social-scientific literature have emerged on this question. The first, represented by Edward Glaeser and Hernando de Soto, presents a "modernization theory" of slums.[47] It contends that poor people are pulled by the wealth of cities and stay in slums transitionally until they begin to participate creatively in urban prosperity and move into formal housing. This perspective presumes that all people can, in principle, be integrated into the economy and thrive as a consequence.[48] The second trajectory regards slums less rosily. Davis's *Planet of Slums* sums up this trajectory. Recent analysis out of MIT has shown that slums are hardly a purgative way into urban wealth; instead, they are poverty traps.[49] Saskia Sassen (along with Pope Francis) falls under this rubric, as she regards slums as sites of expulsion, destinations for outcasts from a shrinking global economy.[50] This trajectory of thought emphasizes push factors, that is, adverse conditions in rural areas that force people to find economic opportunity in cities, whether or not in reality such opportunities are there.[51] Slum proliferation relates inexorably to the neocolonial phenomenon called "land-grabbing," in which Western countries are buying up vast areas of the Global South for industrial-level agricultural production, thereby displacing smallholder farmers who have little choice but to move from their rural homes to urban slums.[52] Any consideration of slums these days must, it seems, decide whether slums are transitional vehicles toward prosperity or poverty traps. In our estimation, one must opt for the latter position.

Vyjayanthi Rao and Ananya Roy have, each in her own way, pointed out that slums are often used as metonyms for twenty-first century (mega) urbanization in the Global South, and consequently that scholarly treatments of slums must tread carefully in how they theorize slums.[53] Alan Gilbert has raised analogous cautions against adopting fully either the positive, de Soto-style narrative of slum opportunity or the negative, Davis-style narrative of slum apocalypse.[54] We are interested in this aspect of slums with regard to neoliberalism, because as with the environmental crisis, even if neoliberals recognize that rapid worldwide urbanization has led to a sharp increase in global slum populations and a consequent rise in human misery, market-friendly theory can dissuade governments from providing services for slumdwellers, can enable companies that rely on slumdwellers' labor from providing them with living wages and health-care, can stifle outcry over rising rents in slums or the bulldozing of slums for real estate development, and can in general contribute to a culture de-sensitized to the fact that a billion or more people live in unacceptable conditions. Neoliberal theory can produce such desensitization by explain-ing away crushing poverty and indignity on the same model as climate change denialism. While avoiding an overly dire tone with regard to slums, we do deem it necessary to point out how a positive theorization of slums has been offered by neoliberals.

The best example of this is the intersection between slum life and human capital anthropology. Slumdwellers are, by some accounts, ideal human capital—completely "free," assuming freedom means freedom from state interference in market projects. For example, an October 2016 report on slums by Thomas Reuters, a neoliberal corporate philanthropic organization, presents the Dharavi slum in Mumbai as a humming econ-omy full of entrepreneurial human capital, entirely untethered from gov-ernmental control.[55] Author Rina Chandran illustrates: "Most homes double up as work spaces, the whirr of sewing machines, the clang of metal and the pungent odour of spices mingling with the call for prayer and the putrid smell of trash." She then speaks ecologically, "Slums are ecosystems buzzing with activity."[56] Such narratives about slums suffuse the finan-cial press, wider media, and, especially, business schools,[57] which have be-gun studying economic activity in places such as Dharavi precisely to gain insight into no-holds-barred entrepreneurial creativity. As with much neoliberal theory and practice, there is some truth to the contention that slumdwellers retain human freedom and, in many cases, make the best of difficult situations. That said, idealization of slum entrepreneur-ialism strikes us as just as deceptive and potentially destructive as human capital anthropology as such. This proves especially true because slum-dwellers are relegated to a second-class status that, except in rare cases of exception, bars them from competition in the "real" marketplaces of neoliberalism.

Earlier we gained from Mirowski the insight that human capital an-thropology and everyday mercilessness go together. While "human capital" designates the ideal neoliberal subject, the model for market success, everyday mercilessness expresses the contempt, ridicule, and exclusion directed toward market failures. Such mercilessness, which is "everyday" in the sense of subtle and subliminal, structures urban landscapes.[58] Close proximity of exorbitant luxury and lurid depravation carries a message: follow the market where it leads, or suffer being left utterly without support, access, anything, with your only promise being an early death.[59] Arundhati Roy gets it right when she chooses petrochemical magnate Mukesh Ambani's billion-dollar home, Antilla, which rises out of the slums of Mumbai, as a symbol of the neoliberal "gush-up" model of economics whereby very few "successes" rise and market "losers" are left quite literally in the dust.[60] We can praise slums as places ideally suited for unleashing human capital's creative potential, but it would be more accurate to see them as decreative ecosystems of annihilation, as disposal systems for the human waste produced by neoliberal economies. Slums are, for all the entrepreneurial cheering, altars of market sacrifice.

The Sacrifices of Neoliberalism

As noted in the introductory discussion of environmental destruction and slum proliferation, neoliberalism necessitates sacrifice and, whether invoked in a religious or secular idiom, sacrifice entails some form of violence. Theologically, sacrifice represents the act of offering something as an immolation to a god and serves as *both* an act of destruction and an attempt to *make* things *holy* or sacred (*sacri-ficium*). In religious sacrifice there exists a dialectic, the goal of which is to restore an order destroyed by sin. The sacrifices of neoliberalism, however, are nondialectical, unholy sacrifices, acts of destructive violence that punish the most vulnerable and marginalized in our world while offering comparatively few redemptive qualities.

We often fail to perceive the violence of neoliberalism because it is neither dramatic nor explosive. We have grown accustomed to associating violence with immediate and visible acts, as with a terrorist attack or an act of war. But, as Rob Nixon persuasively argues in *Slow Violence and the Environmentalism of the Poor*, subtle forms of violence exist that accumulate slowly over time. For Nixon, climate change, environmental destruction, and the displacement of vulnerable populations all result from the capitalogenic transformation of the natural world, which occurs through slow violence. The issue with slow violence is that it is hard to perceive and is easily rendered invisible because it transpires cumulatively over time and tends to adversely affect poor and powerless populations who have little or no political voice. One thinks here of forms of environmental racism that push toxic and polluting industries to the periphery of society where the negative health effects of these industries will slowly sicken and kill poor and minoritized populations. One could argue that climate change itself is a manifestation of global environmental racism, a form of neocolonialism through which the damaging effects of extractivist, fossil fuel–driven capitalism silently impose displacement, destruction, and death on the poorest populations around the world. Whether we look at Flint, Michigan as an instance of environmental racism coordinating with neoliberal austerity policies, or the slowly drowning Island of Nauru in the South Pacific, whose inhabitants are the victims of the slow violence of extractivist capitalism, we find that the earth and its most vulnerable populations have been treated as sacrifice zones.

Slums represent another instance of the same colonizing and sacrificial logic by which surplus and discarded populations are warehoused in substandard and inhumane living conditions at the margins of society. Slums are spaces of social abandonment and systemic neglect where the poor, the disabled, and the marginalized are left to fend for themselves without state protection or support. Slumdwellers live in what Giorgio Agamben calls the "threshold of indistinction," a gray zone between bare life and political citizenship, between legal and illegal status, where they expend all of their resources and energies on mere survival.[61] The structurally generated suffering of slumdwellers, condemned to material deprivation and social death, is the very antithesis of the politics of mercy we sketch in chapter 5.

For these reasons we paired environmental destruction and slum proliferation. When juxtaposed with Pope Francis's plea in Laudato Si', in its subtitle and throughout, for all people of good will to see the earth as a common home, the phenomena of environmental destruction and slum proliferation appear for what they are: evidence of neoliberalism's commitment to a divided home, parceled out into habitable zones for market successes and sacrifice zones for market failures. Environmental destruction and slum proliferation show the sinister side of neoliberal "creativity," the emptiness of its utopianism, and the brazenness of its idolatry.

Racial Neoliberalism, Mass Incarceration, and Mass Deportation

We will now shift from our discussion of global neoliberal crises to domestic crises in the United States of America, a country that is, in many ways, the cradle of neoliberalism. Although Austrian and German economists may be credited with cultivating the seeds of neoliberal theory and ideology, the United States soon became the primary sower of these seeds and the greenhouse for their lasting growth. Therefore, we turn to discuss United States racial neoliberalism, that is, the way neoliberal political economy, political rationality, and culture are inflected by the distinctive racial history of the United States. By analyzing the phenomena of mass incarceration and mass deportation, we will see prime examples of the type of expulsive neoliberal structures outlined by Sassen and Francis.

Racial Neoliberalism

The term *racial capitalism* was developed in South Africa in the 1970s and 1980s to describe the racialization of political and economic structures under apartheid. It was subsequently popularized by Cedric Robinson's *Marxism and the Black Radical Tradition* (1983), which argued that capitalism always operates through existing forms of racism.[62] Against Marx, Robinson argued that capitalism did not dramatically break with feudalism, but rather strategically utilized its racialized categories of exploitation for capitalist purposes. For Robinson, Europe was racialized before the advent of capitalism, so that the proletariat were already racialized subjects (Jews, Roma, Slavs, etc.).[63] Capitalism appropriated existing racial categories as media for pursuing projects of accumulation through the expropriation of indigenous land (settler colonialism), the extraction of labor from those deemed to be nonpersons (slavery), and the racialized oppression of global immigrants. Although there is no stable relation between racism and capitalism, since these realities are interlaced in distinctive ways in every sociohistorical situation, one constant of capitalism is that it deploys race in order to institute hierarchies and normalize the differential value attributed to groups of people.[64]

Racial neoliberalism represents a distinctive form of racial capitalism that extends the basic logic of racial capitalism into new social spaces by deploying a unique set of ideological and practical strategies. This is done in three ways.

First, racism is remade under neoliberalism as colorblind and meritocratic. Neoliberals argue that we live in a postracial or colorblind culture in which individuals are freed from identity constraints and judged solely on the basis of merit.[65] The marketplace is defined as a neutral arbiter of merit. It follows that failure to succeed results from personal faults or limitations and not systemic or structural causes. David Theo Goldberg argues in *The Threat of Race: Reflections on Racial Neoliberalism* that a liberal-conservative consensus has emerged over the past forty years around what amounts to a postracial ideological framework.[66] He describes this as a neoliberal consensus that embraces discourses of "antiracialism" while rejecting any substantive "antiracist" policies. Antiracialism rejects the category of race altogether in favor of meritocratic competition. By way of contrast, antiracism attempts to remedy historical injustices by demanding structural reform (criminal justice reform, expansion of antipoverty programs, etc.). Of course, for those committed to antiracial or colorblind discourses of neoliberalism, these programs are irrelevant because the market is viewed as the primary mechanism for distributing goods to impoverished communities of color.

Second, racial neoliberalism coheres with widespread proliferation of procedures of securitization.[67] "Securitization" means increased state support for the expansion of military, police, and immigration enforcement. Generally, we find that a renewed focus on securitization emerges in concert with the process of neoliberalization. It is often the case under neoliberal austerity regimes, which drastically cut back social spending, expenditures on security, policing, incarceration, and immigration enforcement actually expand.[68] Securitization proceeds in lockstep with neoliberalism by imposing discipline and order on a society that has been destabilized and restructured by market reforms. Historically this increased focus on security has not responded to a dramatic increase in crime, but rather a response to the insecurity generated by wealth inequality, unemployment, and trimming of social programs. It is not a coincidence, therefore, that the expansion of the state security apparatus in the United States coincides with the massive reduction of social spending on welfare in the 1980s.

Of course, this process of securitization—mass incarceration, intensified policing and border security, and mass deportation—does little if anything to respond to underlying structural crises that marginalize both white working-class communities and communities of color. But even if securitization fails to mitigate the social suffering of marginalized populations, it serves two functions under neoliberalism.

It manages the insecurity of the general population. The neoliberal state dispenses with the work of providing economic protections for citizens, but it doubles its efforts to offer protection from racialized criminal threats. The shift to securitization undermines the view that social problems can be dealt with effectively through the maintenance and expansion of social programs. Instead, social problems are criminalized and then managed through enhanced police enforcement and increased focus on detention, incarceration, and deportation.

Similarly, the transformation of the state into a securitized instrument of punishment becomes a means of disciplining surplus populations made obsolete by processes of deindustrialization and globalization. Prior to the neoliberal era, welfare provisions were the primary method for managing surplus populations.[69] But as welfare programs were decimated through neoliberal reforms, the dominant method for dealing with issues such as poverty, mental health issues, and drug addiction became criminalization and punishment. The shift toward securitization justified the neoliberal state's disposal of persons no longer needed by the labor market. Incarceration and deportation have been deployed with increased frequency during the neoliberal era as a means of removing undesirable populations from market society.

Third, privatization, a central neoliberal commitment, has created novel ways of profiting from a politics of punishment and exclusion directed disproportionately toward communities of color. While the rise of private prisons and detention centers is a relatively new phenomenon that emerged in the 1980s alongside neoliberal reforms, it represents one of the clearest instances of the imbrication of neoliberal pursuit of profit with race. In 1984 the first for-profit prison business, Corrections Corporation of America (CCA), won a contract to run a prison facility in Tennessee.[70]

Since then the growth of CCA (now called CoreCivic), as well as other private prison corporations, has exploded. In addition to expanding to immigration detention and deportation services, these corporations set up satellite factories for global corporations to contract low-wage labor from prisoners. Furthermore, even when not privatized, the prison and immigration-deportation complexes rely on vast networks of private firms to function and these firms often actively lobby for higher levels of incarceration, detention, and deportation. As we will see later in this chapter, persons of color bear the brunt of these "creative" market initiatives.

We turn now to mass incarceration and mass deportation as two distinct, and yet overlapping, regimes of control, punishment, and expulsion that intersect with and amplify neoliberalism's racialized mercilessness.

Mass Incarceration

In 1980 the prison population in the United States was approximately 300,000 people. By the 1990s that figure grew to almost 1 million. By the 2000s it had reached 2.4 million people. Presently, one in thirty-five adults in the United States are in prison, on parole, or on probation.[71] The United States accounts for approximately 5 percent of the global population, but warehouses 25 percent of the global prison populations. These statistics are jarring and raise a number of disquieting questions about the rapid development of the United States' vast carceral apparatus. In general, there have been two primary interpretative positions that attempt to account for the explosion of mass incarceration over the past forty years: structural racism and capitalism.

The persistence of structural racism in American history is often pinpointed as the primary cause of the rise of mass incarceration in the United States. Michelle Alexander offers the most famous example of this approach in The New Jim Crow: Mass Incarceration in an Age of Colorblindness (2012). Her book describes how mass incarceration succeeded Jim Crow policies as a new means of social control of African American populations after the end of the formal Jim Crow system. She contends that after the Civil Rights Act in 1964 there emerged a political backlash by disaffected whites who feared that their jobs, educational access, and social standing were threatened by the social transformations associated with the civil rights movement. The Republican Party saw this disaffection as an opportunity for electoral advantage and seized upon it.[72] They successfully deployed the so-called Southern Strategy that utilized coded forms of racism to appeal to whites' racial resentments. After the civil rights movement it was no longer socially acceptable to use explicit forms of racism in public, so politicians employed "dog whistles" to signal to voters that their policies would serve white interests and punish communities of color.[73] Richard Nixon, Ronald Reagan, George H. W. Bush, and Bill Clinton all built a winning electoral strategy around policy proposals to cut welfare, enact a war on drugs, and get tough on crime. As politicians achieved electoral success with dog whistle strategies, they attempted to deliver on their campaign promises by passing legislation that launched the war on drugs and tough-on-crime policies that swept unprecedented numbers of African American men into the criminal justice system. Alexander surveys the results: "more African American adults are under correctional control today—in prison or jail, on probation or parole—than were enslaved in 1850, a decade before the Civil War began."[74]

Alexander argues that the exploitation of racial resentment by politicians drove the rise of mass incarceration. Others have suggested alternative explanations that, without rejecting Alexander's thesis, supplement it by pointing to economic factors behind the expansion of the American carceral complex. Ruth Wilson Gilmore, Angela Davis, Cedric Johnson, and Loïc Wacquant suggest that the crisis of capitalism in the late 1970s and the neoliberal restructuring of society in the 1980s worked in concert with structural racism to create the prison-industrial complex. For these thinkers, the relation between racism and neoliberalism most adequately explains mass incarceration's genesis.[75] There are three notable features of this relation: (1) the management of surplus populations through criminal justice rather than welfare, (2) the management of neoliberal crises through the security state, and (3) the profit-seeking mechanisms of private and public prisons.

First, as a result of neoliberal reforms and the attendant processes of deindustrialization, globalization, and deregulation, sizeable portions of the population have been rendered unemployable and useless by market standards. During the era of industrial capitalism, increases in unemployment were dealt with by expanding the welfare state. Similarly, declines in unemployment meant restriction of welfare benefits in order to push recipients back into the labor market. In their classic work *Regulating the*

Poor (1971), Frances Fox Piven and Richard Cloward argue that this expansion-retraction cycle served to manage the poor and mitigate any social disorder that might result from unemployment.[76] The neoliberal restructuring of economy and the state undermined this approach from two sides by assaulting the Keynesian ideal of full employment and enacting severe cuts to welfare and antipoverty spending.[77] Under neoliberalism, the welfare state has been replaced with a punitive state.[78] It has been estimated that increased prison populations during the rise of mass incarceration shaved almost two percentage points off of US unemployment statistics. Angela Davis detects in mass incarceration something even more insidious: prisons serve to inoculate society from disturbing questions about structural racism and the inequalities generated by capitalism. Prisons "function ideologically as an abstract site into which undesirables are deposited, relieving us of thinking about real issues afflicting those communities from which prisoners are drawn in such disproportionate numbers . . . the prison has become a black hole into which the detritus of contemporary capitalism is deposited."[79] Both spatially and ideologically, prisons warehouse societal problems generated by the nexus between structural racism and neoliberal capitalism.

Second, mass incarceration relates to neoliberalism's tendency to create insecurity for white working-class communities and communities of color alike. A defining feature of neoliberalism is its proneness to constant crisis.[80] The felt sense of precarity produced by neoliberal reforms and their attendant crises, especially among working classes, could be dealt with by resisting neoliberalism and demanding a more extensive redistribution of wealth, greater economic protections, and the revitalization of unions. The alternative, neoliberal approach has been to translate economic insecurity into political insecurity and to reduce the state's function to criminal security provision. Wacquant details this approach: "by elevating criminal safety (*sécurité, Sicherheit, sicurezza*, etc.) to the frontline of government priorities, state officials have condensed the diffuse class anxiety and simmering ethnic resentment generated by the unraveling of the Fordist-Keynesian compact and channeled them toward the (dark-skinned) street criminal, designated as guilty of sowing social and moral disorder in the city, alongside the profligate welfare recipient."[81] In this sense, securitization represents a political strategy of deflection and redirection that immunizes neoliberal policy from critique. Furthermore, it serves as a potent political strategy that assembles white resentment against communities of color.

Third, neoliberalism harnesses the power of capital to profit from incarceration.[82] Prisons have been privatized at an alarming rate during the period of mass incarceration. From 1999 to 2010 the expansion in federal prisoners housed in private prisons grew by 784 percent.[83] At the core of private prison expansion is the claim that private prisons are inherently more efficient and therefore more desirable than public prisons. Contracts are granted on the basis of a bidding process and because these contracts can be terminated, it is argued that privatization offers the most effective means of saving taxpayers' money. But there is a disconnect between the profit-seeking aims and goals of private prisons and the vision that prisons should serve the public good as sites of rehabilitation. The business model of private prisons necessitates ensuring a steady flow of prisoners to fill prison cells. Filled beds mean more profits. Consequently, corporations operating private prisons advocate for policies geared toward higher levels of incarceration. In a 2005 annual report from the Corrections Corporation of America, the authors note that any political or legal attempt to reduce incarceration levels represents a serious threat to their business model:

> The demand for our facilities and services could be adversely affected by the relaxation of enforcement efforts, leniency in conviction and sentencing practices or through the decriminalization of certain activities that are currently proscribed by our criminal laws. For instance, any changes with respect to drugs and controlled substances or illegal immigration could affect the number of persons arrested, convicted, and sentenced, thereby potentially reducing demand for correctional facilities to house them.[84]

Furthermore, private prisons generate profits by spending as little as possible on each individual prisoner. Cost-reduction trumps rehabilitation. Critics argue that private prisons have a vested interest in generating recidivism. This makes sense. The private prison industry needs bodies in beds, and rehabilitation is costly. It follows that privatized prisons are doubly motivated not to rehabilitate prisoners.[85]

The problems lie deeper than individual prison-operating corporations seeking profits. More serious is the existence of a broader network of private entities that profit from public prisons.[86] This nebulous network of government-backed private sector actors is often referred to as the "prison industrial complex." Diverse firms provide food, clothing, medical supplies, and other materials to prisoners in private and public prisons alike. In addition to this vast network, there has been a noticeable shift among other corporations toward using prisoners as cheap labor. This contemporary turn toward "convict leasing" can be traced back to legislation passed in 1979 under the Federal Prison Industries Enhancement Act, which permitted private business to enter into contracts with state prisons.[87] This practice has since expanded to federal and state prisons and is used by Whole Foods, Walmart, AT&T, BP, and many other companies. This practice is often called "insourcing" and is billed as an alternative to outsourcing labor to China, Bangladesh, or other areas in the Global South. Corporations employ prisoners at a rate far below minimum wage (the average rate per hour is between 86 cents and 3.45 dollars).[88] Furthermore, companies paying these rock-bottom wages bear no responsibility for health insurance or other benefits such as sick days, vacation, or retirement. Nor must they deal with unions. We have seen that prisons function as warehouses for market undesirables, which largely is true. But now we must add that, if the price of their labor sinks low enough, prisoners become desirable once more.[89]

None of these issues on their own—structural racism, surplus populations, securitization, for-profit prisons—fully accounts for the phenomenon of mass incarceration. But by analyzing them together we start to see how the perverse convergence of deep-seated racial resentments, dog-whistle politics, disemboweling of social programs, and attempts to manage macroeconomic shifts through expulsion has contributed to a crisis that exposes the lie of contemporary America's so-called colorblindness.

Mass Deportation

The United States is currently in the midst of an immigration-deportation crisis. During the 2016 election this issue served as a flashpoint. Donald Trump inveighed against "illegal immigrants," called for a "Muslim ban," and proclaimed that the construction of a wall at the US-Mexico border would be a central focus of his presidency. Furthermore, Trump announced that it would be necessary to build a "deportation force" in order to forcibly remove 11 million undocumented immigrants from the United States.[90] Although Trump's rhetoric has been more inflammatory than previous presidents, his record is broadly consistent with his predecessors. Trump is on track to deport a similar number of undocumented immigrants to Bush (2 million) and Obama (2.5 million), if current trends continue and he serves eight years in office. The deportation crisis has been building since the late 1990s after the implementation of the North American Free Trade Agreement (1994) and the Illegal Immigration Reform and Immigration Responsibility Act (1996).[91] It has been estimated that more people have been forcibly removed from the United States in the first eighteen years of the 2000s than the entire prior history of the United States.[92]

In what follows we will narrate the emergence of the immigration-mass deportation crisis in the 2000s as the result of the complex interaction between a history of racialized immigration laws with economic-political convulsions associated with neoliberal policy.

The history of immigration policy in the United States is part and parcel of the history of structural racism. The United States first enacted a naturalization law in 1790 that restricted citizenship to "free white persons." Citizenship was refused to Native Americans and African slaves. This restriction remained in place until 1870. In the aftermath of the Civil War the category of citizenship was applied to "white(s)" and those of "African nativity or African descent." This same right of citizenship would not be granted to Native Americans and Asians until the 1940s.[93] And it was not until the passage of the Immigration and Nationality Act (1965) that explicit race-based justification for exclusion was eliminated from American immigration law. The United States replaced race-based exclusions with a quota system that permitted 120,000 persons annually from the Western hemisphere and 170,000 persons from the Eastern hemisphere to immigrate to the United States irrespective of their race and ethnicity.[94] The 1965 legislation limited immigration to 20,000 persons from any individual country in the Eastern hemisphere. And in 1976 this 20,000-person limit was applied to the Western hemisphere as well. Finally, the Immigration Act of 1978 eliminated the quotas based on hemisphere with a global quota of 290,000 per year and a limit of 20,000 from any one country.

While race-based exclusions were officially eliminated with the 1965 reform, it created a new set of problems. Mexican migrant workers had long served as seasonal farm laborers in the West and Southwest regions of the United States. The Bracero Program formalized seasonal migration of Mexican laborers to the United States from 1942 to 1964, bringing almost 500,000 laborers to the United States every year. Following the reforms of 1965, 1976, and 1978 the need for inexpensive, seasonal labor remained, but the mechanism for delivering this labor had been eliminated. The restriction of immigrants to 20,000 per year from countries in the Western hemisphere was particularly problematic for Mexico, since it had provided the United States almost half a million migrant workers each year during harvest season. Thus, Mexican laborers were forced to return to the informal system that existed before the Bracero Program. Now that informal system has been outlawed. Those who returned for work were labeled "illegals" and excluded from legal protections.

This complex history of racist and exclusionary immigration law interrelates with neoliberalism in three ways, which should sound familiar given our discussion of similar phenomena in conjunction with mass incarceration: (1) the creation of exploitable labor, (2) processes of securitization, and (3) the expansion of for-profit immigration, detention, and deportation services.

One of the structural causes for accelerating migration of Mexicans to the United States after the reforms of 1965, 1976, and 1978 was the 1994 North American Free Trade Agreement (NAFTA). This policy had a devastating effect on rural Mexican farmers by permitting heavily subsidized American corn to flood the Mexican market. In the two years after the implementation of NAFTA the poverty rate in Mexico jumped from 52 percent to 69 percent. The introduction of cheap American agriculture into Mexico displaced approximately 15 million Mexican farmers from their land. This displacement led to massive waves of migration into Mexican urban centers and into the United States. The end result was that the undocumented population in the United States swelled from 2.2 million before NAFTA to over 11 million by 2005, where it has remained ever since.[95]

The social dislocation created by NAFTA, qua neoliberal reform, benefited US corporations by providing agricultural and other industries with a steady pool of exploitable labor. In this sense, the situation is markedly different than that of mass incarceration. With mass incarceration the processes of deindustrialization and globalization created a surplus labor population that was managed by the criminal justice system. After the reform of 1965 and subsequent immigration reforms, it is not a surplus of labor but rather a lack of exploitable labor in certain sectors that was the problem.[96] American industries continued to need laborers willing to work in undesirable jobs for pay below minimum wage, but these workers could not be found among US citizens. This situation was remedied by exploiting a reserve of laborers rendered exploitable precisely because of their status as "illegal."[97]

The construction of illegality and the threat of deportation reinforce the vulnerability and exploitability of this population. The threat of deportation generates docile laborers with few legal protections and little or no access to social entitlements. Nicholas de Genova contends that deportation serves an economic purpose, even if it is unrealizable as a political project: "it is deportability, and not deportation per se, that has historically rendered undocumented migrant labor a distinctly disposable commodity. There has never been sufficient funding for the INS to evacuate the United States of undocumented migrants by means of deportations, nor even for the Border Patrol to 'hold the line.'"[98] Although deportations have increased since de Genova wrote this in 2002, the analysis remains valid insofar as the primary function of deportation is not literally to expel undocumented migrants from the country. Rather, it serves as a means of ensuring the continued marginalization and exploitability of those who remain in the United States. That said, in times of recession, as the one brought about by the 2008 financial crisis, deportation is employed to expel surplus labor. Tanya Golash-Boza observes: "The mass deportation of men of color is part of a U.S. policy response designed to relocate surplus labor to the periphery and to keep labor in the United States compliant."[99] Beyond these economic functions, deportability serves at a political level to rally certain constituencies around the perceived need for intensified (racialized) security enforcement.[100]

Perhaps neoliberalism's central paradox is its demand for expanded state security regimes set alongside calls to eliminate most government programs. While this paradox may remain unresolvable, it makes more sense once one realizes that deregulation and globalization undermine economic sovereignty, thus stoking nostalgia for national (and racial) sovereignty. Such nostalgia emerged with particular clarity in the 2016 election with Trump's incessant talk about a prospective wall along the

US-Mexico border. But this case is by no means unique. It fits with broader, transnational agitation for intensified securitization at borders including in Europe and the Middle East. Current demands for walls differ from those of previous epochs, when walls were erected to claim territorial sovereignty and prevent foreign countries from invasion. Currently the demand for walls responds largely to nonstate actors: migrants and terrorists. Incongruously, these walls rarely constitute an effective means of interdicting, monitoring, or controlling the flow of goods and peoples across borders.[101] But walls—even when just imagined and promised—supply the state with tangible evidence that it cares for its citizens' security. And even in the absence of real security, walls potently symbolize national sovereignty in an age of its widespread dissolution.

The migration crisis interweaves with the prison industrial complex, since neoliberalism has created a vast carceral and security apparatus that profits from immigration enforcement and deportation. This apparatus has been described as the "border-industrial complex" (Akers Chacón and Mike Davis) and the "immigration industrial complex" (Deepa Fernandes, Golash-Boza).[102] As with the military-industrial complex and the prison-industrial complex, critics of the immigration-industrial complex analyze the collusion between state agencies and private corporations in the expansion of methods of securitization, enforcement, and punishment of vulnerable populations. For instance, in 2009 Congress passed appropriations laws that mandated a detention bed quota at thirty-four thousand beds per year. Every day that an individual is detained costs taxpayers 120 dollars. Over the course of a year, this detention bed quota costs taxpayers approximately 2 billion dollars—thus providing revenue in the same amount to companies operating detention centers.[103]

The detention bed quota is just the tip of the iceberg of the profit-seeking motives that align state agencies with private corporations. Roxanne Doty and Elizabeth Wheatley describe four features that interlock to sustain the immigration-industrial complex. First, the legal apparatus, represented by laws that range from the Illegal Immigration Reform and Responsibility Act (1996) to Arizona's S.B. 1070 (2010), augments measures to identify, punish, or expel undocumented migrants from the United States. Second, the expansion of prison corporations accommodates intensified focus on enforcement. The two largest prison corporations in the United States, CoreCivic and GEO Group, garner over 10 percent of their revenue from

Immigration and Customs Enforcement (ICE) by providing a broad array of detention services. Third, the ideologies of neoliberalism and securitization have supported the expansion of the immigration-industrial complex. The neoliberal commitment to privatization and to the market as a more efficient and cost-effective method for delivering social services has been the central ideological justification for growth in detention sectors. Doty and Wheatley point to criminalization as a critical ideological component that legitimates rising costs associated with the immigration-industrial complex. By stoking fear about criminality among immigrant populations— when, in point of fact, immigrants on average commit fewer crimes than native-born populations—politicians and media enable targeting of these populations for containment and expulsion (with their attendant costs) rather than reform and inclusion.[104] Fourth, private corporations that profit from detention and deportation commit significant resources to lobbying efforts that attempt to influence legislation and funding priorities and direct them toward the strategic priorities of their business model.[105]

With this we see that, in ways similar to mass incarceration, the immigration industrial complex combines a variety of factors, threaded together by neoliberal economics and political common sense and braided with racial animus and racist structures, to yield a crisis that threatens millions of people in the United States—all that so a tiny fraction of the population can profit handily from their precarity.[106]

The Politics of Racial Neoliberalism

Let us return briefly to Alexander's argument. She contends that mass incarceration amounts to a thoroughgoing redesigning of old Jim Crow-style legalized discrimination. Once Jim Crow was outlawed with the Civil Rights Act of 1964, imprisonment became the new method for reinstating legalized discrimination and disenfranchisement. The racial caste system was reconstituted in response to shifting labor needs within American society. After the eras dominated by slavery, sharecropping, and manufacture, the new era of mass unemployment for African Americans became the era of mass incarceration of African Americans and other expendable populations no longer needed by the labor market.

Aviva Chomsky maintains that a similar operation is at play with the current immigration-deportation crisis among Latinx persons in the United

States. The legal discriminations against immigrants outlawed with the Immigration and Nationality Act (1965) were redesigned through the invention of "illegality." Once migrants are labeled as "illegal," all manner of exploitation becomes permissible. Chomsky describes the experience of undocumented immigrants as one of "internal exile" and "civic death," since "illegal" status excludes them from voting rights and public benefits.[107]

Neoliberalism's rise coincides with new "colorblind" forms of discrimination. Given neoliberalism's everyday mercilessness and its penchant for securitization, it becomes perfectly reasonable (per neoliberal political rationality) to aid and abet discrimination in the forms of criminalization, punishment, imprisonment, and deportation of market "losers." Marketized colorblindness has masked racial animus in politics, thus offering proponents of mass incarceration and mass deportation plausible deniability regarding their politics' driving urges.

Neoliberalism has intersected with, exacerbated, and sought to profit from crises generated by structural racism. Neoliberalism has redesigned structural racism to create systems predicated on the logic of exclusion and expulsion, barring vulnerable populations from access to work, housing, community life, healthcare, education, and various state benefits and protections.[108] Having considered racial neoliberalism, we can see the logic of neoliberal mercilessness in a new light, as attaching itself to ongoing histories of racialized exclusion while profiting from the social misery produced by these forms of exclusion.

From a Catholic perspective, racial neoliberalism is an ethos that follows from a stunting of people's capacity for seeing the truth of human dignity (through reducing people to racial categories and dog-whistle labels) and a perversion of people's capacity for compassion (through reducing our sensibilities to the need for security above all else, dulling our ability to feel disturbed at the suffering of others), resulting in a way of life predicated upon corrupt structures and institutions such as mass incarceration and mass deportation that, almost as evidence of their objective falsity, are largely kept hidden from the public.

Neoliberalism as Culture of Indifference

The question we are left with after examining the four crises of environmental destruction, slum proliferation, mass incarceration, and mass deportation is this: How are these crises not causing widespread outcry, to the extent that neoliberalism would be discredited and alternatives eagerly embraced? How, more briefly, can people be indifferent to the crises of neoliberalism?

While Pope Francis does not pretend to be able to answer such questions completely, his cultural diagnoses demonstrate that he has asked and reflected upon them. We began this chapter with Francis's analysis of faceless economy and its relationship to a culture of exclusion in which persons are pushed to the margins and expelled from the social order. In *Evangelii Gaudium*, in the section "No to an Economy of Exclusion," Francis suggests that the dominant economic system generates both intolerable forms of "exclusion" and "inequality." The market enforces the rule that everything that is not of short-term financial value can be sacrificed, including the earth and its most vulnerable inhabitants. Francis declares: "In this system, which tends to devour everything which stands in the way of increased profits, whatever is fragile, like the environment, is defenseless before the interests of a deified market, which become the only rule" (*EG*, 56). Thus, a culture of exclusion, or a throwaway culture (*LS*, 16 22, 43), is born in which "everything has a price" and persons and things not deemed valuable by market standards can be discarded, expelled, or eliminated. Those without "value" are market "losers." Society, following the protocols of market logic, punishes these losers; "this way of thinking has room only for a select few, while it discards all those who are unproductive."[109] A culture of exclusion, then, represents an inevitable consequence of a faceless economy insofar as it forces individuals to focus on abstract and impersonal metrics rather than the preservation of dignified life and sustainability.

This culture's other profile is a culture of indifference (see *LS*, 25, 53, 92, 246). This side of the economy of exclusion affects even those who succeed according to its standards. As we discussed in chapter 1, Francis maintains that a new idol has emerged in the world, the idol of money. He argues that "we calmly accept its dominion over ourselves and our societies" (*EG*, 55). The acceptance of this idol's power over us is not a mere cognitive matter (though such ill thinking would be bad enough), but instead represents a reality that shapes us affectively, forms us as subjects, and trains us to engage in the world in very specific ways. In particular, Francis maintains that it forms us to be inordinately attached to the imperatives of the market and indifferent to exclusion and social suffering. Francis observes:

> To sustain a lifestyle which excludes others, or to sustain enthusiasm for that selfish ideal, a globalization of indifference has developed. Almost without being aware of it, we end up being incapable of feeling compassion at the outcry of the poor, weeping for other people's pain, and feeling a need to help them, as though all of this were someone else's responsibility and not our own. The culture of prosperity deadens us; we are thrilled if the market offers us something new to purchase. In the meantime, all those lives stunted for lack of opportunity seem a mere spectacle; they fail to move us. (EG, 54)

Our capacity to feel and be affected by the suffering of others has been dulled, even deadened, through our capitulation to market culture. Francis proposes that an alternative culture, a culture of encounter, is needed to contest this culture of indifference. We will say a bit more about this in chapter 4 in conjunction with Francis's interpretation of the parable of the Good Samaritan. But before we move to that chapter, we should deepen our understanding of the culture of indifference by examining Francis's comparatively little-known essay "Corruption and Sin."[110]

The essay was originally published in 1991, amid a scandal in Argentina centering on a politically impeded rape-and-murder investigation in the Catamarca province. It was republished in 2005; then-Cardinal Bergoglio intended it to be read as an Advent examination of conscience.[111] The essay does not concern neoliberalism directly. But it includes a set of theological reflections on personal and political corruption that can provide a theological framework for criticizing neoliberalism as an ethos. Furthermore, the language that Bergoglio uses to describe corruption resonates strongly with many critical phrases he directs against "the economy that kills."

Bergoglio draws a fundamental distinction in this text between sin and corruption. In the 2005 preface he deems it unfit to "accept the state of corruption as just another sin."[112] The distinction lies in this: sin is something that a person (eventually) recognizes about himself, both inwardly and outwardly; ultimately it is ordered toward a request for God's mercy.[113] Corruption, however, is not ordered toward God's mercy, but rather consists in being "tired of asking for forgiveness," and in considering oneself "sufficient for [one's] own salvation."[114] Corruption is not mere hypocrisy, according to Bergoglio. Instead, he views it as an attack on truth itself that promises disaster for the corrupt person: "In setting themselves up as the measure of all things, there is an underlying danger: no one can twist reality so much without running the risk of that same reality turning against them."[115] He continues: "Being is transcendentally *verum*, true, and I can twist it and wring it like a towel, denying the truth; but being will continue to be true, even if, in the context of a particular situation, someone manages to present it otherwise."[116] In this way Bergoglio construes corruption as a kind of sick, constructivist project. Corruption brings with it an air of triumph, of being the standard of judgment (above truth). Corrupt people divide others according to this standard. One is "either an accomplice or an enemy."[117] Corruption becomes common sense—it is purveyed as the only realistic way. It is more than contagious, as sin and temptation are; it "actively proselytizes."[118] It becomes socially acceptable, and its effects can be easily shrugged off, through "social cosmetics."[119] This is all to say, if we switch briefly from Bergoglio's lexicon to Wendy Brown's, that corruption is sin qualitatively intensified into a political rationality: a constructive form of reason that ousts what would otherwise be recognized as truth, presenting itself as bedrock for judgment and as the common sense that all people should hold, and to which all people (in principle) are brought through dissemination and reeducation.

Bergoglio relates his description of corruption to a meditation from St. Ignatius's *Spiritual Exercises* called the meditation on the Two Standards. In this meditation, Ignatius instructs the person making the Exercises to imagine life as a battlefield, where the armies of Christ and Lucifer vie for souls to add to the forces fighting under their respective battle flags, or "standards." Lucifer's soldiers, or demons, seduce people through a progressive set of temptations, starting with riches, proceeding through worldly honor, and on to pride.[120] The point of these temptations "is not to make them commit sins, but rather to ensnare men in the state of sin, in the state of corruption."[121] The devil plans "to create a condition strong enough to resist the invitation to grace."[122] Christ invites people into a share in God's life; the devil actively resists people accepting this share in God's life, precisely by locking themselves into their own high self-estimation and, consequently, their disregard for or mercilessness toward others. This small section on Ignatius should be underscored: Bergoglio depicts corruption as demonic.

It should also be highlighted, in keeping with Bergoglio's criticism of "social cosmetics," that corruption is not only an individual phenomenon, but a collective one. Bergoglio declares: "Corruption is not an act but a state, a personal and collective state, to which people get accustomed and in which they live. The values (or non-values) of corruption are integrated into a real culture, with a capacity for its own systematic doctrine, its own language, and its own particular way of acting."[123] The state of corruption habituates people into being corrupt. This "state" becomes a culture, defined by corrupt values, bolstered by an ordered set of teachings on truth, a way of speaking, and a set of practices. In this way, corruption becomes global, comprehensive, a political rationality.

Lest it seem like we are extrapolating too far, pushing Bergoglio in Brown's direction, his further analyses of corruption can be marshalled along the same trajectory. Bergoglio identifies a dual dynamism at play in corruption that, as we see it, gives it the air of a (perverse) political rationality. The dual dynamism has to do with two classic philosophical dyads: appearance–reality and transcendence–immanence. Corruption distorts both, at least from the point of view of Catholicism. Corruption takes no interest in reality breaking out as truthful appearance. Instead, corruption constructs reality "in such a way that it can be imposed and accepted as widely as possible in society" (i.e., making it *appear* attractive, often through deception); it takes away reality and replaces it with appearance.[124] Hence Bergoglio's deployment of the potent phrase "social cosmetics." Corruption renders all transcendence immanent, reducing it to "at most, an armchair transcendence."[125] Being, which for Bergoglio is truth, is "ill-treated through a kind of socially acceptable shamelessness."[126] These may seem like very heady accusations, steeped perhaps in outdated Catholic metaphysics—unless one takes into account a new example (far more recent than Bergoglio's essay) that corroborates his concerns: the Trump administration's complete unconcern with truth, its purveying of "alternative facts," its promotion (in word) and often enforcement (in deed) of a nostalgic, "conservative" table of values that its figurehead (Donald Trump himself) clearly does not follow, all to give the sheen of a moral, Christianity-friendly government that is nothing of the sort. Corruption consists in a political rationality without discernible reason, an ontology without recognizable being. If political rationality is, as we argue in chapter 2, a gatekeeper for reality, we could say that corruption as political rationality makes everything unreal; reality itself is merely a function of cosmetics, of manipulation, of the art of the deal.

Corruption breeds a culture of shamelessness. Catholic hope holds out that even great sinners can avoid becoming corrupt, so long as they remain open to forgiveness.[127] So long as sinners feel their hearts' weakness, they stand on the threshold of possible salvation. This is the difference between the sinful and the corrupt. The corrupt no longer feel their hearts' weakness. They no longer perceive their need to be forgiven. They close themselves to mercy.[128] The heart of the corrupt one becomes a "root of bitterness" (see Heb 12:15). Sinful people can remain open to transcendence; the corrupt become self-contained. Like Ananias and Sapphira, the couple who knowingly withheld for themselves money they had promised to the community for the benefit of all, the corrupt attempt to seal themselves off from God and others, thus "testing the Spirit of the Lord"—potentially with the same catastrophic results (Acts 5:1–11).[129]

With Bergoglio's idea of "corruption," we gain an important diagnostic tool for examining neoliberalism theologically. When he calls corruption a "state," he means a condition of the depth dimension of individuals and a whole society. When he first penned this critique of corruption, he directed it against an Argentine culture that had degenerated into allowing police brutality and negligence, widespread violence and wrongdoing of various sorts, and betrayals of Argentina's ostensive Catholic heritage. We have already begun to point out how his critique of corruption has wider applicability for examining twisted political rationalities, which operate at the same level as does corruption, and with the example of the Trump administration, which we have designated as an example of neoliberalism's latest degeneracy, we opened the lines of communication still more.

Several insights emerge from this reading of Francis's "Corruption and Sin" as it may be applied to neoliberalism and its concomitant culture of indifference. First, neoliberalism is a system that constructs the market as above truth, just as corruption is a constructivism that wrings the life out of truth. Evidence for this abounds, even if we take into account only the crises this chapter has treated: climate change denialism as performing an agnosticism that disregards scientific fact; the obscuring of dire conditions in slums through entrepreneurial rhetoric; and the distortion of human dignity through enhanced racism and a hidden carceral and deportation complex. Second, neoliberalism is triumphalist in the way that Francis says is endemic to corruption. Neoliberal slogans such as "there is no alternative" and "the end of history" (the neoliberal refrain after 1989) and the spirit of victory that carried neoliberalism through the global financial crash of 2008 (and more local ones, such as the collapse of the "Asian tiger" economies in 1997 or Argentina's depression from 1998 to 2002) serve as ample evidence. Third, as with corruption, neoliberalism sets itself up as common sense and assiduously sets to educating people in this common sense. Nothing forestalls action on crises like a system that autoimmunizes by teaching people to assume it as natural. Such naturalization may be a constitutive feature of capitalism in all its forms, or even beyond that systems of power generally, but neoliberalism has been distinctively effective at promoting itself as common sense. Fourth, for this work of theology, the specifically theological valence of Francis's category of corruption commands serious attention as well. Francis's allusions to the Ignatian meditation on the Two Standards levels a grave charge against corruption, namely that it is demonic or Luciferian, the result of human freedom being tempted by and capitulating to an ethos that twists truth, triumphalistically brandishes this twisted truth as a viable guide for living, and then presents such contorted living as a common standard, an ethos stamped by the devil, the deceiver.[130] Fifth, all of this may be tied together by one more theological valence, which relates to mercy, the chief theological topic of this entire book. A corrupt life is a life that regards itself as beyond mercy, that views mercy as no longer possible. Surely neoliberalism remains at best agnostic with regard to mercy and forgiveness. We suspect, though, that at least in its performance, exemplified by the four crises described in the current chapter, neoliberalism attempts definitively to leave mercy behind.

Given all this we can confirm Francis's diagnosis of the culture of indifference, and using one of his own texts, we can sharpen that charge. Neoliberalism breeds an extraordinarily pernicious kind of indifference. This indifference is apathy, for sure, but a creative-destructive apathy perfectly primed *not* to address neoliberalism's crises.

Part III: Catholic Mercy in a Neoliberal Age

4   A Theology of Mercy

Undergirding and impelling the papal critique of economism that we set forth in chapter 1 is a theology of mercy. We indicated this preliminarily in the introductory remarks to our presentations of each pope's social teachings. Now that we have spent two chapters considering neoliberalism as our world's dominant form of economism we can return to the theology of mercy that we pointed to in chapter 1. We mean here to use certain elements of systematic theology to counter neoliberalism. This exercise in discursive resistance arises from our attempt to take neoliberalism seriously not just as an approach to political economy but also as a political rationality that gives shape to a new reality and an ethos that deforms everyday life.[1]

We argue that the neoliberal account of reality must be resisted as much as the facts of neoliberalization and that systematic theology provides necessary tools for thinking, imagining, and enacting a distinctively anti-neoliberal, Catholic politics that befits the Catholic ethos of mercy.[2] A theology of mercy must oppose neoliberalism's central devotion to the impersonal market, its human capital anthropology, its assembly of human capital around an ethic of competition and mercilessness, and its culture of sacrifice to the market as the new golden calf. Such opposition will support and coordinate with what we call a politics of mercy. This chapter opens this opposition by presenting Catholicism's central devotion to the merciful Trinitarian God, its anthropology of "being neighbor," its assembly (ekklesia) of people around an ethic of Christic mercy and hospitality, and its culture of charity, which, again, we see as primed to give rise to a politics of mercy.[3]

We link this chapter's systematic theological intervention with our presentation of the popes' critiques of economism in chapter 1 by drawing Trinitarian, anthropological, and ecclesiological ideas from the popes' writings and, in some places, supplementing those with ideas from theologians with whom the popes associate themselves (the prime example being Francis's collaboration with Walter Kasper). When we discuss the works of mercy, the popes have something to say as well. But as we move toward elucidating a politics of mercy, we converse with several voices beyond the popes to do two things they do not do with adequate thoroughness: (1) reimagine the works of mercy as ramifying structurally and (2) indicate how these ramifications can bear upon neoliberalized economies, politics, and cultures in particular. By carrying the popes' theological legacy forward into thinking about a politics of mercy, we intend to follow the trajectory that they have already established and that, given how CST has developed from John Paul's earliest social encyclical to Francis's latest social pronouncements, is beginning to emerge within papal teaching as well as in wider Catholic discourses and practices. The systematic theological reflections on mercy we record here are not only meant to deepen our critique of neoliberalism but also to provide resources for those who want to imagine and build a world beyond neoliberalism, a world marked foremost by mercy rather than by market sacrifice.

Trinity, Mystery, and Mercy

Neoliberalism's bedrock commitment is to the market, which, as an information processing and distributing system beyond human comprehension, must be honored with silence. Hayek influentially refers to the market as a "cosmos," or a cosmic process that cannot be second-guessed and that demands human submission. For instance, in his pivotal *The Mirage of Social Justice*, Hayek declares: "It is precisely because in the cosmos of the market we all constantly receive benefits which we have not deserved in any moral sense that we are under an obligation also to accept equally undeserved diminutions of our incomes. Our only moral title to what the market gives us we have earned by submitting to those rules which makes the formation of the market order possible."[4] Even more, we have "the obligation to abide by the results of the market also when it turns against us."[5] It is hardly a stretch to sound out the theological resonances of these statements. The market bears sovereign freedom, which it uses to bestow graces on undeserving recipients. These graces impose certain obligations, as if in a covenant. And even when these graces are withdrawn, the market demands loyalty since, the implication goes, the market knows best. In the same text, Hayek depicts "social justice" as the phrase that encapsulates the main infraction against people's obligations to the market. Demanding equitable distribution of goods and services fundamentally misunderstands what occurs in a market economy, and this error stems from a misconception regarding what the market is. The market is not a personal "distributive agent."[6] Instead, the market is an "impersonal process" that cannot be held to account for supposed "injustice."[7]

We have, then, a paradox: the market bestows all but is not a distributive agent. This is the central mystery—that the market must be honored with submission—but not related to as "personal," for such a relation would bring dishonorable demands from the *demos*. The market seems to desire sacrifice; but as an impersonal agent, it would likewise seem entirely apart from justice, let alone mercy. And there is a further paradox, which we know well from chapter 2: although the market is presented as sovereign, the market is ever in need of protection, encasement, even production. Certainly, it is a mystery why such a sovereign should command silence, submission, and sacrifice. Because of these paradoxes at the heart of neoliberalism, it is more than reasonable that scholars such as Slobodian should describe it as a "negative theology."[8]

Christianity has a different bedrock commitment: to the plural unity of a merciful God who is honored through personal prayer and love of neighbor, and by a people that assembles around the person who reveals God's mercy in the flesh, Jesus Christ. This God is not a cosmos but the One who made the cosmos, loving it into being and never hating anything God made (Wis 11:24). In a way akin to the neoliberal market, although superior to it in creative power, this God's distribution of graces carries with it a set of obligations that center on the injunction to "be merciful." Unlike the neoliberal market, this God does not shy away from being a personal distributive agent, and what God gives personally sets the standard for justice. This God does not need protection or encasement from any earthly agent or institution. Because of God's exalted wisdom, which God freely bestows, God remains a mystery, but this God is unlike the "god" of the market, which fails to communicate, remains inscrutable, and gives no wisdom. Far from an impersonal process (or information processor), this God is a God of love (1 Jn 4:16), rich in mercy (Eph 2:4), the one who desires mercy, not sacrifice (Hos 6:6; Mt 9:13), and whose steadfast love endures forever (Ps 136).

We mean to suggest that the conflict between the neoliberal market and the Trinitarian God is over what reality is at its fundamental level. If reality is inconstant, inscrutable, with no discernible connection to justice (other than market rules), then a neoliberal order of class warfare, diminished substantial freedom, de-democratization, theaters of cruelty, accelerated environmental destruction, slum proliferation, mass incarceration, and mass deportation, at the very least, makes some sense. However, if reality is fundamentally love, mercy, and steadfast kindness, the crises of neoliberalism to which we have just pointed make no sense and should be decried as false and, indeed, evil. In order to provide some ingredients for such an outcry, we sketch a Trinitarian theology.

The Trinity

Trinitarian theology provides a mercy-centered view of reality. We commence with Walter Kasper, whose book *Barmherzigkeit* (*Mercy*, 2012) received a prominent endorsement during Pope Francis's first Angelus blessing (March 17, 2013).[9] Reflecting upon Kasper's work, Francis proclaimed, "A little mercy makes the world less cold and more just. We need to understand properly this mercy of God, this merciful Father who is so patient. . . . Let us remember the Prophet Isaiah who says that even if our sins were scarlet, God's love would make them white as snow [Is 1:18]. This mercy is beautiful!" Kasper devotes *Mercy*'s central chapter to systematic theological reflections that embed the theme of mercy within the theology of God.[10] He does this in reaction to what he perceives as a "catastrophic" failure to integrate mercy into systematic theology.[11] We concur with his insight that mercy should enjoy a more central position in systematic theology, especially as systematic theology responds to neoliberalism in light of CST. Kasper roots his treatment of the Trinitarian God and mercy in the social writings of John XXIII, John Paul II, and Benedict XVI and aims to present a composite account of the theology that inspires their teachings on peace, development, and social logics.

Kasper contends that a Trinitarian theology centered on God's mercy testifies to God's sovereign freedom, by which God decides to bestow on humanity forgiveness, help in trials, redemption, and love.[12] As Kasper sees it, Trinitarian theology begins with exegesis of 1 John 4:8 and 16, "God is love."[13] Drawing out the meaning of this statement, one discovers that "the one and only God is no solitary and dead God, but rather that God, in himself, is life and love."[14] And this God is intrinsically self-communicating, always sharing God's very self, each Trinitarian person, Father, Son, and Holy Spirit, with the other. Christians make sense of God's outward expression of mercy by way of discovering God's free, gracious, inner life of love, revealed so potently in the First Letter of John, which in turn gives readers of the Gospels a sense of the relation between Jesus, the one he calls Father, and the Spirit he claims will be sent after him (see Mt 11:27, 28:18; Lk 10:22; Jn 3:35, 10:30, 13:3, 14:9, 14:26, 14:28, 19:30). Kasper contends, "The triunity of God is, therefore, the inner presupposition of God's mercy, just as, conversely, his mercy is the revelation and mirror of his essence."[15] Kasper clarifies that God does not self-actualize (implying a change in God) when God's mercy becomes a reality for creation. Instead, this constitutes the event by which people are invited to take their place "beside God's heart."[16] Kasper plays a bit here on the German word *Barmherzigkeit* (mercy), which has the word *Herz* (heart) at its center. Central to mercy is the heart.

With the theme of "heart" raised, let us depart momentarily from Kasper's theology of mercy to the encyclical John Paul II wrote just before *Laborem Exercens*, whose title, *Dives in Misericordia (Rich in Mercy)*, points to the divine Father as the source, the heart of mercy. John Paul's presentation of the Father's mercy hinges on his exegesis of the prodigal son parable from Luke's Gospel (Lk 15:11–32). John Paul sets up his exegesis by briefly considering how Jesus makes manifest the Father's mercy in his preaching. He names the parables of the prodigal son and the Good Samaritan (Lk 10:30–37), and by contrast the parable of the merciless servant (Mt 18:23–35) as evidence (*DM*, 3). Through such parables, Jesus reveals that people "should be guided in their lives by love and mercy"; this "constitutes the heart of the Gospel ethos" (*DM*, 3).

John Paul's interpretation of the prodigal son parable delineates with striking insight the exact contours of love and mercy that should guide human life. The love and mercy shown by the father toward his wayward son defy common expectations. Normally people evaluate mercy "from the outside," thus roughly equating it with paternalism, where mercy would "belittle the receiver" and "offend" human dignity (*DM*, 6). But the mercy of the father in the parable is different. Effusive generosity defines it. Far from being diminished, the son's enduring value is recognized, "restored" in the sense of being acknowledged once more (*DM*, 6). The son has squandered his monetary inheritance and, so he thinks, displaced himself from the dignity of being son to his father (*DM*, 5). But his father's deeply affectionate reaction to the son's return from his dissolute living tells another story. The father conducts himself with compassion from the heart that displays the kind of faithful love (*hesed*) that God enacts throughout the Old Testament (*DM*, 6). John Paul presents the father's love and mercy as "fidelity to himself," to his own fatherhood—thus, as we read John Paul, to the father's promises to the son whom he values beyond number. The father remains faithful to himself as father precisely by valuing his son, upholding his son's dignity. He takes joy in the son's return, thus testifying to the son's abiding dignity (*DM*, 6). Far from discounting the son's own dignity, the father's fidelity underscores it.

John Paul regards the father in the parable as an analogy for the God Jesus calls "Father." From the parable we learn about the mercy of the one now called the first person of the Trinity. John Paul explains, "The true and proper meaning of mercy does not consist only in looking, however penetratingly and compassionately, at moral, physical or material evil: mercy is manifested in its true and proper aspect when it restores to value, promotes and draws good from all the forms of evil existing in the world and in man" (*DM*, 6).[17] "Restores to value" is the key phrase. Mercy meets evil, which here is figured as degradation of value, by putting value (back) in place. God the Father's mercy reveals itself through Jesus's preaching, and indeed Jesus's life, as recognizing the dignity of God's creation, especially human persons.

It is worth briefly contrasting the picture John Paul paints of the Father's mercy with the mercilessness of the neoliberal market. The market is fickle, inscrutably parsimonious, and recognizes no dignity or constant value of any sort, instead reducing all people to things and all things to variable prices, rates, and indexes. The discrepancy between the first person of the Trinity and the neoliberal *primum ens* could not be plainer.

The theme of the "heart" also relates to the second Trinitarian person, Jesus Christ. The reference to "heart" we noted in Kasper's *Mercy* leads him into an excursus on a classic Catholic devotion: veneration of Jesus's Sacred Heart.[18] Despite its recent decline, this devotion, properly understood, provides a pathway for understanding the Trinity as free, personal, and self-communicating. Kasper observes, echoing Bonaventure, "In the heart of Jesus, we recognize that God himself has a heart (*cor*) for us, who are poor (*miseri*), in the broadest sense of the word, and that he is, therefore, merciful (*misericors*)."[19] The Sacred Heart proves emblematic of intra-Trinitarian love—and mercy, as exemplified in the devotion to divine mercy initiated by Polish sister St. Faustina Kowalska (1905–38) and championed by John Paul II.

In a 1999 letter to commemorate Pope Leo XIII's consecration of humanity to Jesus's Sacred Heart, John Paul relates the Sacred Heart devotion to what he had written of the Father's mercy in *Dives in Misericordia*.[20] He recalls that the Father's mercy is professed in a special way in the Catholic Church when Christ's heart is venerated. Through the Heart of Jesus, divine mercy becomes accessible on a human level, thus giving hope. John Paul argues, looking ahead to the new millennium, that the person "of the year 2000 needs Christ's Heart to know God and to know himself; he needs it to build the civilization of love."[21] The fact that Jesus revealed God's mercy by working with human hands and loving with a human heart should not be lost on Jesus's followers; in fact, it should be put front and center. The Sacred Heart devotion helps to do that. John Paul recognizes that, in 1999, this devotion does not have the currency it did even a half a century before. Nevertheless, he encourages the study and practice of it "with language and forms adapted to our times."[22]

Kasper provides similar encouragement. He engages the Sacred Heart devotion within the horizon of modern, European secularization. He notes that "the modern veneration of the sacred heart of Jesus became pervasive in the context of the dawning Enlightenment and secularization, and in connection with the strengthening sense of the absence—indeed, the death—of God."[23] Kasper deems it telling and hopeful that as the Western world grew obtuse and apathetic toward God's love, many Christians took solace precisely in God's long-suffering love, symbolized in the heart of Christ.

Echoing John Paul and Kasper, we suggest that the Sacred Heart devotion be given attention in twenty-first-century Catholic theology and life. It may seem that the Sacred Heart would not apply to our current real-world predicament. It could be objected that the heart of Jesus is less suited to theology than it is to private spirituality. But as we see it, Jesus's heart has currency for theology and life (not just *private*, religious life) in light of Pope Francis's criticisms of neoliberal heartlessness. We quote again words from early in his pontificate: "We have created new idols. The worship of the golden calf of old (see Ex 32:15–34) has found a new and *heartless* image in the cult of money and the dominance of an economy which is faceless and lacking any truly humane goal."[24] Hardly a devotional abstraction, the Sacred Heart of Jesus symbolizes the material concreteness of God's revelation in Jesus as we know it from the Gospels. It symbolizes Jesus moved in his viscera by the crowds who followed him seeking guidance; then he teaches them and heals their sick (Mk 6:34; Mt 14:13). It symbolizes Jesus brought to such anger that he calls his opponents in a dispute a "brood of vipers" (Mt 12:34). It symbolizes Jesus disturbed to the core by the death of his friend, Lazarus (Jn 11:33, 35, 38). It symbolizes Jesus so consumed by zeal for God's house that he drives the money changers from the Temple (Mk 11:15–19; Mt 21:12–17; Lk 19:45–48; Jn 2:13–16). And it symbolizes Jesus looking upon the wealthy young man with love, then commanding him to go and sell all his possessions (Mk 10:21). The Sacred Heart brings concretely to expression that Jesus, the second person of the Trinity, is a person of heart who lives with and from the heart, and who commands any who would follow him to love as he does (Jn 13:34).

The doctrine of the Trinity, expressed in the Sacred Heart devotion, could apply to the heartlessness of the neoliberal era and its culture, which we regard as distinct even though not entirely removed from the secularized-atheistic period and culture addressed by John Paul and Kasper. The "heartless image" of the "cult of money" emblematizes the neoliberal commitment to impersonality, against which we are directing Trinitarian theology.

Devotion to Jesus's heart leads us to the third Trinitarian person. As John Paul puts it, "The Heart of Christ is alive with the action of the Holy Spirit, to whom Jesus attributed the inspiration of his mission (Lk 4:18; see also Is 61:1) and whose sending he had promised at the Last Supper."[25] Kasper plumbs the Trinitarian depths of these biblically attested events, as well as Jesus's death on the cross, where he breathes out the Spirit (Jn 19:30): "The inner reality of God as self-emptying and self-communicating love, which has become decisively and unsurpassably revealed on the cross, does not remain in itself, but is bestowed on us in the Holy Spirit."[26] He adds the statement that has propelled our Trinitarian reflections: "In his mercy, God lets us not only see into his heart; he creates space for us beside his heart and in his heart through the Holy Spirit."[27] Put otherwise, if the one Jesus calls Father is the source of divine life *within* God, the Spirit functions as the divine source of eternal life given to people through and as divine indwelling. John Paul discusses the Holy Spirit in such terms in the encyclical he publishes the year before *Sollicitudo Rei Socialis*, a meditation on the Spirit called *Dominum et Vivificantem* (1986).[28] He reflects upon Jesus's words when he encounters a woman at a well, where Jesus tells her that he can provide water that "will become . . . a spring of water welling up to new life" (*DV*, 1; Jn 4:14). John Paul associates this phrase with descriptions of the Holy Spirit elsewhere in John's Gospel, the New Testament more widely, and, of course, the Nicene-Constantinopolitan Creed, from which comes the encyclical's title, "Lord and Giver of Life."

But more important for our Trinitarian theology centered on mercy is John Paul's interpretation of another Johannine passage, the Last Supper discourses, where Jesus promises an Advocate who will be sent after his death to testify to the truth and to "convince the world concerning sin and righteousness and judgment" (*DV*, 27; Jn 16:8).[29] John Paul explains: "Convincing concerning sin means showing the evil that sin contains, and this is equivalent to revealing the mystery of iniquity. It is not possible to grasp the evil of sin in all its sad reality without 'searching the depths of God'" (*DV*, 39).[30] Sounding resonances between Paul's teaching in 1 Corinthians 2:10 that the Spirit searches all things including God's depths and Jesus's proclamation that the Advocate will be the Spirit of truth, John Paul finds that the Spirit's role is to confront people with the contrast between a sinful "mystery" and the true mystery of God.

The Spirit reveals sin to be that which opposes life and truth and causes suffering (*DV*, 39). The Spirit can lay bare that which opposes life and truth, that is, death and lies, because the Spirit is the "eternal source of every divine giving of gifts to creatures" (*DV*, 39). The mystery of evil, John Paul implies, is its ultimately futile attempt to undo the divine giving of gifts. The remedy for such attempted undoing is, in a word, mercy. In the Spirit, John Paul teaches, "we can picture as personified and actualized in a transcendent way that mercy which the patristic and theological tradition following the line of the Old and New Testaments, attributes to God." He continues, "In God, the Spirit-Love expresses the consideration of human sin in a fresh outpouring of salvific love." Then he expresses it more pointedly, and with greater interest for our theology of mercy: "Whereas sin, by rejecting love, has caused the 'suffering' of man which in some way has affected the whole of creation, the Holy Spirit will enter into human and cosmic suffering with a new outpouring of love, which will redeem the world" (*DV*, 39). The meaning of "convincing of sin" takes on wide-ranging significance. It means the way that the Spirit works to unmask sin from the dawn of humanity and ultimately to overcome sinful rejections of love and gift wherever and whenever they occur.

Pneumatology crowns, therefore, our approach to Trinitarian theology, because it witnesses to how the value-recognizing generosity of the one Jesus calls Father and the heart-filled compassion of Jesus Christ transform God's creation. A creation that, because of sin, bends toward rejecting God is directed back toward God by the Spirit who gives new life, filling the whole universe with the gift of God's love (*DV*, 54). John Paul alludes here to the book of Wisdom 1:7, which proclaims that God's Spirit "fills the world, / is all-embracing" (NAB) or "holds all things together" (NRSV). In chapter 5 we consider a practical principle from CST that follows from such a pneumatology: the universal destination of goods, meaning that the "goods of this world are originally meant for all" (*SRS*, 42). The goods of this world, which are all God's creations, must be shared as the father effusively shares his goods with the prodigal son and as Jesus outpours love from his heart, in such a way that their sharing reflects the Spirit's holding of all things together.

Negative Theology

We have referred a few times, especially in our presentation on the Holy Spirit, to the *mystery* of God. That topic bears a little more attention as we direct Trinitarian theology against neoliberalism. We recall here Quinn Slobodian's contention that neoliberalism (at least in its "Geneva School" variety) is a "negative theology."[31] It regards the market, its bedrock reality, as indescribable, indecipherable, and incomprehensible. This unknowable market can command devotion and sacrifice in the forms of encasement by all social institutions, which are built around the market like a temple, and of social exclusion, because the market cannot be made to answer to the needs and desires of the *demos*. Regarding the global economy as unknowable became the "starting point for designing the order within which the world economy could thrive."[32]

It may seem that the Trinity shares with the neoliberal market the characteristic of unknowability, so that all our contrasting of neoliberalism's with Catholicism's bedrock reality may be seen as misplaced. There is, after all, a long biblical tradition from the book of Job (Job 11:7, 36:26) through Paul's First Letter to Timothy (1 Tim 6:16), that insists upon the unsearchability of God's ways and the inability of human persons to see God (see also Ex 33:20; Jn 1:18; 1 Jn 4:12). So, too, is there a long tradition of apophatic mysticism, which in the persons of Dionysius the Areopagite and Meister Eckhart commanded the attention of many throughout the second half of the twentieth century, especially thinkers who worked at the intersection of postmodernism and Christian theology. Benedict XVI acknowledges in his *Introduction to Christianity* that Trinitarian theology in particular would seem to teach us more about God's unknowability than God's knowability, inasmuch as presentations of Trinitarian doctrine had long focused as much on rejecting heresies as presenting positive statements about God.[33] To say God is Trinity would seem to express more what God is *not* than who God is.

Add to the fact that "Trinity" is consistently referred to as "Mystery," and the case against contrasting the inscrutable neoliberal market and the mystery of God would seem settled in favor of their rough equivalency. There are, though, decisive differences between the two that must be highlighted as we conclude our remarks on Trinitarian theology. Far from exhibiting the market's caprice, the Trinity is the God of *hesed*, steadfast love, as we have already noted above. This quality of God is widely attested throughout both Testaments of scripture and in innumerable people's lives. Surely God's ways remain, properly speaking, unsearchable, but more so for the granularity of God's faithfulness ("Even the hairs of your head have all been counted," teaches Jesus in Lk 12:7) than the indecipherable whims of a dispassionate pretender-deity like the market. Far from the impersonal force that, supposedly, doles out economic graces, God is "personal," even if God is "person" not in precisely the same sense that we customarily mean by "person."[34] This has the implication that God, though incomprehensible, is also knowable. As we have already seen with Kasper, God self-communicates, robustly, effusively, and *in person*. Benedict elaborates, poetically, "God is wholly and only love, the purest, infinite and eternal love. He does not live in splendid solitude but rather is an inexhaustible source of life that is ceaselessly given and communicated."[35] And he adds (with ideas that gesture toward our discussion of the universal destination of goods in chapter 5): "The 'name' of the Blessed Trinity is, in a certain sense, imprinted upon all things because all that exists, down to the last particle, is in relation; in this way we catch a glimpse of God as relationship and ultimately, Creator Love."[36] Creative communication and gift-giving defines God through and through, *and* God's creation through and through. Ceaseless giving rather than parsimonious partitioning define a Trinitarian vision of life.

These few examples mean to indicate that, even though God is mystery (so some measure of negative theology is necessary in order to rule out what God is not and to chastise those who would claim to know too much), God is mysterious in a vastly diverse sense from the incomprehensible neoliberal market. In brief, a divinity to which no positive theology applies is false. So goes it with what Francis rightly calls the "faceless economy."

Anthropology, Ecclesiology, and Mercy

John Paul II's critique of economism began with his rejection of how human labor (thus human subjectivity) is reduced to its economic valence only. For John Paul, this was not just a matter of how we think about ourselves and others when we look for work or go to the workplace. Instead, the topic of labor implicates the whole range of human life, and labor's economization threatens the same range. John Paul's concerns developed immediately with regard to communism, but we learned in chapter 1 that the economization of human labor effected by communism resulted from its imitation, somewhat in reverse, of the early error of capitalism, namely, conceiving of the vast majority of people as labor power to be bought through a wage. Chapter 2 considers how neoliberalism transforms this commodification of human labor by reeducating the human person about herself, convincing her that she is no longer a substantial person (even a commodity has some remaining substance) but rather an ephemeral, only *potentially* valuable, bit of human capital. Coterminous with this, confirming John Paul's worst fears, significant dimensions of human life have been economized, but instead of on the model of a commodity to be bought with a wage, on the model of an investment that has value only inasmuch as fickle investors esteem it. Chapter 2's closing discussion of "everyday mercilessness" indicated the major downside of the neoliberal human capital anthropology: human capital's craving for esteem often manifests itself as a craving for the failure, punishment, and expulsion of others, over whom one's own human capital can assert its inconstant value. Put more pointedly, the narcissistic drive of human capital often entails mercilessness toward other bits of human capital.

An anti-neoliberal theology must provide a countereducation regarding the human person. We suspect that, given the proclivities of Catholic theologians and theological ethicists, they would recommend a "relational" anthropology to rectify the atomistic and narcissistic proclivities of human capital anthropology. This is necessary, but insufficient. What must be established even more firmly is the constancy of value of each and every human person, which should relate to the human person's status as *imago dei*, the image and likeness of God (Gen 1:26–27, 9:6; Ps 8:5; Is 64:8; 1 Cor 11:7). We discuss the *imago dei* in greater detail in chapter 5. But here, in the face of human capital's mercilessness (see chapter 2), the *imago dei* must be defined in terms of the *merciful* God (*Deus*). So the *imago dei* is a relational subject, but even more particularly, the *imago dei* is a merciful subject, an image of the merciful Trinity. Or in Jesus's language, to say that a person is *imago dei* is, at the same time, to say that each person is a neighbor to all others. Jesus illustrates this with the parable of the Good Samaritan (Lk 10:25–37), which we take to be the locus classicus for a theological anthropology centered on mercy.

Neighbor Anthropology

To approach the meaning of this parable we examine some of Pope Francis's reflections on it, as he has returned to it frequently, whether as Archbishop of Buenos Aires or as pope. In a text composed for the World Meeting of Popular Movements in 2017, Francis wrote that the primary threat or danger in the world is that we "disown our neighbors" and by doing so deny both their humanity as well as our own.[37] He uses the Good Samaritan parable to shed light on this denial of humanity and, by contrast, to define what, on a Christian account, humanity is. He raises the same question as the lawyer who asks Jesus what is needed to inherit eternal life: "Who is my neighbor?" (Lk 10:29). Jesus responds with a parable that depicts what it means to "be neighbor." A man who has been waylaid by robbers and left to die at the side of the road is ignored by two religious "elites," who, although they see the man in this dire strait, pass by on the road's other side. A Samaritan, who Pope Francis describes as a "foreigner, a pagan and unclean," does something different; he shows "true mercy" to the man: "he binds up the man's wounds, transports him to an inn, personally takes care of him, and provides for his upkeep." He draws near to the man, "to the point of identifying with him." Francis relates this parable to the current global economic system, which "has the god of money at its center." This system acts like the robbers and globalized society often acts like the religious elites, looking "the other way with the pretence of innocence." Or at best one looks at the world's wounded through a screen, from a distance. In either case, global society "manifests an absence of true commitment to humanity." Jesus's parable teaches a different way, which responds not to the question "who is my neighbor?" but "to whom should I be neighbor?" Francis appeals to his audience to struggle against a system that classifies others "in order to see who is a neighbor and who is not." Authentic humanity consists in having compassion in one's heart, "that capacity to suffer with someone else." Such humanity "resists the dehumanization that wears the livery of indifference, hypocrisy, or intolerance."

A year prior, during an Angelus blessing in St. Peter's Square, Francis ties together the Lukan parable of the Good Samaritan with the Matthean parable of the sheep and the goats (Mt 25:31–46). He recommends that his listeners ask themselves, "Am I 'the neighbor,' or do I simply just pass along? Or am I among those who select people according to their own pleasure? It's good to ask ourselves these questions and often because, in the end, we will be judged on the works of mercy."[38] He evokes the parable where Jesus the Judge announces his presence in the "least of these":

> The Lord will say to us: But you, you remember that time on the road from Jerusalem to Jericho? That man was me half dead. Do you remember? That hungry child was me. Do you remember? The migrant whom many want to drive out, it was me. Those grandparents alone, abandoned in nursing homes, it was me. That sick person alone in the hospital, that no one goes to see, was me.[39]

Francis presents the Christological valence to his neighbor anthropology. He cites specific examples of those our current world tends to deem worthless, even less than human: the hungry child, the migrant, the elders, and the sick. All of these people are equated with Christ. Jesus himself is the man by the side of the road, abandoned by robbers and ignored by many passersby. He identifies with those who need mercy, the implication being that those who treat these people mercifully show mercy to Christ, fulfilling his law (see Gal 6:2). This Christological lens is important to keep in mind as we consider our last example of Francis's interpretation of the Good Samaritan parable.[40]

Even before he was named Pope Francis, Archbishop Jorge Bergoglio made similar links between the parable of the Good Samaritan and contemporary social situations, yielding insights for a theological anthropology centered on Christ's mercy. A prime example is in his "Te Deum" address of May 25, 2003.[41] Bergoglio delivered this public address on Argentina's National Day (commemorating the revolution of 1810) in the aftermath of a devastating, neoliberal-policy-induced depression in the country (1998–2002). This particular homily offers, for our purposes, an important meditation on human fragility and the need to address it by rebuilding civil society.[42] It includes, moreover, fruitful instruction regarding the kind of theology, and indeed theological anthropology, encapsulated in the parable:

> The story of the good Samaritan . . . does not introduce a teaching of abstract ideals, nor does it confine itself to the instrumentality of an ethical-social moral. Rather it is the living Word of God, who humbled himself and came near enough to touch our most quotidian fragility. This Word reveals to us an essential characteristic of the human person, so often forgotten: that we are made for the fullness of being; we cannot, therefore, live indifferent in the face of pain, we cannot allow that anyone remain "off to the side of life," cast out of his dignity. This should disgust us.[43]

The parable, as is true of the best of Christian theology generally, confronts its hearers with the living Word—Jesus Christ himself—through its earthly words. This living Word challenges its hearers far more than a wooden "moral of the story." And this living Word discloses something about God: that the living God comes near to fragile and broken people to heal them. This lesson about God reveals the intelligibility and truth of the human person, that we are created for wholeness. Such orientation toward holism proves pivotal for how people should process what they experience in the world, particularly when they come face to face with someone who is suffering.

Bergoglio then relates these exegeses to social life, an integral component of theological anthropology. Jesus's parable, with its image of the dying man on the roadside, provokes pivotal questions. Bergoglio states them declaratively: "The inclusion or exclusion of the wounded one on the side of the road defines all economic, political, social, and religious projects. They all confront us daily with the option to be Good Samaritans or indifferent travelers who pass on by." We pose them interrogatively. Does social life in today's world include or exclude the wounded? Does it decide for the merciful touch of the Samaritan, or the indifference of the elites? Clearly Francis has in mind that social life currently excludes more than includes, representing the elites' indifference. But a culture of exclusion and indifference, while contemptible, is an "opportunity to grow." Francis exhorts the people of Buenos Aires, "Let's stop dissembling the suffering of the lost and take care of our crimes, carelessness, and lies, because restorative reconciliation alone will raise us, and [thereby] we will have lost fear of ourselves. It's not about preaching a triumphalist ethic, but about facing up to things from an ethical perspective, which is always rooted in reality." This reality, Francis contends, is "marked very deeply by fragility: the fragility of our poorest and excluded brothers, the fragility of our institutions, the fragility of our social bonds." He exclaims, "Let's care for the fragility of our wounded people (*Pueblo*)! . . . Let's care for each man, each woman, each child, and each elder with the Good Samaritan's solidaristic and attentive attitude of neighborliness." Francis concludes with an appeal to Mary, Our Lady of Luján, that she will inspire people to follow the example of Christ, "who carries our fragility on his shoulders."

In chapter 3 we noted Pope Francis's appeal for a culture of encounter. Now we should be able to see that this appeal flows from his neighbor anthropology and its concomitant awareness of each person's fragility and mutual vulnerability with others.[44] And it is worth pointing out how Francis's exhortation to encounter, with its roots in theological anthropology, also coheres with the Trinitarian insights we gathered from John Paul II, particularly with regard to the first person of the Trinity. Encounter restores people to dignity, just as the prodigal son's father

restores his dignity, at the son's moment of weakness, through an effusively generous welcome home—face to face. A neighbor anthropology
holds that people are ineluctably dignified, so each person must be
neighbor to each other by recognizing that dignity. Such an anthropology completely contravenes a human capital anthropology, where no
one bears inherent dignity or worth, so one must constantly produce
and manage one's worth or portfolio value, and each person must be a
"brand" to every other, trying to attract the other as an investor, hardly
as a neighbor.

Innkeeper Ecclesiology

A theology that stands against neoliberalism must also include an ecclesiology. When we think of the church, the *ekklesia*, we have in mind the
assembly of the faithful, and thus bring people together as an assembly.
What assembles the Christian people is Christ Jesus, whom Francis describes, using a classic formulation, as "the face of mercy" (*misericordiae
vultus*).[45] What assembles people under neoliberalism is human capital anthropology's ethic of competition and everyday mercilessness and, as a
consequence, expulsive sacrifice. Devotion to Christ must break such an
assemblage, putting in its place an *ekklesia* of mercy.

Francis's account of the Good Samaritan parable includes a striking ty-
pological ascription. He reads the innkeeper in the parable as a type for
the church. One could say that the neighbor anthropology exemplified by
the Good Samaritan coordinates with an innkeeper ecclesiology, a standard for assembly in which hospitality is predominant. Francis teaches
during a general audience in 2014: "The suffering person is entrusted to
an innkeeper, so that he might continue to care for him, sparing no expense. Now, who is this innkeeper? It is the Church, the Christian community—it is us—to whom each day the Lord entrusts those who are
afflicted in body and spirit, so that we might lavish all of his mercy and
salvation upon them without measure" (see 1 Pet 2:10).[46] Of course to be
generous with others in sharing God's mercy, "to be instruments of God's
mercy," the church presupposes that "it was we who first received mercy
from God."[47] The twofold profile of agent of mercy and receiver of mercy
corresponds to a similar structure in Kasper's book: the Church as sacrament and recipient of mercy.[48]

Francis provides us with the image of the innkeeper to get an ecclesi-ology up and running. Elsewhere, famously, he proposed the image of the church as a "field hospital." In an interview with fellow Jesuit Antonio Spadaro, Francis said:

> I see clearly that the thing the church needs most today is the ability to heal wounds and to warm the hearts of the faithful; it needs near-ness, proximity. I see the church as a field hospital after battle. It is useless to ask a seriously injured person if he has high cholesterol and about the level of his blood sugars! You have to heal his wounds. Then we can talk about everything else. Heal the wounds, heal the wounds. . . . And you have to start from the ground up.[49]

These remarks resonate with the theological material we have covered so far. It imagines an ecclesiology patterned on the Trinity's loving, stead-fast nearness to creation and on the Good Samaritan's accompaniment of wounded people (the Good Samaritan is invoked just two paragraphs later). Whether innkeeper or field hospital, the church must signify to and embody in the world the mercy it has received from God (see 1 Pet 2:10).

Kasper sketches just such a view of the church, citing a precedent in John Paul II's *Dives in Misericordia.*[50] The church witnesses to God's mercy in three ways: proclaiming God's mercy, providing mercy sacramentally, and revealing and realizing God's mercy in its whole life.[51]

The church's primary task is proclaiming a message of mercy. Kasper discusses this task in two remarkable, interlaced ways befitting our con-cern with neoliberalism. First, he advises that the church use the Letter to the Hebrews as a guide for insisting upon the contemporaneity of the church's message of mercy (its "today" character; Heb 3:7–8, 13, 15, and 4:7). One could go even further than Kasper does, and notice that the "today" repeatedly referred to in Hebrews not only suggests the ever-new applicability of the Gospel message (summed up with "Jesus Christ is the same yesterday, today, and forever," Heb 13:8), but that the "today" referred to is the sabbath day of rest (Heb 3:11, 18, and 4:1, 3–5, 8–11). Ecclesiology today, in the face of a merciless system that allows no sabbatical for human capital in its attempts to attract investors, must focus on God's mercy spec-ified as sabbatical rest. *This* is what proves so contemporary, because it's so necessary, yet so contrary to our current time.

Second, Kasper firmly places the church's kerygmatic task within the program inaugurated by Pope Paul VI, vigorously pursued by John Paul II, continued and strengthened with Benedict XVI, and renewed with Francis: the new evangelization.[52] The new evangelization, even though it recognizes both that every age has been marked by multitudinous problems and that the Gospel exists as eternal truth, resolutely takes up the challenge of preaching the Good News of salvation in Jesus Christ in a new situation.[53] Rather than professing timeless dicta, the church of the new evangelization aims to "speak of God concretely, in light of people's hardships and woe, and help them to discover the merciful God in their own life story."[54] Kasper recommends, following John Paul II, whose famous refrain was "Be not afraid," a shift in kerygmatic style: "We must attend to the present situation with mercy and say that, above all of the fog and frequent gloominess of our world, the merciful countenance of a Father prevails, who is patient and kind, who knows and loves each individual, and who knows what we need (Mt 6:8, 32)."[55]

Should the church combine concrete proclamation and merciful style, it could present an attractive vision arrayed against neoliberalism, with its abstract faith in the impersonal market and its chief proclamation, "be afraid of market judgment, of being left behind; even today your brand could become irrelevant and your investors abandon you." To people suffering under neoliberalism, whether materially or spiritually, the church can offer truth, which lends intelligibility to human life as communal. Kasper writes, "When the church attests to the mercy of God, it not only proclaims the deepest truth about God, it also proclaims the deepest truth about us humans."[56]

Kasper does not stop with this proclamation. The church's sacramental life offers a real-symbolic, embodied, lived signification of mercy. This is especially true of the sacrament of penance. This sacrament, at least in principle, dovetails perfectly with the church's proclamation of mercy. It puts into action the "today" of the Letter to the Hebrews, in the sense of the continuous renewal of God's bestowal of mercy: "The sacrament of reconciliation is the genuine sacrament of the mercy of God, who repeatedly forgives us anew and grants us time and again a new chance and a new beginning."[57] The sacrament coheres with the Christian church's insistence upon God's personal proximity to people, and the injunction that people draw near to one another as neighbors. The sacrament's culmination, Christ's absolution of sins through the words of the priest, is concrete and personal rather than anonymous and general.[58] Through an act of personal proximity, guilt and division are released and peace conferred. In his bull of indiction for the Jubilee Year of Mercy, Pope Francis adds palpable heft to Kasper's proposal: "Let us place the Sacrament of Reconciliation at the centre once more in such a way that it will enable people to touch the grandeur of God's mercy with their own hands. For every penitent, it will be a source of true interior peace."[59] As he concludes his section on penance in the church, Kasper presents a hopeful estimation of the sacrament as a gift for the church and the world, submitting that "it could assist in giving Christian humility a new lease on life, establishing more merciful dealings with one another in the church and thereby helping the church to become more merciful."[60] In a neoliberal world that seems more unforgiving every day, a church of mercy that imitates and embodies the God who constantly grants new chances, like the prodigal son's father, certainly looks preferable.

But we would be remiss to ignore possible objections to Kasper's estimation. He himself acknowledges that the sacrament of penance is met with suspicion by many people today, even many faithful Catholics. People regard it as a "coercive instrument of control" that, for some, has contributed to "downright traumatic experience[s]."[61] Kasper deflects such objections. He has some justification, as they can sometimes be overblown. But he does so too facilely, chalking them up, for the most part, to contemporary delusions of innocence or impulses to offload guilt onto "the system."[62] It is worth staying open to critical questions about the sacrament—while at the same time remaining faithful to it.[63]

The Second Vatican Council teaches: "While Christ, holy, innocent, and undefiled knew nothing of sin, but came to expiate the sins of the people, the Church, embracing in its bosom sinners, at the same time holy and always in need of being purified, always follows the way of penance and renewal."[64] Kasper recognizes that the sacramental mediation of mercy affects the church first. Critical reflection can, too. In this way, the church can rise above neoliberalism, which admits of no self-critical impulses. The answer to perceived market errors and collapses is not to confess failure or to change course but to add more markets, to double down, to entrench market rules. Thus, markets are made to appear invulnerable. By contrast, through the church's practices of examination of conscience and conversion, it testifies to its own vulnerability. This coordinates with the human fragility that Pope Francis highlights in his neighbor anthropology. Witness to vulnerability opposes the church to neoliberalism, which recognizes communal vulnerability only inasmuch as this vulnerability can be parlayed into the neoliberal system of sacrifice.

The Works and the Politics of Mercy

Theological doctrines like Trinity, anthropology, and ecclesiology must issue in a life. Specifically, a theology of mercy should issue in works and, we argue, a politics of mercy that can counteract in word and deed neoliberalism. We commend the corporal and spiritual works of mercy as the medium for redirecting Catholic action away from the neoliberal practices that habituate Catholics into the deformed and unacceptable ethos we described at the end of chapter 2 and the culture we engaged at the end of chapter 3. The works of mercy can, if practiced consistently and with firm intention, help to restore societal structures. The works of mercy, properly practiced, sympathize with and address another's distress;[65] but also, they effect conversion in their practitioners and in the cultural milieu in which they are practiced. In both cases, the works of mercy reform—or better, convert—human subjectivity, especially its freedom.[66] But we wish to go even further and recommend that the works of mercy be reimagined first structurally and then as a distinctive politics in order to face up to the comprehensive threat that neoliberalism presents to Catholic faith and life, and, of course, the milieu of diverse human cultures and planetary systems in which Catholic faith is held and life is led. We start, then, with a traditional account of the works of mercy as charity and continue with a reimagination of these works tailored toward the crises of neoliberalism.

The Works of Mercy as Charity

We will not recount a history of the works of mercy; suffice it to observe that these works represent a long, venerable, and continuous tradition stretching back from our day all the way to Jesus himself—and beyond him to the Law, the prophets, the psalms, and Hebrew wisdom. Thankfully

James Keenan has provided a summary narration of the works of mercy that has become a standard in the literature over the past decade-and-a-half.[67] As systematic theologians, we focus more closely on the works' role today.

The works of mercy are of two kinds: corporal and spiritual.[68] The corporal works of mercy, which address the needs of the body, feed the hungry, give drink to the thirsty, clothe the naked, ransom the captive, shelter the homeless, visit the sick, and bury the dead. The spiritual works of mercy, which address sufferings of the spirit, admonish the sinner, instruct the ignorant, counsel the doubtful, comfort the sorrowful, bear wrongs patiently, forgive all injuries, and pray for the living and the dead. Though ancient, these works, like the Christian *kerygma*, bear a striking contemporaneity. This owes itself not only to distresses of various sorts being a constant in human life. Theologically, these works perform Christ's mercy (Jesus, yesterday, today, and forever, Heb 13:8) and give concrete shape to the grace of the Spirit, whose gifts enable the works of mercy (see Lk 4:18–19; Isa 61:1–3). Even more, they set a framework for Catholic living supple enough to address forms of suffering specific to each age, and they consist of a sort of list of "best practices" that could unravel dominant modes of conduct in our particular neoliberal era.

Among many notable apologists for the works of mercy in twentieth-century Catholicism (a list that includes John Paul II and Mother Teresa of Calcutta), Dorothy Day was incomparably vocal with regard to the works' potential for transforming individuals and society. She found them attractive because of their personalism, as opposed to their impersonality, because they are "help given from the heart at a personal sacrifice."[69] The works of mercy, empowered by God's gift of charity, function to enlarge the hearts of those who practice them, so they may "love each other . . . [their] neighbor . . . and [their] enemy as well as [their] friend."[70] A Catholic transformed by practicing the works of mercy no longer needs the externally imposed "goad of duty" to help others in need, but comes to do these things gladly. The "total Christian," as Day calls such a person, feels in her heart that such help is rendered to Christ, and "it is not a duty to help Christ, it is a privilege."[71] Far from a set of practices based in my advantage, the works of mercy construe the only advantage worth pursuing as the meeting of another's needs, which is tantamount to serving the Son of God himself. In addition to converting individuals' hearts, the works of mercy are "the best revolutionary technique . . . for changing the social order rather than perpetuating it."[72] Not state intervention, not market mechanisms for poverty reduction, but direct and personal action to address another's distress is demanded by the Gospel and is the optimal way to turn this world toward a new heaven and new earth.[73] Day's vision for social change through the works of mercy, so powerfully implemented in the Catholic Worker movement from her day through ours, anticipates Benedict XVI's similar vision of integral human development through charity (penned, we repeat, in the aftermath of the neoliberalism-induced 2008 global economic crisis). Benedict writes, "As the objects of God's love, men and women become subjects of charity, they are called to make themselves instruments of grace, so as to pour forth God's charity and to weave networks of charity" (CV, 5). Subjects of charity, trained through embodied and spiritual exercises of mercy (paired with the sacraments and devotions of the church[74]) and working in communion with one another, promise a revolution. Pope Francis speaks similarly: "The works of mercy affect a person's entire life. For this reason, we can set in motion a real cultural revolution, beginning with simple gestures capable of reaching body and spirit, people's very lives."[75]

Although we have reservations with regard to the sort of vision for social transformation we have just briefly considered, we acknowledge the potency of Day's charity-centered, direct-action model in general and in the particular situation of the neoliberal era. Day's adoption of the "little way" that she learned from St. Thérèse of Lisieux (called "the little flower"), which shows mercy to lives deemed least appreciable, quite obviously presents a challenge to an economic system that has consolidated enormous wealth and power into fewer and fewer hands while excluding more and more. But at a less obvious yet perhaps ultimately more important level, the little way of charity, with its simple gestures, bears possibilities for unraveling neoliberal cultural formation, which proceeds just as much through little-by-little daily activities as by large-scale class warfare. To neoliberalism's subtle centrifugal force, exerted on human capital to set one bit against another, the little way of charity opposes the centripetal force that brings human persons together as they approach Christ and the Kingdom through the activity of the Spirit. To neoliberalism's responsibilization, which swaps authentic personal responsibility for marketized guilt and shame, the little way of mercy opposes reawakened personal responsibility rooted in Christ who suffers in the distress of the least of these and joy in Christ fed, sated, clothed, visited, ransomed, housed. To neoliberal governance, set and kept in motion by "best practices" of market competition and optimization, the little way of mercy opposes the works of mercy, which shape people who hunger and thirst for righteousness (Mt 5:6).

The works of mercy were developed before the advent of globalization and offer a localist, charitable response to social exclusion. Therefore, in an era of globalization we must acknowledge that many of the most pressing problems we face require a more comprehensive response than charity is capable of offering. This is not to reject the central role that charity has played—and should continue to play—in Catholic life (an error often made by the Left in its desire to replace charity with more extensive structural reform). It is simply to recognize the enormity of the institutional frameworks that reproduce human misery on a global scale.

The danger of a charity-centered view of the works of mercy lies in their tendency toward what David Harvey calls "conscience-laundering."[76] Under neoliberalism, charity has been stripped of its Christian signification, even among many Christians, so it has become a synonym for giving money and excess goods to "charitable" organizations; furthermore, such a turn has, with neoliberalism's ubiquitous marketization, produced a vehicle for perpetuating a world unacceptable by the standard of mercy.[77]

Our concern here, given that Catholic theology, social teaching, piety, and practice emphasize the charity dimension of the works of mercy, read as occasional, individual acts of addressing specific needs, is to direct these works toward the "political" half of "the personal is the political." Given neoliberalism's ersatz holism, resistance to it cannot rely solely on personal transformation, however much it must begin there.

Mercy as Structural Principle

In chapter 1 we discussed how CST reads the personal and the political-structural together. A key term is *social sin*. John Paul II introduces it in *Sollicitudo Rei Socialis* (SRS, 36), and his successors take it up in their own social teachings. Even before John Paul, Latin American liberation theologians and feminist theologians had already been thinking and writing about social sin and structures of sin.[78] At the prompting of Catholic ethicists such as Kristin Heyer, we look to Latin American theologians as a corrective for John Paul's view of social sin, in order to take more seriously the nonvoluntary and unconscious aspects of social sin. For Heyer, the contrast between John Paul's teaching on social sin (and magisterial doctrine more generally) and liberation theology is that the latter has "been concerned less with safeguarding continuity with the theological tradition" than with "a primarily pastoral concern for distinctive contexts."[79]

We regard it as slightly more accurate to say that Latin American liberation theologians strive for continuity with a deeper and different tradition than one marked by individualistic, act-oriented moral theology and legalistic approaches to social justice. In particular, liberation theologians' sensitivity to nonvoluntary and unconscious dimensions of sin, which yield a more complex view of social sin than John Paul's, stretches all the way back to St. Paul. If we link up Paul's writing about the law of sin that dwells in him, preventing him from doing the good that he wants and impelling him to do the evil he does not want (Rom 7:17–25) and the (deutero) Pauline literature's references to the "power of darkness" (Col 1:13) and "principalities, powers, and world rulers" (Eph 6:16), we have no reason to doubt the scriptural veracity of a view of sin as, in addition to individual, social and structural. Traditional resources can also be discovered in Christian theologies of concupiscence, so long as concupiscence is not understood in a narrowly sexual sense.[80] We need not chalk up liberation theologians' attention to social and structural sin to pastoral concerns only. Deep theological tradition is in play. Furthermore, commonsensical theoretical considerations obtain. Just as one would do much better to calculate the volume of a solid using calculus rather than counting on one's fingers, one can make greater theological sense out of social phenomena like neoliberalism and the massive crises to which it contributes with the type of notion of social sin that Heyer seeks and Latin American liberation theologians develop. Such a notion of social sin would prove more applicable to resisting neoliberalism's deformation of economy, politics, and culture. Neoliberalism, like the "flesh" or "principalities" in Paul, or like "concupiscence" in later theological tradition, has found increasingly innovative ways of systematically dulling personal freedom, responsibilizing subjects while bereaving them of the resources needed to enact real responsibility, and, once more, shaping individuals and social structures marked by indifference or even outright vindictiveness.

Jon Sobrino's collection of essays, *The Principle of Mercy: Taking the Crucified People from the Cross* (1992), succinctly and powerfully expresses the notion of social sin we seek.[81] Sobrino's essay, "Five Hundred Years: Structural Sin and Structural Grace," uses such a notion of sin to examine the quincentenary of colonialism in Latin America and to diagnose the most recent mutation of this structural sin in a renewed, post-1989 world of Northern-industrialized countries' plundering of the South.[82] He illustrates social sin by summarizing the relations between Europe and Latin America: "They oppress and threaten life; they seek ideological and theological justifications; they hold, as an unspoken fundamental premise, the human inferiority of some in relation to others. We can call all that structural evil in a very precise sense."[83] The overarching phenomena Sobrino names obviously result in some way or are perpetuated by individual choices and sins, but to chalk them up simply to that is gravely misleading. The structural dimension of oppression, the construction of hierarchies, and the ideologies that legitimate these mechanisms of exploitation have lives of their own. They must be contested at a structural level. Sobrino assesses the situation further by quoting from several economists who attempt dispassionately to describe conditions in the global economy. Their descriptions amount to the following conclusions: (1) poor countries today (1992) are important only for providing raw materials and labor, but (2) given the new economy that depends more on technical knowledge than old-fashioned land and labor, the Third World is rendered largely extraneous, except (3) as a dumping ground for poisonous waste.[84] Again, this entrenched, five-hundred-year-old structure outpaces simple individual contestation. And, it must be noted, Sobrino writes comparatively near the *beginning* of neoliberalism's rise on the global stage.

Against structural sin, Sobrino finds that the only viable antidote is structural mercy, or what in another essay he calls "the principle of mercy."[85] Sobrino defines mercy as "a re-action to someone else's suffering, now interiorized within oneself."[86] Adding further nuance he observes, "Mercy is a basic attitude toward the suffering of another, whereby one reacts to eradicate the suffering for the sole reason that it exists, and in the conviction that, in this reaction to the ought-not-to-be of another's suffering, one's own being, without any possibility of subterfuge, hangs in the balance."[87] We should accent here the "basic" character of this attitude, with "basic" designating a primordial stratum not relegated to individuals alone. Whole communities, from small to enormous, can share such an attitude. We have already underscored the aspiration of all Christians to share in the merciful and compassionate attitude of Christ. The same goes, Sobrino reminds us, for the church, a personal reality never fully reducible to an aggregate of its members or their discrete actions, however inseparable it is from these. The "principle of mercy" enunciates a "*pathos . . .* that ought to 'inform' that church—give it its specificity, shape and mold it."[88] The principle of mercy, as the basic attitude for the corporate (as opposed to individual) reality of the church positions it with regard to reality, toward a reality shot through by social (again not simply aggregated) sin. Sobrino uses the Good Samaritan parable—as does Francis in his theological anthropology—to depict the church's positioning through the principle of mercy: "the place of the church is with the wounded one lying in a ditch along the roadside."[89] The church that shares in the attitude of Christ aligns itself with those expelled to the roadside, rather than adopting a posture of indifference toward this suffering. To do so entails a real and painful change of heart and transformation of practice—not just individually, but collectively and at the level of (often vast) structures. The Catholic Church especially, being itself a vast structure, should be able, at just as imposing a level, to live as the "Samaritan church."

This will involve a recalibration of the works of mercy as structural. Mercy is "more than a categorical practice of 'the works of mercy,'" Sobrino reports, and we concur.[90] We certainly do not discourage their practice, nor will we disagree with Benedict XVI, his papal predecessor and successor, or Dorothy Day that personal transformation must drive and support structural transformation. That said, given our contemporary condition of structural deformation and devastation, we must read and implement the works of mercy as principles—structural guides for social reality. In particular we are interested in Catholic resistance to the economization of the works of mercy. Somehow, out of a visceral commitment to Christ, to the humanity in which we can see Christ's face, and in the creation that God spoke into being through Christ the Word, Christians must resist the takeovers of their hospitals by for-profit businesses, of their schools by "school choice" politics, of religious orders by the interests of their wealthy donors. Catholics, who historically have been closely involved with labor organizations, but whose support for them has flagged

in the neoliberal era, must renew this support. And Catholics who in relatively recent history have supported environmental and racial justice
organizations must increase this support—and repent from Catholics' environmental and racial sins of the past and present. The works of mercy,
to care for others' bodies and souls, must not be economized, and the det-
rimental effects of economization must be remediated with Catholics at
the forefront, not only as a matter of individual choice but as a matter of
deep decision by a Samaritan church.

The Politics of Mercy

Beyond structural mercy, which is prophetic condemnation, a demand
that structures of sin be eliminated, and a call for the church to reformulate itself in the process, we propose a politics of mercy which would be
more deliberate—and more closely tailored to neoliberalism—about how
to build an alternative world. As we begin to reflect on the politics of
mercy, we would do well to recall once more that just forty years ago neoliberalism still languished as an obscure ideology debated among relatively marginal figures in economics. It was, by the Keynesian standards
of the time, a full-blown utopian project with little chance of emerging as
a viable alternative, let alone as serving as its replacement. But it should
be clear by now that neoliberalism is the dominant common sense in the
world today. The neoliberal revolution was successful, in part, because it
combined a utopian vision of market society with concrete reforms that
subtly pushed society toward realizing this vision. Mirowski, though a
critic, finds this almost admirable:

> The genius of the Neoliberal Thought Collective has been to appreci-
> ate that it is not enough to dangle a utopian vision just beyond reach as
> eventual motivation for political action; the cadre that triumphs is the
> side that can simultaneously mount a full set of seemingly unrelated
> political proposals that deal with the short-, medium-, and long-term
> horizons of action, combining regimes of knowledge and interim out-
> comes, so that the end result is the inexorable movement of the *polis*
> ever closer to the eventual goal.[91]

Neoliberals recognized that it was necessary to pursue multiple ideological, economic, and political projects at the same time to prepare the ground

for the time when the circumstances were ripe for dramatic social change. In *Capitalism and Freedom* (1962), Milton Friedman reflected on the role that crisis plays in social change and the preparatory work needed before a crisis: "only a crisis—actual or perceived—produces real change. When that crisis occurs, the actions that are taken depend on the ideas that are lying around. That, I believe, is our basic function: to develop alternatives to existing policies, to keep them alive and available until the politically impossible becomes politically inevitable."[92] Neoliberalism has strategically exploited crises—natural disasters, war, financial crashes—as opportunities for reorganizing society and further entrenching neoliberal policies of privatization, deregulation, and financialization. Conveniently enough, many of the crises exploited by neoliberals were caused directly or indirectly by neoliberal policy.

Neoliberal strategy consists of a multilayered attempt to manage crises so as to economize society more and more. As Mirowski suggests, this involves short-term, middle-term, and long-term tactics and strategies that offer a complex array of ideological, policy, and social interventions that appeal to different constituencies. Together these tactics and strategies work to bend the arc of history toward the market. We engage in a comparable operation with respect to the works of mercy, hoping that Catholics in concert with all people of good will and in cooperation with divine grace can bend history's arc toward God's justice. We share with neoliberals the view that crises often open possibilities for social change and affirm a multifaceted strategy. Accordingly, in the analysis of the works of mercy in chapter 5 as ingredients for resistance to neoliberalism, we reimagine them using a fourfold schema: we examine each work in view of a theological ideal and social principle, and then recommend short-term, middle-term, and long-term responses.

We begin with theological ideas and a practical principle from CST (universal destination of goods or a secular analogue, in the absence of a firm CST principle, namely, abolitionism), that provide an indication of God's will for creation to which people should aspire. Put basically, we mark the positive reality pointed to by Catholic theology in order to reveal how deficient our neoliberal world is by contrast. This starting point is crucial because, as we suggested earlier in this chapter, Catholicism and neoliberalism diverge sharply in their description of reality itself. We have laid out theological ideas in this chapter to provide a

Catholic systematic vision of mercy; in chapter 5 we choose specific Catholic ideas and principles that are best suited to address the specific crises we discussed in chapter 3. Another justification for this approach is that neoliberalism has achieved its most decisive victories at the level of the imagination. Neoliberalism's success has been so comprehensive that it is virtually impossible to imagine a society not organized by market principles. And while this restriction of imaginative possibility has affected Catholics and non-Catholics alike, Catholics have foundational reasons for contesting neoliberal hegemony because they profess mercy, not markets, as the basis for life. Following this key profession, we will describe a theological idea—the doctrine of creation, *imago dei*, the freedom of Christ, and the hospitality of Christ—set against the world that neoliberalism has produced. Our theological descriptions of a merciful alternative to neoliberalism may seem utopian. But it must be acknowledged that the process of preparing for social change always appears utopian by the reigning standards. Even so, social change does take place. And the form it takes, as Friedman argued and as neoliberalism's rise has demonstrated, depends on the preparatory work of imagining alternative worlds.

Discursive and imaginative resistance therefore represent critical tools for contesting neoliberalism, even as they alone are inadequate to produce broad societal transformation. In the background, we assume and continue to affirm the traditional aim of the corporal works of mercy— feeding the hungry, visiting the sick, ransoming the captive, welcoming the stranger—as a charitable response to social suffering. But here we attempt to reimagine their significance in a viable and holistic politics.

Our short-term responses focus on the process of conscientization, since neoliberal responses to crises begin with epistemic tactics such as the sowing of doubt. For many of these crises either the severity of the situation is diminished (environmental destruction) or the very existence of the crisis is hidden (mass incarceration). Accordingly, a fundamental task that makes possible a substantive response to these crises is a description and recognition of their root causes and effects. Surely in the short term (or for even longer) works of mercy such as visiting the sick can be practiced to alleviate symptoms of concrete crises, but a more thorough program of building a merciful society befitting the Trinity's mercy, the authentic meaning of human life, and the fruitful enactment of catholicity demands more, and this *more* must be based on adequate knowledge of the crises at hand.

Middle-term proposals will vary by case, but they have the aim of preparing for holistic societal transformation. We recognize that these works must involve political and economic reforms that support a broader politics of mercy. In effect, the middle-term responses to the crises aim in different ways tailored to the crisis under view to prepare a social space for long-term transformation. Topics discussed will include, depending on the issue analyzed, the CST principle of subsidiarity, governmental reforms (where subsidiarity properly understood demands them), expanding our understanding of human rights and international law, and a critique of United States interventionism. Because the middle-term reforms will vary by case, we leave the details to chapter 5.

Finally, we describe a long-term horizon for social transformation by responding to the following question: What should a society look like if we take with grave seriousness the political implications of a Catholic theology of mercy? As we work toward answers to this question, we keep in mind Benedict XVI's Augustinian wisdom, which reminds Catholics that the Kingdom of God will never arrive fully on earth until Christ's Second Coming. We aim not for a fully realized eschatology, but rather for a social order organized to prevent the advance of hell upon the earth (Benedict XVI). Such an order should rightly be called, as Pope Francis has persuasively argued, a culture of mercy. In chapter 5 we describe the universal destination of goods and abolitionism as long-term social visions that seek to eliminate structures built on neoliberal sacrifice and to create structures that reflect God's mercy.

5   The Politics of Mercy against Neoliberal Sacrifice

In chapter 3 of *Laudato Si'*, Pope Francis argues that nothing short of a "bold cultural revolution" is needed in order to confront the interconnected crises of environmental destruction, global poverty, and global migration. It is evident from the context of Francis's remarks that he thinks that this revolution should not be limited to civil society alone but must extend to the economic and political orders as well. On the basis of the Catholic vision of mercy elaborated in chapter 4, this chapter seeks to describe some of the features of this cultural revolution, which will have to be an anti-neoliberal revolution in terms of a politics of mercy.

After having set conceptual coordinates and analyzed four neoliberal crises in chapter 3 (environmental destruction, slum proliferation, mass incarceration, and mass deportation) and having expounded upon a theology of mercy in chapter 4, we can now examine constructive Catholic theological responses to these social crises of neoliberalism. We address the four neoliberal crises by retrieving the corporal works of mercy: environmental destruction—visit the sick; slum proliferation—feed the hungry, give drink to the thirsty, clothe the naked; mass incarceration—ransom the captive; and mass deportation—welcome the stranger. These pairings may seem counterintuitive. But we hope in light of the last chapter's argument in favor of a politics of mercy to show how the pairings make sense and how they help to outline a distinctively Catholic politics.

We address the first two crises—environmental destruction and slum proliferation—through the theological ideas of creation and *imago dei* and the practical maxim from CST that coheres with them and sets the standard for the long-term goal for the transformation of civilization: the universal destination of goods. We set these ideas and this maxim against the neoliberal deformation of private property. We address the other two crises—mass incarceration and mass deportation—through a Christological lens, with theological ideas of freedom in Christ and Christic hospitality, which we align, because of the lack of applicable CST principles, with the secular maxim and long-term goal of abolitionism. We set these ideas and this maxim against neoliberal practices of punishment and exclusion.

The chapter's thesis ties together all the work we have done so far. Given CST's criticism of economism; neoliberalism's character as a distinctive economism that perpetuates and exacerbates devastating, large-scale crises; and the Catholic theological commitment to mercy, a Catholic response to neoliberalism must address the crises of neoliberalism as a politics of mercy. With our argument here we return to the theme with which we opened the book: neoliberal sacrifice, which God rejects, versus holistic mercy, which God desires.

Universal Destination of Goods

In his public remarks, Francis has characterized neoliberal globalization as a new form of colonialism that often "appears as the anonymous influence of mammon: corporations, loan agencies, certain 'free trade' treaties, and the imposition of measures of 'austerity' which always tighten the belt of workers and the poor."[1] Free trade, structural adjustment policies, and massive cuts to social spending (under the auspices of "austerity") represent the basic elements of neoliberal policy, and Francis views these policies as fundamentally tied to a new colonialism that extends the modern colonial project of constructing a center and a periphery, with the peripheries serving as sacrifice zones. "By placing the periphery at the service of the center," Francis avers, "it denies those countries the right to an integral development."[2]

In response, Francis maintains that Catholics must not only resist "ideological colonization" but also demand structural changes that transform the global economy's basic mode of operation. During his speech to popular movements in Bolivia in 2016 he proclaimed, "Let us not be afraid to say it: we want change, real change, structural change," against the backdrop of a global order that "has imposed the mentality of profit at any price, with no concern for social exclusion or the destruction of nature."[3] Social exclusion—specifically the "dreadful injustice of urban exclusion" that Francis denounced during his visit to the Kangemi slum in Nairobi, Kenya, in 2015[4]—and the destruction of nature serve as the most obvious sacrifices of this new colonialism. Accordingly, as we explore visiting the sick and giving food, drink, and clothing to the dispossessed as works of mercy responsive to environmental destruction and slum proliferation, we also recognize the need to attend to the societal transformation necessary to remedy the social ills produced by neoliberal globalization. Furthermore, we claim that to do so demands that we recognize that globalization is not neutral, but rather an extension of modern colonization through which the Global South has been plundered by the North.

We address this situation theologically by retrieving the doctrines of creation and *imago dei* as resources within the Catholic tradition that support the defense of life against the neoliberal ethos of sacrifice. We coordinate them with the universal destination of goods, a maxim from CST that we take as a long-term civilizational claim that supports the works of mercy of visiting the sick and giving food, drink, and clothing which, if reimagined as a politics of mercy, can assist in resisting and building alternatives to the neoliberal global order. Our basic contention is that if you do not respect these ideas (the doctrine of creation and *imago dei*) and this practical principle (the universal destination of goods), the earth will be sickened, and people will be deprived of life. Conversely, if the ideal is respected, what would follow in the long term is healing and dignified life.

The doctrine of creation and *imago dei* will be described later, but before moving on we should provide a brief introduction to the universal destination of goods. This phrase denotes the proper relationship between private property and the just use of creation. This traditional formulation is rooted in the Bible and finds expression throughout the history of Christian theology (Ambrose, Chrysostom), but has been revitalized in the twentieth and twenty-first centuries by Vatican II, Paul VI, John Paul II, and Francis. What has become a central claim of modern CST—the proposition that the universal destination of goods should serve as the first principle of the social order—was first formulated by John Paul II in *Laborem Exercens* and has been repeated by Francis in *Laudato Si'*. In *Laborem Exercens*, John Paul II observes: "[The church's tradition has never viewed the right to private property] as absolute and untouchable. Quite the contrary, it has always seen it in the broader framework of the common right of all to enjoy the goods of the creation; in other words, the right of private property is subordinate to the right of common usage, the destination of goods for all" (*LE*, 14).[5] Put otherwise, the goods of creation were intended to provide life for every human person and our task is to ensure that each individual has their basic needs met and has the capacity to live a dignified life. We find it interesting that both the works of mercy and the universal destination of goods are filed under the seventh commandment in the Catechism of the Catholic Church: thou shall not steal. Our constructive proposal for a politics of mercy that addresses the neoliberal crises of environmental destruction and slum proliferation follows this cue. Private property in general is not theft, but neoliberalism has produced a social order that has thoroughly undermined the universal destination of goods and, as we noted in chapter 2, has defined private property in a way dangerously close to theft.[6]

Visit the Sick

Jesus's first miracle in the Synoptic Gospels is healing the sick (Mk 1:21–31; Lk 4:31–39; Mt 4:23).[7] On the basis of the scriptural evidence it appears that attending to the sick and curing those afflicted with disease was central to Jesus's ministry. It is little wonder, therefore, that visiting the sick would become a central practice of mercy throughout the church's two-thousand-year history, from the earliest apostles (Mt 10:1; Mk 16:18; Lk 9:1; Acts 5:12–16, 28:8–9; 1 Cor 12:9) through the present-day Catholic operation of hospitals and health care organizations. We must also remember that beginning with the scriptures Catholics have turned to metaphors of healing to explicate salvation in Christ, most notably with the Christological reading of Isaiah 53:5, "by his wounds we were healed" (1 Pet 2:24). Pope Benedict XVI evoked this passage in his message for the 2011 World Day of the Sick.[8] And in view of extreme sickness of the planet—in *Laudato Si'*, Pope Francis observed that we have turned creation into "an immense pile of filth" (*LS*, 21)—we think it fitting to apply the work of mercy of visiting the sick even more widely to the environmental crisis.[9] Francis has suggested that the climate crisis necessitates the articulation of a new work of mercy: care for creation. He locates this work among the seven spiritual works of mercy—this work calls Catholics into a relationship of "grateful contemplation of God's world which allows" them "to discover in each thing a teaching which God wishes to hand on to us"—and the corporal works—it "requires simple daily gestures which break with the logic of violence, exploitation and selfishness and makes itself felt in every action that seeks to build a better world."[10] But we choose here to reflect on visiting the sick from an environmental perspective, because we wish to continue to focus on the traditional corporal works of mercy as a Catholic response to neoliberalism. We reimagine what it means to visit and heal the sick in an age of environmental destruction. It entails not only direct restoration to health (which is needed) but also protection of those harmed and sickened by the ill effects of privileging private property over common health.

We begin theologically with an examination of God's intention for our world, precisely as God's creation. The doctrine of creation is crucial for contemporary Catholic reflection on the environmental crisis, as is evidenced by the substantive contributions of the three most recent popes in "Peace with God the Creator, Peace with All of Creation" (John Paul II, 1990), *In the Beginning: A Catholic Understanding of the Story of Creation and Fall* (Benedict XVI, 1985), and *Laudato Si'* (Francis, 2015). John Paul's reflection on the World Day of Peace draws the link between the Catholic doctrine of creation and the ecological crisis, marking this crisis as a moral one, characterized by "the indiscriminate application of advances in science and technology," which does not attend properly to responsibility or future consequences, thus threatening health and life itself.[11] John Paul proposes recovering the ideas of a "harmonious universe" and "common heritage" as impetus to a salutary vision and shared work geared toward healing the earth.[12] Benedict XVI followed John Paul's line of inquiry in his message for the World Day of Peace in 2010, "If You Want to Cultivate Peace, Protect Creation," in which he insisted, consistent with his long-standing emphasis on this theme in *In the Beginning* and *Caritas in Veritate*, that it is absolutely critical to recognize the world as creation and not as the result of evolutionary determinism or chance.[13] The failure to acknowledge that creation is a gift from God and, as such, contains within it a prescribed order, has produced a situation of uncertainty about its purpose and has led to its instrumental use (CV, 48). While Benedict never makes this point explicit, the neoliberal restriction of something's value to its market value is itself a symptom of a broader failure to recognize creation's transcendent significance. Benedict maintains that it is vital to reject any attempts "at total technical dominion over nature, because the natural environment is more than raw material to be manipulated at our pleasure; it is a wondrous work of the Creator containing a 'grammar' which sets forth ends and criteria for its wise use, not its reckless exploitation" (*CV*, 48). In *Laudato Si'* Pope Francis extended this papal critique of a technological and market-driven comportment toward the natural world and offered a constructive template for following the Gospel of Creation (*LS*, 62–100). The Catholic doctrine of creation supports sacramental engagement with the natural world: "The universe unfolds in God, who fills it completely. Hence, there is a mystical meaning to be found in a leaf, in a mountain trail, in a dewdrop, in a poor person's face. The ideal is not only to pass from the exterior to the interior to discover the action of God in the soul, but also to discover God in all things" (*LS*, 233). The popes' teachings on creation, including their rejection of violence toward and domination of nature, point toward a Catholic ethos rooted in healing, reconciliation, and genuine appreciation of creation as gift. Catholics who wish to observe papal teaching must reflect in a comprehensive way the healing touch of Christ in their behavior toward all of creation, since all things are connected, God is in all things, and all creation cries out for redemption (Rom 8:22). Given creation's current woundedness, Catholics are called to visit the sick, which under a politics of mercy means recognizing the inherent link between the Catholic doctrine of creation and the CST principle of the universal destination of goods.[14]

In the short term, "visiting the sick" must first entail a robust recommitment to truth, which means in this case recognition of the widespread destruction that neoliberalism has unleashed upon our common home. At its most basic level, this involves contesting the widely disseminated idea that there is no significant relationship between human activity and environmental destruction. This sort of denialism, which, we clarified in chapter 3, is not necessarily held by the individuals in neoliberal think tanks who constructed it, is nevertheless widely prevalent in American society. Even in the wake of *Laudato Si'*, one-third of Catholics in the United States deny that climate change is caused by human beings.[15] Near the end of chapter 3 we identified neoliberal corruption as an attack on truth, and there could hardly be a better illustration of this than climate change denialism. Neoliberalism weaponizes doubt. This prevents any curative action toward God's creation.

In *Laudato Si'* Francis emphasized the centrality of "ecological education" as a formative environmental practice urgently needed to confront this collective crisis. His conception of this "education" is expansive, carrying beyond simply introducing Catholics to the basic scientific facts of environmental degradation. It includes aesthetic and sacramental formation that enables individuals "to see and appreciate beauty" and to "reject self-interested pragmatism" (*LS*, 215). Additionally, in the short term, Francis proposes a series of practices that range from lifestyle changes (*LS*, 203–8) and voluntary simplicity and limiting consumption (*LS*, 209–10) to individual and community action (*LS*, 216–20).

The issue with individual action, however necessary and praiseworthy, is that it tends to individualize the response to environmental destruction and could play into the neoliberal playbook of responsibilization. As a result, it is critical that these short-term responses are pursued alongside middle-term, communal responses to environmental destruction that push for broader structural reforms. Neoliberals have proposed market-based solutions such as trading carbon credits as the most effective middle-term response for mitigating the adverse effects of climate change. In principle there is no reason for CST to oppose market-based solutions as a piece of a broader package of policies. But the reality is that carbon credits have served to mask (and even profit from) the carbon emissions problem rather than to remedy it. They deflected any call for a substantive reorganization of the economy and in the process have bought time for the creation of long-term market-based solutions like geoengineering.

The middle-term task is to prepare for long-term global solidarity based on the universal destination of goods by contesting the market-driven logic from the local level upward. We must recall that neoliberalism began as globalist utopianism and was enacted as globalization, which often ran roughshod over local interests, needs, desires, and health. From a Catholic perspective it is necessary to retrieve subsidiarity as a localist attempt to take back the earth from private corporations bent on destroying creation for the purposes of profit-seeking activities. Experiments in civil society should be privileged in order to limit the power of the market and to resist the hold that big oil and other extractive industries continue to have over governments. The recent case of the French town of Vittel, whose water has been divvied between Nestlé and Ermitage (a cheesemaking company), is a case in point. As a result of Nestlé and Ermitage's extractive practices, the local groundwater has recently run dry. In 2016 three local environmental groups with representatives on the Local Water Commission formed a group called Collectif eau 88 to resist further degradation of local resources. They made several demands, including halting authorizations to Nestlé and Ermitage for water extraction, more of a say for local civil society (as opposed to corporate power brokers) in debates regarding water use, and that "water should again be considered as a 'common good,' and not the monopolistic privilege of a multinational company uniquely preoccupied by its own profit."[16] This should be seen as a cautionary tale: neoliberal-style extraction poses an existential threat to people and ecosystems that demands serious and immediate change in corporate and governmental policy.[17] The demands of Collectif eau 88 are consistent with the principle of subsidiarity, which concerns, perhaps first and foremost, freedom for local decision-making. Likewise, it concerns addressing problems at levels properly scaled to their magnitude and extent.[18] With hope, the Local Water Commission in Vittel could turn away from its evident goal of preserving the interests of international capital at the expense of the local population and ecosystem. But should this local body be disinclined to make such a change, a larger scale effort, likely led by a higher level of government, would prove necessary. While government is not the answer to every problem, it can answer some problems. When corporations are writing environmental policy and when corporations fail to engage in sustainable practices, it becomes imperative that the government intervene and regulate industries. The challenge of neoliberalism is precisely that big corporations and big government are synergistic and work in concert to deregulate the market. As a consequence, we need different types of governmental action, just as we need new forms of corporate responsibility (CV, 37–38).

Finally, in the long term the goal must be to create a society not predicated on extraction, pollution, and the heedless embrace of economic growth at the cost of life itself, but rather on the principle of the universal destination of goods, which defends creation as intrinsically valuable and as our common home. There is a great deal that is packed into the phrase "our common home," and if we take its implications seriously it demands a renewed commitment to the cultivation of an ethos that can protect and preserve this commonality.

We began our description of neoliberalism in chapter 2 by quoting one of the founding figures of neoliberalism stating that he wanted a market friendly utopianism. We need to recall that moment now. Our judgment is that the neoliberal approach to the environmental crisis is a destructive form of utopianism. We seek to offer an alternative to market-based solutions alone. We recognize that offering the universal destination of goods as an alternative will be seen as utopian by today's political common sense. But as Hayek strove against long odds in the 1940s to develop an alternative politics based on the principle of market society, we strive today to do a similar thing under a different standard.

What we seek are creation-based solutions to a market-generated problem. The ambition of neoliberalism is to encase the market against people's demands for equality and redistribution. We seek to protect creation from market domination. The ambition of a politics of mercy is to heal the planet and people of the ravaging effects of neoliberalized markets and a perverse conception of private property, where even life itself can be claimed as private property.[19] The earth has been parceled and privatized, and from this it needs healing. It stands to reason that the response should involve the restoration of the commons and the universalization of creation's use for the benefit of all peoples.

Shortly after the publication of *Laudato Si'*, Francis observed in Bolivia: "The universal destination of goods is not a figure of speech found in the church's social teaching. It is a reality prior to private property. Property, especially when it affects natural resources, must always serve the needs of peoples."[20] In chapter 3 we discussed the way in which neoliberalism contradicts this teaching. The issue with the neoliberal prioritization of private property over the commons is straightforward: profits are concentrated, and ill effects are distributed with gross unevenness, falling disproportionately on those who profit least from neoliberal extractivism. While virtually every human being is complicit in the destruction of the environment in some way, we noted earlier that it is unambiguously the case that some persons and corporations bear more responsibility than others. Kate Aronoff sets this forth: "Just 100 companies have been responsible [for] over two-thirds of greenhouse gas emissions since the Industrial Revolution, and the richest 10 percent of people worldwide account for more than half of emissions from lifestyle choices."[21] Naomi Klein adds that fossil fuel companies have an enormous stake in the economy continuing to operate exactly as it does today (at 2014 market prices, fossil fuel in-the-ground reserves were worth $27 trillion).[22] The huge payoffs involved in mass-privatization yield neoliberal opposition to anything even resembling the universal destination of goods.

There are many possible creative remedies to the ecological crisis we face. Two possibilities that cohere with what we have already said are affluent countries taking the lead in reducing carbon emissions (as opposed to forestalling any reductions whatsoever), and what Thomas Pogge calls the "global resource dividend."

First, Francis believes that the affluent world (Global North) owes the global poor (Global South) an "ecological debt" because of its disproportionate use of natural resources. The prosperity that the Global North enjoys also saddles it with a responsibility. Northern countries must limit consumption, curb emissions, and offer resources to poorer countries to support sustainable development. Francis admonishes: "We must continue to be aware that, regarding climate change, there are differentiated responsibilities" (LS, 52). This is an important claim because the primary impediment to global climate treaties has been the refusal of affluent countries to take greater responsibility in reducing emissions.[23]

Second, because the natural resources of the earth disproportionality benefit the elite—in production as well as consumption—we should advocate for a mechanism that could more broadly distribute wealth generated from the goods of creation. Pogge has proposed a "global resource dividend" as a means of redressing the imbalances created by the global resource extraction and the consumption of natural resources, because the global poor rarely benefit from either resource extraction in their native lands (the wealth generated goes to national and global elites) or from the consumption of these resources (historically, the Global North has been the primary beneficiary). Furthermore, because the global poor will be the population most adversely affected by the effects of climate change, it stands to reason that some compensatory mechanism should be created in order to remedy this situation. Pogge recommends a 1 percent resource dividend—technically, it is a dividend and not a tax because "it is based on the idea that the global poor own an inalienable stake in all limited natural resources"[24]—that would be paid any time a country decides to allow resources to be extracted from its land. Because this 1 percent dividend would be passed on to the consumer, it would ultimately amount to a "tax on consumption."[25] The money collected from the global dividend would then be redistributed to the global poor, who have not received adequate benefit from the mechanisms of the current system. From the perspective of CST, this type of creative remedy follows quite logically from the universal destination of goods insofar as it attempts to ensure that all human beings benefit from the goods of creation. A dividend on resource consumption would have the positive side effect of incentivizing a shift away from fossil fuels and toward more sustainable forms of energy consumption. Even more attractively, this dividend would use an incentive that resembles a neoliberal one, a market-based solution of sorts, to help undo neoliberal destruction.

Obviously, both of these remedies demand the creation of a regulatory and distributive international body. *The Compendium of the Social Doctrine of the Church* argues: "If it is true that everyone is born with the right to use the goods of the earth, it is likewise true that, in order to ensure that this right is exercised in an equitable and orderly fashion, regulated interventions are necessary, interventions that are the result of national and international agreements, and a juridical order that adjudicates and specifies the exercise of this right" (#173). In this regard, Benedict XVI's proposal for a global regulatory body in *Caritas in Veritate* should be revisited and defended.[26] Arguably, the neoliberal era culminated with the formation of the World Trade Organization, a massive international organization tasked with making the world safe for trade and for the extraction of fossil fuels. A politics of mercy should strive in the long term for an equally massive international effort to recover the health of our planet. We already have large, global cooperation. It is a matter of which master this cooperation will serve, the impersonal market or the merciful Trinity (see Mt 6:24).

Pope Francis repeatedly remarks that *Laudato Si'* is directed toward all persons of good will (*LS*, 3, 62). Its larger audience fits with the enormity of the climate crisis it addresses—a crisis similar to the nuclear arms crisis faced by John XXIII in *Pacem in Terris*, which also was addressed to all people of good will. Francis argues that because the reach of environmental destruction is global it requires a global response, inclusive of religious *and* nonreligious communities. A diverse array of strategies should be employed to conscientize, to reform individual patterns of behavior and reduce consumption, to advocate for policy and structural reform at both national and international levels, and to pursue an overarching politics rooted in the commitment to protecting our common home and its most vulnerable inhabitants. Francis framed our situation accurately: "if we destroy creation, creation will destroy us."[27] Even though the "us" in Francis's phrase certainly refers to all of humanity, we must not forget—we cannot emphasize it enough—that lives sacrificed will number disproportionately among indigenous populations and the racialized urban poor, even as this capitalogenic crisis stems largely from the excesses of affluent populations in the Global North.[28]

Give Food, Drink, and Clothing

The proliferation of slums across the globe threatens the very possibility of dignified life for a rapidly growing population and as such represents a grave violation of human dignity. Catholic tradition has insisted on the protection of human dignity, because it is committed to the vision of the human person found in the Book of Genesis, the Psalms, and the prophets that human beings are created in the image and likeness of God, as the *imago dei* (Gen 1:26–27, 9:6; Ps 8:5; Is 64:8; 1 Cor 11:7). Likewise, the Catholic tradition condemns encroachment on human dignity, especially (as happens too often today) among those who outwardly profess Christian faith while doing violence to their neighbors (see Jas 3:9).

The centrality of the theme of human dignity has become increasingly pronounced since the Second Vatican Council, where it was pervasive. Its importance reached a crescendo in *Gaudium et Spes*, whose first chapter is devoted to the dignity of the human person and whose second chapter provides a vision for human community centered on this inviolable dignity.[29] These chapters succeed an introduction in which, among other modern world problems, the council fathers put front and center the issue of economic inequality, especially between the Global North and nations attempting to extricate themselves from their pasts of colonial exploitation and domination.[30]

John Paul II shares the council's emphasis on human dignity, making this theme the pivot for his papacy. Perhaps John Paul's single favorite text from the council is *Gaudium et Spes* 22, which proclaims the foundation for human dignity in the Incarnation of Jesus Christ, in whom humanity achieves its perfection. John Paul cites this text at auspicious moments in his pontificate, from his first encyclical *Redemptor Hominis* (RH, 8) through his social writings, including *Sollicitudo Rei Socialis* (SRS, 47n86) and *Centesimus Annus* (CA, 47n99). Human dignity serves as the lodestar for any social or economic order.

Benedict XVI follows in the same line, providing particularly forceful reflections on human dignity in *Caritas in Veritate*, where he contrasts human dignity and the demands of justice with widening wealth inequality (*CV*, 32). Later he insists, in a statement that Catholics must reflect on deeply in light of growing slum proliferation and other neoliberal structures of expulsion, "On this earth there is room for everyone: here the entire human family must find the resources to live with dignity, through the help of nature itself—God's gift to his children—and through hard work and creativity" (*CV*, 50). One should note the ecological tone of this statement, which continues in the remarks that follow it.[31] The conjunction of human dignity and the worth of creation is a constant throughout Benedict's papal writings and pronouncements, as with his opening address at the 2008 World Youth Day in Sydney, Australia.[32] Francis, too, makes contributions along this line, as we discuss below.

The theological tradition of the *imago dei* and respecting human dignity points us toward a political rendering of the corporal works of mercy that provide not just for the basic necessities of life of food, drink, and clothing but also, as Francis has argued, for a broader set of "sacred rights" that includes land, lodging, and labor. Such expanded provision, which facilitates dignified living and not just mere survival, would be anti-neoliberal. It disallows neoliberal celebration that survival has been provided, because survival should be *assumed*, not lauded. What should be celebrated is a world in which dignified, abundant life is the universal norm. As with visit the sick, we read these works of mercy with an eye toward the universal destination of goods. A politics of mercy configured like this can help us think and act anew with respect to slums.

In the short term, the politics of mercy applied to slums will involve conscientization. This must start with recognition of the crisis of global slum proliferation and the sharp contrast between this and the near daily creation of billionaires at the other extreme of the socioeconomic spectrum. But it will rapidly become more complex from there if conscientization is to address slum proliferation as a specifically *neoliberal* crisis. Chapter 3 treated neoliberal ideas that attempt to legitimate the vast wealth disparities in contemporary urban life, which allow some people to live in skyscrapers and many more to live in slums. Catholics must turn against legitimating discourses such as the neoliberal principle that (extreme) inequality is necessary for the healthy operation of economies, even to the extent that inequality must be fostered and protected; modernization theories of slums, which insist that slums are way stations toward urban prosperity; business-school admiration for slum entrepreneurship; and various justifications for entrepreneurial poverty reduction through microfinance and other mechanisms. Although these discourses exhibit varying levels of toxicity, their central assumption—that slumdwellers should be seen through an optic of market valuation and entrepreneurial practice—should at the very least be met with a hermeneutics of suspicion informed by the robust Catholic idea of human dignity centered on creation *in imaginem dei*. The added benefit of this hermeneutics of suspicion, which is directed primarily toward overly positive readings of the conditions of slumdwellers, is that it can avoid the opposite extreme, which, in chapter 3, we identified in works such as Mike Davis's *Planet of Slums*. Rather than depicting slums as hellscapes that deprive people of all freedom and self-worth, an account of slums and consequent praxis coordinate with a theology of the *imago dei* would recognize the enduring freedom of people who live in slums and affirm their labor, creativity, and social organization as reflective of their enduring and incalculable dignity.

In the middle term, a critical task is to advocate for the expansion of human rights to include a broader commitment to economic rights and material equality. In *Not Enough: Human Rights in an Unequal World*, Samuel Moyn argues that during the period of neoliberal ascendency the human rights movement was focused on the protection of civil and political rights. Because human rights were construed as individual, political, and legal, the demand for economic and social rights was marginalized. In particular, the antipoverty movement focused on minimal provision rather than equality. This allowed neoliberals to claim victory by reducing global poverty in raw numbers (providing minimum provision) without touching the issue of soaring inequality. Moyn suggests that by focusing on only one dimension of social justice (minimum provision) the human rights movement allowed "the distributional victory of the rich" to go largely uncontested.[33] The consequences of this distributional victory is on full display with the rise of populism throughout the Global North as well as the wave of new migrations throughout the Global South. Moyn contends that if the human rights movement aspires to be more than a mere palliative that seeks only to mitigate the most extreme pathologies generated by the neoliberal order, then it must take up the distributive challenge and work toward a more substantive equality.[34]

Notably, Francis has pressed for this type of project in his focused criticism of inequality—"inequality is the root of social evil"[35]—as well as his advocacy for the expansion of human rights to include what he characterizes as "sacred rights"[36]: "The Bible tells us that God hears the cry of his people, and I wish to join my voice to yours in calling for the three 'L's' for all our brothers and sisters: land, lodging and labor. I said it and I repeat it: these are sacred rights. It is important, it is well worth fighting for them. May the cry of the excluded be heard in Latin America and throughout the world."[37] Francis further emphasized the centrality of this demand to CST during his speech in the Kangemi slums in Nairobi, Kenya. To build a more merciful social order it is critical "that every family has dignified housing, access to drinking water, a toilet, reliable sources of energy for lighting, cooking and improving their homes . . . that basic services are provided to each of you; that your appeals and your pleas for greater opportunity can be heard; that all can enjoy the peace and security which they rightfully deserve on the basis of their infinite human dignity."[38] The excluded people of the world should have these three basic needs met as rights, and this should be the baseline focus for daily struggle. Francis approves of the quotidian actions of popular movements that aim to provide the three Ls, and with them, food for the hungry, drink for the thirsty, and clothing for the naked, and reminds Christians that their charge to distribute the fruits of the land and of work is stronger than philanthropy and moral obligation; "it is a commandment."[39]

In this, Francis offers an approach to rights that exceeds that of the dominant juridical framework under neoliberalism insofar as it extends the responsibilities of local and international communities beyond the impersonality of policy, law enforcement, and bureaucracy and into a vision of sociality predicated precisely upon sustaining and facilitating *personal* lives, so *families* may flourish, *people* with appeals, pleas, and aspirations can enjoy abundant life. And all this precisely because human persons are *sacred*. No human person is ever just a label, a number, a "beneficiary."

The long-term alternative would be a social order centered not on capital accumulation and encasing the market against people's demands for food, drink, clothing, lodging, land, and labor but on the provision of these conditions for life so that people may live abundantly. In Francis's words, it would mean moving toward a world where social life is defined by the "adequate administration of our common home (*casa común*)."[40] It would be to develop a communitarian economy rooted in the CST idea of the universal destination of goods. The perdurance of concrete living bodies and the protection of the right to land, labor, and lodging should be prioritized as the fundamental task of every sociopolitical order and, as such, should displace capital as the organizing principle. This teaching prioritizes the universal distribution of goods over the individual right to private property because the right to private property is not absolute and must always be set in relation with and viewed as subordinate to the universal destination of goods.[41]

We have presented Pope Benedict XVI's social vision as particularly fructifying for an anti-neoliberal vision of the state, where the political sphere could be reclaimed from marketization and restored as a proper sphere unto itself. *Caritas in Veritate* points to a multiplicity of tactics for creating a new social order that involves the reform of the political sphere along with civil society and the economy. As discussed above, Benedict even goes so far as to call for a global political authority with the power to regulate the economy and to ensure food security and basic economic rights for the global population (*CV*, 67). Although this suggestion was dismissed by the political and religious Right as impractical,[42] this is precisely the type of creative thinking necessary to confront extreme inequality in a neoliberal era. And it fits exactly with a proper understanding of the principle of subsidiarity: given the global extent and severity of wealth inequality, including the proliferation of slums amid the crowning of new billionaires, a global political solution has become inevitable. Furthermore, in response to those who would object to ceding too much authority to a centralized body that nullifies national sovereignty, one could respond that this is precisely what neoliberalism has done over the past forty years. It has displaced national sovereignty and imposed policies that have disproportionately enriched global elites, while only marginally improving material conditions for the global poor (outside of China).

In a world in which we witnessed the largest increase in billionaires in history in 2017 (the world now has 2,043 billionaires),[43] while 1 billion people continue to live in slums, and in which 26 people possess as much wealth as the bottom 50 percent of the global population (3.8 billion people),[44] can the protection of the sacred rights of the poor (Francis) mean anything other than the massive redistribution of wealth in the realm of civil society (charity) and political life (redistribution)? Whether we term this a society built upon the foundation of the logic of the gift (Benedict XVI) or a culture of mercy (Francis), what is evident is that real and substantive change is not only *possible*, but *necessary* for the victims of neoliberal sacrifice.[45] The long-term alternative is a true slum-free city that, if necessary, will also be a city without skyscrapers. While it is rarely stated in these terms, this is a clear implication of CST on the priority of the universal destination of goods over private property. Let us conclude by taking note of how Francis describes the duty of justice in this context: "we can no longer sustain unacceptable economic inequality, which prevents us from applying the principle of the universal destination of the earth's goods. We are all called to undertake processes of apportionment which are respectful, responsible and inspired by the precepts of distributive justice." He continues: "One group of individuals cannot control half of the world's resources. We cannot allow for persons and entire peoples to have a right only to gather the remaining crumbs. Nor can we be indifferent or think ourselves dispensed from the moral imperatives which flow from a joint responsibility to care for the planet, a shared responsibility often stressed by the political international community, as also by the Magisterium."[46]

Abolitionism

We now apply our discussion of the works of mercy to the context of the United States of America. As in chapter 3, we engage the distinctive US crises of mass incarceration and mass deportation through the lens of race. This entails discussing how the works of mercy apply—or historically have failed to apply—to the realities of race and racism. There have been significant shortfalls in this respect in the US Catholic Church. Having acknowledged these shortfalls, though, we move on to provide a sketch of how US Catholics could practice what they preach by grappling with mass incarceration and mass deportation, using the traditional corporal works of mercy of ransoming the captive and welcoming the stranger as guides. Like we did with the first two crises, we provide a brief program here for a politics of mercy, which with respect to these crises would take shape as an antiracist politics guided by the long-term civilizational principle of abolitionism.

Bryan Massingale observes in *Racial Justice in the Catholic Church* that the most important thing to note about CST on the issue racism in society is that there is very little of it.[47] Outside of Pius XI's 1937 document, *Mit Brennender Sorge: On the Church and the German Reich*, which denounced the racism of Nazi anti-Semitism, and the US Catholic Bishops' statement on *Discrimination and Christian Conscience* (1958), there is no official statement on racism in the Catholic tradition prior to Vatican II. Even at Vatican II, the only document to explicitly raise the issue was *Gaudium et Spes*, which mentioned race only a handful of times in the context of discussions of broader social divisions in the world.[48] After Vatican II, the Pontifical Council for Justice and Peace produced two important analyses of racism: *The Church and Racism: Toward a More Fraternal Society* (1988) and *Contribution to World Conference Against Racism: Racial Discrimination, Xenophobia, and Related Intolerance* (2001). Additionally, various episcopal conferences in Africa, Asia, Europe, Latin America, and North America have published criticisms of racism in society.[49]

In view of our prior analysis of racial neoliberalism in the United States, we have a specific interest in the US Conference of Catholic Bishops' statements on racism. During the civil rights era and its immediate aftermath, the Catholic bishops published two statements on racism in American society: *Discrimination and the Christian Conscience* (1958) and *The National Race Crisis* (1968). The 1958 document called for overcoming racial division but offered no clear policies or strategies for achieving this aim. In contrast, the 1968 document, released in response to the race riots of 1967 and Martin Luther King Jr.'s assassination (three weeks before its publication), emphasized the importance of political responses to racial problems in the areas of jobs, education, welfare, and housing. In 1979 the US Conference of Catholic Bishops released *Brothers and Sisters to Us*, a statement on the Catholic Church's approach to racial justice in a new situation in which the "external appearances" of racism had shifted, but the problem remained the same. In a distinctive contribution to CST on the matter, the document proclaimed that the battle against racism "demands an equally radical transformation, in our minds and hearts as well as in the structure of our society."[50] At the same time, it provided no substantive analysis of the structures of American racism. In a remarkable document published on the tenth anniversary of *Brothers and Sisters to Us*, the US Bishops' Committee on Black Catholics admitted that the document "made little or no impact on the majority of Catholics in the United States."[51] A study on the twenty-fifth anniversary of *Brothers and Sisters to Us* revealed that only 18 percent of US Catholic bishops had issued statements condemning racism since its publication in 1979.[52] In Massingale's analysis of subsequent remarks on race by individual US bishops, he concludes that the overall tendency is to view racism as little more than "personal prejudice."[53]

Massingale's judgment agrees with James Cone's blistering critique of the Catholic Church's response to racism in the United States in "A Theological Challenge to the American Catholic Church" (1986).[54] Cone contends that while the Catholic Church in the United States has often focused on raising awareness about the suffering of the poor in Central America, it has not confronted the United States' own history of racial exclusion. This oversight leads Cone "to question the quality of [the Catholic Church's] commitment to justice in other areas."[55] Even though Cone does not understate Catholic contributions to struggles for justice, he argues that the church's mixed message with regard to race cannot be overlooked. In a 2006 interview, Cone adds: "The solidarity of North American white theologians with the struggles of the poor in the developing world should only be taken seriously if they make a similar solidarity with the poor in the United States. You cannot help the poor out there [in Latin America] without first siding with the poor here."[56] Cone says this of white Catholic theologians, but the same goes for the hierarchy of the US Catholic Church. Theologians and bishops alike have failed to seriously confront the sin of white supremacy and offer a *structural* analysis of its effects in US history. In view of this, Massingale determines it "difficult *not* to conclude that Catholic engagement with racism is a matter of low institutional commitment, priority, and importance."[57]

The anemia of the US Conference of Catholic Bishops' response to structural racism carries over into statements on the migration crisis in the United States. Despite the pastoral letter, *Welcoming the Stranger Among Us: Unity in Diversity*'s (2000) twelve thousand words, the word *racism* appears only four times. Although bishops characterized racism as "America's 'original sin,'" they attribute this sin mostly to its creation of "stereotypes about people whose facial features or skin color identify them as Asian, Arab, African, or Mexican," maintaining somewhat weakly that "in some instances, racism has been so deeply engrained that an institutional racism prevails."[58] Even with this acknowledgment, the bishops fail adequately to confront the history and effects of structural racism in US immigration policy or its bearing on the current crisis. Vague motions toward the existence of systemic racism without specifying the enthronement of white citizenship are hardly enough.

There are some causes for hope. In their joint pastoral letter, *Strangers No Longer: Together on the Journey of Hope* (2003), the Catholic Bishops of Mexico and the United States advocated for concrete policy reforms focused on (1) addressing the root causes that generate migrants and refugees (they specify war and poverty as primary causes); (2) transforming immigration law by creating a path to citizenship for undocumented migrants and labor protections for temporary workers; and (3) restoring due process for migrants (which was taken away in 1996 by the Illegal Immigration Reform and Immigrant Responsibility Act). Since the publication of this joint statement, the US Conference of Catholic Bishops has continued to promote dramatic immigration reform centered on earned legalization, immigrant worker programs, and prioritizing family-based immigration.[59] In the wake of the 2016 election and the Charlottesville riots in 2017, the conference formed a committee on racism (the only other two committees of similar rank focus on religious liberty and the defense of traditional marriage) and promised a pastoral letter on racism in 2018.[60] This committee was announced at the conference's fall assembly in 2017, which opened with speeches by Bishop Joe Vasquez of Austin, Texas, and Archbishop José Gomez of Los Angeles, regarding immigration. These bishops stated their formal opposition to various dimensions of Trump's immigration policy and described the efforts of the Catholic Church in the United States to protect migrants' rights.[61]

The resulting document was approved for publication on November 15, 2018 and released soon after. Positively, *Open Wide Our Hearts: The Enduring Call to Love* describes the struggle against racism as a "life" issue and acknowledges the Catholic Church's complicity in America's racist history through its participation in the colonization of indigenous populations and the trans-Atlantic slave trade.[62] The Bishops straightforwardly recognize: "the truth is that the sons and daughters of the Catholic Church have been complicit in the evils of racism."[63] Additionally, the document offers a more sophisticated analysis of the different forms of racism than previous documents by narrating the histories of oppression and exclusion that have shaped the lives of generations of African American, Latinx, and Native American communities.[64]

But even as *Open Wide Our Hearts* represents a significant improvement from previous church documents, it is still plagued both by an inadequate understanding of racism as well as an anemic response to it. In the document, the bishops describe racism as the conscious and unconscious act of holding one's "own race or ethnicity as superior" and other races and ethnicities as "inferior and unworthy of equal regard."[65] And while the document does periodically recognize that racism exists within structures and institutions, the focus remains on racism as an interpersonal transgression that demands a personal response ("open wide our hearts"). In one of the final sections of the document, "Changing Structures," the bishops resort to bland generalities about the need to promote policies that confront "racism and its effects in our civic and social institutions."[66] The refusal to name concrete and very specific structures of sin *as* structures of sin (prisons, detention centers) is a significant weakness. Thus, while this document avoids the problems associated with colorblind discourses, it does not rise to the level of an antiracist response.

Although there has been a more concerted effort to confront issues of xenophobia and racism after the Second Vatican Council, the Catholic Church has not lived up to its own name during this period. Instead of signifying divine universality (catholicity) to the world, it has inscribed all-too-human exclusion into ecclesial structures and practices. This is unacceptable; it is a sin, a stain, corruption, and demands repentance.[67] Racial neoliberalism represents an assault on catholicity. Catholics must treat it as such and struggle for a true universality that folds all particularity into itself without exclusion or cancellation. As we discussed in chapter 2, the neoliberal ethos proves so unacceptable and appalling precisely because it pretends to universality and globalism, but through a shortcut respecting only market metrics and practices, and only people who are market successes (all other people and the environment be damned). Neoliberalism is a universalization of markets that necessarily excludes persons and creation both in principle (chapter 2) and in fact (chapter 3) with devastating effects for thought and life. If Jesus says that we should have life and have it abundantly, racial neoliberalism wipes away abundance for most, walling it off in privatized reserves for the scanty few.

Catholics must take with dire seriousness Paul's statement in Galatians 3:28 that in Christ there is no Jew or Greek, slave or free, man or woman.[68] While this verse has a contested and fraught history, it sums up the true universalism of the New Testament, evident in passages such as Jesus's interaction with the Syrophoenician woman (Mk 7:24–30; Mt 15:21–28), the story of Pentecost (Acts 2:1–4), Peter's baptism of the Roman Cornelius and his household (Acts 10:1–11:18), and Paul's ministry to the Gentiles (Rom 15:14–16). The point is that God's mercy extends to all.[69] By the standard of catholicity and God's mercy, the Catholic Church has every reason to oppose racial neoliberalism and to attempt to take an antiracist stance toward social structures that marginalize communities of color. Race ought never to be hidden, as neoliberalism has done with its "colorblindness." Instead, Catholic thought and life must become antiracist, foregrounding the racialized nature of structural exploitation in our world.

What is true of the Catholic Church in general is also true of the works of mercy in particular. There is no explicit mention of racism in official formulations of the works of mercy and very little, if any, commentary on the relationship between the works of mercy and the sin of racism.[70] The traditional focus of the works of mercy has been on suffering produced by material deprivation and social isolation. It is incumbent on us to reimagine the works of mercy in view of the history of structural racism, and quite specifically, the Catholic Church's own complicity and silence in this history. We stand convinced that the reimagined works of mercy could function as an antiracist politics of mercy. To ransom the captive and to welcome the stranger in our world today must mean supporting explicitly antiracist initiatives and policies, given the formidable racialization of the prison and immigration industrial complexes. Racially reimagined works of mercy would also take aim at slum proliferation and environmental destruction. In formerly colonized regions of Latin America, Africa, and Asia, slums have emerged as sites to warehouse surplus populations. Furthermore, environmental racism is a central practice of racial neoliberalism. The Flint, Michigan, water crisis (2014 to present), for example, was generated by the nexus between neoliberal reform (an unelected "emergency manager" aiming to cut costs) and structural racism (costs were cut in a mainly African American city). Coherent, earnest, and genuinely contemporary practice of the works of mercy today simply cannot ignore the racialized character of neoliberal exclusion.

With regard to environmental destruction and slum proliferation, we used the CST principle of the universal destination of goods as a civilizational commitment to orient a politics of mercy aimed at addressing these crises. Our presentation of the shortfalls of CST's treatment of race and racism should suggest that no principle apposite to the universal destination of goods yet exists to confront mass incarceration and mass deportation. For this reason, we recommend abolitionism as a civilizational claim taken from secular discourses but consistent, as we will show, with Christic freedom and hospitality. This civilizational claim demands a restructuring of the social order so that all persons are free and welcome. This civilizational claim, enriched by Christological ideas of freedom and hospitality, can help us to articulate an antiracist politics of mercy set against the sacrifices of racial neoliberalism.

We discuss Christ's freedom and Christ's hospitality later in this chapter, in connection with our discussion of ransoming the captive and welcoming the stranger. For now, we should say a bit about how abolitionism functions as the long-term goal that animates an antiracist politics of mercy. As we have seen, the politics of mercy demands that society be restructured so that its policies and programs take root in mercy rather than punishment and sacrifice. Abolitionism, as we employ it, refers to the attempt to eliminate neoliberal institutions of racial securitization and to replace them with institutions that protect the dignity and authentic freedom of all persons.[71] The contemporary abolitionist project which we invoke here entails both destructive and reconstructive elements. First, it lays bare the structures of neoliberal securitization (prisons, detention centers, etc.) for what they are: systems of racialized punishment and exclusion. Second, it recognizes that if an abolitionist politics has as its goal the elimination of carceral structures, it is necessary to generate different policies and build different institutions that respond humanely to the issues of poverty, structural violence, and forced displacement. Taken in an abolitionist sense, ransoming the captive and welcoming the stranger entail not only the work of freeing the incarcerated and providing sanctuary for migrants but also the structural work of building a society in which social problems are dealt with mercifully (welfare, healthcare, education, fair trade, noninterventionism) rather than punitively (impris-onment, detention, deportation).

Even though abolitionism is a secular political discourse, it exhibits re-markable resonances with pronouncements by Pope Francis regarding the relationship between prisons and mercy. In a speech given to inmates in a prison in Ciudad Juárez, Mexico, in 2016 he said the following:

> Divine Mercy reminds us that prisons are an indication of the kind of society we are. In many cases they are a sign of the silence and omis-sions which have led to a throwaway culture, a symptom of a culture that has stopped supporting life, of a society that has abandoned its children. Mercy reminds us that reintegration does not begin here within these walls; rather it begins before, it begins "outside," in the streets of the city. Reintegration or rehabilitation begins by creating a system which we could call social health, that is, a society which seeks not to cause sickness, polluting relationships in neighborhoods, schools, town squares, the streets, homes and in the whole of the social spec-trum. A system of social health that endeavors to promote a culture which acts and seeks to prevent those situations and pathways that end in damaging and impairing the social fabric. . . . The problem of secu-rity is not resolved only by incarcerating; rather, it calls us to intervene by confronting the structural and cultural causes of insecurity that im-pact the entire social framework. Jesus' concern for the care of the hungry, the thirsty, the homeless and prisoners sought to express the core of the Father's mercy. This becomes a moral imperative for the whole of society that wishes to maintain the necessary conditions for a better common life. It is within a society's capacity to include the poor, infirm and imprisoned, that we see its ability to heal their wounds and make them builders of a peaceful coexistence. Social reintegration be-gins by making sure that all of our children go to school and that their families obtain dignified work by creating public spaces for leisure and recreation, and by fostering civic participation, health services and ac-cess to basic services, to name just a few possible measures. The whole rehabilitation process starts here.[72]

Francis makes three important points that overlap with an abolitionist vi-sion of the social order in this passage. First, he condemns prisons as symptoms of a throwaway culture that no longer values life and manages social problems through expulsion. Second, he argues that a Catholic commitment to mercy demands that we resist the tendency to deal with social insecurity primarily through processes of securitization and punishment. Third, he observes that we must ensure that mercy is made structural by working so that "the entire social framework" is built on Jesus's concern with "care of the hungry, the thirsty, the homeless and prisoners." This, and not securitization, is the merciful approach to dealing with insecurity and disorder in society. In short, Francis provides us with a theological justification for adopting abolitionism as our civilizational claim.

Ransom the Captive

Visiting the prisoner and ransoming the captive emerge as central practices of mercy in response to the persecution and imprisonment of the earliest Christians.[73] Jesus himself was a prisoner and his earliest followers spent a great deal of time in prison, as the Acts of the Apostles and Paul's letters amply attest (Acts 5; Acts 12; Acts 16; 2 Cor 6:5; 2 Cor 11:23; Col 4:10; Eph 4:1; 2 Tim 1:16–18; and 2 Tim 4:16–18). The God of Israel is praised numerous times in the scriptures for letting captives free (paradigmatically throughout Exodus, but also in Ps 69:33, 79:11, 102:20, 142:7, 146:7; and Is 42:6–7, 49:9, 61:1). Giving comfort and consolation to prisoners became a practice of mercy and encouragement for persecuted Christians. And ransoming or liberating the captive became a central imperative of Christian ministry in the early church. Later, when Christians were no longer imprisoned for their beliefs, the emphasis was placed on attending to the spiritual needs of the imprisoned and the demand that those placed in debtors' prison be freed.[74] This Christian concern with the criminalization of poverty relates to the project of mass incarceration, which criminalizes poverty and then imposes what often amounts to a lifetime of debt on the imprisoned through fines, fees, interest, and restitution.[75]

In view of this history, Catholics should be scandalized to discover that the neoliberal era has brought an explosion of prison populations in the United States and, even more chillingly, has spawned an industry dedicated to earning private profit off of mass incarceration. The emergence of a vast, unparalleled carceral apparatus in the United States requires that Catholic theology and life actively and radically retrieve the merciful work of ransoming the captive.

This retrieval should be rooted in a substantive vision of freedom in Christ. Pope Francis's practice of washing the feet of prisoners in a detention center every Holy Thursday during his pontificate provides a site for Christological reflection. In particular Francis's homily from a recent Holy Thursday (March 29, 2018) offers a radical vision of Christ's freedom.[76] He suggests that there is real freedom expressed in Jesus's washing of the disciples' feet inasmuch as Jesus transgresses the boundaries between master and slave, wealthy and poor, teacher and student in order to show that true life is a life of freedom without regard for social standing. The freedom that Jesus reveals calls us to live beyond structures of exclusion and social death, which is the obverse of neoliberal freedom.

We have consistently critiqued neoliberalism's commitment to the impersonality of the market, which allows for and has facilitated social crises such as mass incarceration, which is in large measure attributable to a disregard for persons and their dignity. Freedom in Christ means living beyond such callousness and mercilessness. Francis puts this poetically, evoking Jesus's passion and concatenating this with the classic image of Jesus as the Good Shepherd: "Understand this: Jesus is called Jesus; he is not called Pontius Pilate. Jesus does not know how to wash his hands of people: he only knows how to take a risk! Look at this beautiful image: Jesus bent down among the thorns, risking to hurt himself by picking up the lost sheep."[77] Neoliberalism washes its hands of people and exhorts people only to risk investment to increase their human capital value and not to risk loving as Jesus does by eliminating social hierarchies and mechanisms of social exclusion. During his visit to the United States, Pope Francis linked the washing of feet to an ethos of inclusion at the Curran-Fromhold correctional facility in Philadelphia:

> It is painful when we see prison systems which are not concerned to care for wounds, to soothe pain, to offer new possibilities. It is painful when we see people who think that only others need to be cleansed, purified, and do not recognize that their weariness, pain and wounds are also the weariness, pain and wounds of society. The Lord tells us this clearly with a sign: he washes our feet so we can come back to the table. The table from which he wishes no one to be excluded. The table which is spread for all and to which all of us are invited.[78]

Freedom in Christ is, ultimately, freedom for radical fellowship and inclusion. Francis makes eminently clear that this inclusion has a structural dimension. It must be performed as healing the "weariness, pain, and wounds of society." Mass incarceration as a product of racial neoliberalism causes massive weariness and pain and inflicts gaping wounds on society (see chapter 3). The theological idea of freedom in Christ as envisioned by Francis guides the program we now suggest for reimagining ransom the captive under the rubric of a politics of mercy.

In the short term, a wide array of individual and local initiatives exists to respond to the structural sin of mass incarceration. Because the works of mercy aim to alleviate the suffering and social isolation of the marginalized, the act of visiting the incarcerated represents a central practice of mercy in an era of mass incarceration. But this act should be accompanied by the recognition that mass incarceration represents a highly racialized act of social exclusion. It is easy to avoid this fact for two reasons. First, the new Jim Crow differs markedly from Jim Crow segregationist racism during the post–Civil War era (1865–1965) because the new Jim Crow's racialized mechanisms of exclusion are hidden from public view. Prisons are set apart from society and rarely seen by anyone other than the incarcerated, their relatives, and those who work in the prison industry. Most people are simply unaware that the expansion of prisons and the number of those incarcerated has proceeded at an alarming pace over the past forty years and that those most affected by this increase are from communities of color. Second, the project of mass incarceration has been sold to the public as a colorblind attempt to make society safe for law-abiding citizens. People commonly assume that if a person is incarcerated, they committed a crime and deserve punishment—race, evidently, need not be a consideration. Therefore, the state and politicians can wash their hands of the racialized character of the US criminal justice and prison systems.

Reimagining ransoming the captive as a political and antiracist work of mercy must begin with raising awareness of the fact of mass imprisonment in the United States and of mass incarceration's racial character. This issue is particularly pressing for Catholic churches in the United States, as James Cone and Bryan Massingale have forcefully and rightly declared. To raise racism and incarceration as theological issues, as topics of central importance to CST, constitutes a critical discursive act of conscientization about structures of sin in our world.[79]

In addition to visiting the prisoner and the work of conscientization, it is also necessary to propose middle-term structural reforms that can support the broader goal of decarceration and provide support for constructive projects focused on restorative rather than punitive or retributive justice. Because decarceration and the reconstruction of the social order constitute interrelated projects of reform directed toward the ultimate abolition of prisons—a goal we deem theologically imperative in view of the biblical and magisterial teachings we have already consulted—we will treat these middle-term projects and the long-term goal together.

If Catholic theology witnesses in an authentic way the freedom of Christ, the long-term goal should be abolition of prisons. In critical prison studies literature and activist circles, the tension between reform and abolitionism remains a central debate. Where abolitionism calls for the complete eradication of the prison system, reform attempts to work within the system to transform it and to mitigate its most pernicious effects. Because these strategies appear to grate against one another, critics have argued either that reform is insufficiently radical (abolitionists) or that abolitionism is unrealistic and utopian (reformists). We follow Angela Davis here by rejecting the binary between reform and abolitionism.[80] The critical question is which types of reforms are pursued, and whether in the long-term they serve to weaken or strengthen the prison-industrial complex. Davis astutely notes: "The history of the very institution of prison is a reform. Foucault points this out. Reform doesn't come after the advent of the prison; it accompanies the birth of the prison. So prison reform has only created better prisons. In the process of creating better prisons, more people are brought under the surveillance of the correctional and law enforcement networks."[81] Reform on its own can lead to subtle improvements, the effect of which historically has led to the entrenchment and expansion of prison as a social institution. In this regard, it is critical to link short-term responses and middle-term reforms to the long-term goal of abolitionism to ensure that charitable and reformist responses do not support the expansion and continuation of the prison-industrial complex.

W. E. B. Du Bois first coined the term "abolition democracy" in *Black Reconstruction in America* (1935), when he argued that the abolition of slavery demanded the creation of new democratic institutions that could support material and political freedom of liberated slaves. As Du Bois theorized it, abolitionism should have entailed not only the elimination of slavery but also the creation of new institutions that would support the inclusion of former slaves into society. The United States failed at this reconstructive task and, as a consequence, after the formal abolition of slavery new institutions of social control emerged that created new ways to supervise, exploit, and punish African Americans: debt peonage, convict leasing, Jim Crow, ghettoization, redlining, and finally mass incarceration.[82] Of particular concern was the fact that a link was established between slavery and criminality with the Thirteenth Amendment. This amendment abolished slavery with the exception of convicts, and, as a result, "felons" were created as a new enslavable class of people. The effect of this provision has been that the criminal justice and prison systems have emerged as institutions through which "the vestiges of slavery have persisted."[83] Davis concludes that prisons "have become a receptacle for all of those human beings who bear the inheritance of the failure to create abolition democracy in the aftermath of slavery."[84]

Davis adopts the unfinished task of Du Bois's abolitionist democracy as the starting point for her reflections on prison abolitionism. As with abolitionist democracy, prison abolitionism combines destructive (decarceration) and creative (reconstruction) elements. Although decarceration and reconstruction can be separated conceptually, these elements are materially inseparable. Taken together they contour an abolitionist vision for society.

Decarceration refers to reforms aimed at reducing the number of prisoners, restricting the number of persons entering prisons, and preventing the growth and expansion of the prison-industrial complex. It attempts to reverse the trend of mass incarceration and redress the enormous harm that it has inflicted on US society and specifically communities of color. Furthermore, decarceration would dismantle not only sociopolitical structures that support mass incarceration—the privatization of the prison-industrial complex projects, mandatory minimum sentences, and other related practices of criminal justice—but also the ideological formations that make prisons and punitive violence seem inevitable.

Reconstruction involves "the creation of an array of social institutions that would begin to solve the social problems that set people on the track to prison."[85] Davis suggests that the task of reconstruction is fundamentally to reshape the social order that generated mass incarceration. Along with Ruth Wilson Gilmore and Loïc Wacquant, Davis points to the connection between the rise of mass incarceration and neoliberalism.[86] The rise of austerity policies in the early 1980s, which led to severe cuts to welfare and other antipoverty programs, emerged alongside the proliferation of security regimes aimed at the management of impoverished and racialized populations. Criminalization replaced welfare. Reconstruction would turn this tide.

Although neoliberalism and mass incarceration emerged as successful political projects fewer than forty years ago, imagining a world beyond neoliberalism and the American prison system is often dismissed as utopian. Davis maintains that such dismissals underscore the ideological construction of prisons as "natural" features of social life and essential to society's functioning.[87] Reconstruction must stem from revealing the contingency and revisability of what has been constructed as natural and necessary. Prisons only emerged as the dominant method of punishment two hundred years ago. Mass incarceration has yet to turn forty. It is possible to imagine alternatives to both prisons and a punitive model for responding to social problems. Importantly, though, Davis argues that the possibility of an alternative future will be realistic only if we move beyond the neoliberal organization of society: "I do think that a society without prisons is a realistic future possibility, but in a transformed society, one in which people's needs, not profits, constitute the driving force."[88] Only by working toward the total transformation of society—beyond market value as the central organizing principle—does it become possible to build social institutions that do not rely on incarceration to deal with the issues of racism, poverty, and illness. Davis's insistence that abolitionist projects should be rooted in "socialist rather than capitalist conceptions of democracy" is critical here because it offers a view of citizenship that not only includes political rights but also economic rights (employment, public housing, education, and healthcare).[89] This claim might very well be viewed with suspicion by some American Catholics. But it was Benedict XVI himself who observed that "in many respects, democratic socialism was and is close to Catholic social doctrine and has in any case made a remarkable contribution to the formation of a social consciousness."[90] Socialism need not denote a state-driven economic order (although neoliberalism is, in many respects, state-driven, inasmuch as states are among the institutions encasing the global economy) but rather an economic, political, and civil order that is person-centered (*social* in a straightforward sense). Independent of labels, the decisive point is that an abolitionist social order is constitutively anti-neoliberal, entails a commitment to both antiracist policies and more inclusive and egalitarian forms of economic democracy, and, as we see it, is coherent with CST because of its anti-neoliberalism and antiracism.[91]

To adopt an abolitionist stance in relation to both neoliberalism and the American prison system is to confront two of the most intransigent social systems in twenty-first-century America. But, as we have argued throughout this book, Catholic teaching and theology calls Catholics to strive for the seemingly impossible and to labor to realize a social order rooted in mercy, forgiveness, and inclusion rather than profit, punishment, and exclusion. The prospects for abolitionism may appear bleak at the current sociopolitical juncture; but unexpected—often dramatic—social upheaval and change occur frequently in our world. Gilmore noted the following in the wake of the 2008 financial crisis:

> The two biggest reasons that people are in prison are issues around income and issues around illness. That's the reason most people in prison are in prison. These are things we can address without putting people in cages and employing other people to watch the people in cages. So yes, we are talking about a wholesale restructuring of society. Now some people say to me, and I'm getting old I'm in my late 50's, "this will take forever." That may be true, but anyone who has been paying the least attention to the news in the U.S. in the last week and a half, sees that things that take forever can happen overnight. The U.S. nationalized two major mortgage banks and the biggest insurance company in the world and in some way shape or form put up 700 billion dollars to bail out investment banks and Wall Street. If that can be done overnight, then a lot of things that we are talking about can also happen overnight if we had the political will.[92]

From a Catholic point of view, such political will should come from an application of the work of mercy of ransoming the captive and the theological reality of the freedom of Christ, which is offered to each and every human person. Jesus Christ died as a "ransom for many" (Mk 10:45; Mt 20:28), having led a life of service to *all* his fellow persons. A politics of mercy arises from reflection on this Christological reality and its anthropological implications: to ransom the captive means to cooperate with the saving freedom of Christ, helping to set societal conditions for the exercise of true freedom, which entails addressing the imposed unfreedom among those deemed market failures, the leftovers, those destined to be warehoused. An anti-neoliberal, antiracist, pro-ransom ethos is exactly what the Catholic ethos of mercy, patterned on Christ's life and death as a ransom for many (and his resurrection, with breaks all death-bound structures), prescribes. Catholics must will it.

Welcome the Stranger

Neoliberals have been adept at exploiting social crises to solidify, reinforce, and even expand their market vision for society. We must ask how to attack the insidious racial neoliberalism at the center of the crisis of mass incarceration and mobilize effective resistance to it. Put otherwise, how do we undermine both neoliberalism and structural racism and build a social order that refuses to accept the sacrifices of neoliberalism as both natural and necessary? The answer, we have been suggesting, is by pursuing a multiplicity of discursive, reformist, and abolitionist strategies simultaneously, and by linking resistance against mass incarceration to other social crises generated by neoliberalism. So that just as mass incarceration and mass deportation represent fundamentally interrelated manifestations of racial neoliberalism, ransoming the captive and welcoming the stranger constitute connected forms of an antiracist and abolitionist politics of mercy.

As we turn to the practice of welcoming the stranger, a work of mercy made all the more urgent in the face of the current threat of mass deportation in US society, we must focus on the relation between prisons and border walls, between systems that manage social inequalities by warehousing and expelling surplus populations, and we must confront these systems of exclusion as intersecting structural violations of human dignity and human freedom.

Catholics should not forget that Jesus and his earliest followers were regarded as foreigners, alien to the great urban center of Jerusalem (e.g., Mk 14:70; Mt 26:73; Lk 22:59; Acts 2:7). Furthermore, in the Book of Exodus God instructs the people of Israel, "Do not oppress the foreigner; you yourselves know how it feels to be foreigners, because you were foreigners in Egypt" (Ex 23:9). Even more ominously, Jesus describes the fate of someone who was inhospitable to the stranger in the final judgment scene of the Gospel of Matthew (Mt 25:43). Early Christian theologians, such as Cyprian, Tertullian, and Clement, urged their fellow Christians to practice the hospitality of welcoming and sheltering strangers.[93]

Perhaps the most prominent tradition of welcoming strangers is the Benedictine tradition, following St. Benedict of Nursia's counsel that "all guests who arrive be received as Christ, because He will say: 'I was a stranger and you took Me in' (Mt 25:35)."[94] Pope Francis has invoked this tradition in his own teaching on hospitality to migrants: "the encounter with the other . . . is also an encounter with Christ," because Christ is the one "with ragged clothes, dirty feet, agonized faces, sore bodies, unable to speak our language."[95] If Catholics remember this tradition of hospitality well they should be scandalized to discover that the neoliberal era has forced numerous populations to migrate from their homes, only to be met where they arrive with widespread, vitriolic anti-immigrant animus. From a Catholic theological point of view, steeped in the same imagination as St. Benedict, rather than being viewed as "illegal," migrants should be viewed as Christ, as opportunities to love another as Christ and to welcome Christ as Christ has welcomed us (1 Jn 4:12 and 13:34–35; Rom 15:7). A response to migrants, then, should proceed in view of the full gravity of the situation described in the final judgment scene of Matthew's Gospel (Mt 25:35).

As with mass incarceration and abolitionism, in the case of the migrant crisis, a long-term maxim provides the proper optic for envisioning short-term and middle-term strategies for enactment of structural mercy. In the long term, the goal must be to build a social order in which no one is viewed as illegal, a social order in which persons are not exploited, terrorized, detained, and forcibly expelled on the basis of class, race, and ethnicity. We can hardly emphasize it enough: the long-term goal is to enact a politics of mercy by taking seriously the counsel of Jesus himself and the entirety of the Catholic tradition that to welcome the stranger is to welcome Christ himself. Where we described the long-term goal with respect to mass incarceration as abolitionism, with respect to mass deportation we specify it as a sanctuary politics, even as it mimics abolitionism in its call for desecuritization and reconstruction. A sanctuary politics structurally embodies the inclusive hospitality of the Catholic tradition in response to the plight of migrants and refugees.

This theological ideal of an inclusive, Christic hospitality is contradicted every day, often violently, through the routine punishment and expulsion of migrants. These ongoing systemic acts of violent exclusion have been made possible, above all else, by Americans' failure to remember their own history, and to practice *memoria passionis*.[96] In the United States, we have failed to remember that the current crisis has taken its form as a result of a complex history of racist exclusion, exploitative capitalism, and state-sanctioned violence. US history has involved a history of sacrifice: a history of settler colonialism, of foreign interventionism and alliances with brutal dictatorships (from Guatemala and Chile to El Salvador),[97] and of neoliberal policies that sustain a global order in which the center (the United States) benefits from policies that exploit the periphery (the Global South).

To fail to recognize this history is, Pope Francis argues, a failure of Christian compassion: "Christian compassion—this 'suffering with' compassion—is expressed first of all in the commitment to obtain knowledge of the events that force people to leave their homeland, and where necessary, to give voice to those who cannot manage to make their cry of distress and oppression heard. They are all elements that dehumanize and must push every Christian and the whole community to concrete attention."[98] Of course, obtaining knowledge of the cause of migration requires a specific form of memory that remembers the persecution and suffering of others and faces up honestly to complicity in a history of exclusion and oppression.

In the short term, Catholics should cultivate *memoria passionis*, which specifically necessitates that we narrate history differently by focusing our attention on the fate of the oppressed and vanquished in history. Contrary to the dominant narrative that celebrates an inclusive US immigration policy toward immigrants, with Ellis Island and the Statue of Liberty as its central symbols, we must narrate the complete history, a history that includes not only Ellis Island, but the Chinese Exclusion Act (1882), the Bracero Program (1942–64), and countless other policies of racialized exclusion. Even more basically, US history is a history of deportation (a history to which Christ would respond, "I was a stranger and you did not welcome me" [Mt 25:43]). Settler colonialism enacted a broad and sweeping displacement of Native Americans, who were expelled (or, in the current language, deported) from their land and denied the rights of citizenship in 1776, 1868 (the Fourteenth Amendment) and 1870 (the Naturalization Act). Although the Fourteenth Amendment opened citizenship to formerly enslaved Africans, it continued to deny citizenship to other racial groups: Native Americans, Asians, and Mexicans. And, as with Native Americans, both Asians and Mexicans have been subjected to the cycle of tolerated migration for the purpose of labor exploitation and then deportation during times of either economic downturn or heightened racial animus. As recounted above, this complicated history of racialized exclusion would only be resolved—or better redesigned—in 1965, when the Immigration and Nationality Act passed and excluded immigration restrictions on the basis of race or ethnic origin.[99]

When US history is narrated in this way, it recasts the entire debate and undermines any attempt to frame the issue in terms of the citizen-illegal binary. Citizenship has been racially constructed in US history, and deportation and expulsion have served as potent mechanisms for sustaining the privileges of white citizenship. When it is recognized that migrants have been historically excluded on the basis of their race and ethnicity, that they have been disempowered by free trade agreements and exploitative labor practices and that they have been displaced by US foreign policy, any attempt to label these persons as "illegal" becomes not only inaccurate but unconscionable. Such a term with its attendant meanings, practices, and social structures should be rejected.

If our engagement with the migrant crisis and the threat of mass deportation is guided by this narration of US history, it follows that short-term and middle-term responses should work to build a social order in which no person is branded as illegal and the threat of deportation is eliminated once and for all for the approximately eleven million undocumented migrants who currently reside in the United States. Obviously, we are currently in the midst of the opposite of this vision, in which the term *illegal* is employed by politicians and citizens alike to marginalize vulnerable racialized groups in America. What it is to be done?

This short-term project of conscientization enables middle- and long-term responses because it works to correct misinformation about why migration occurs, who migrants are, what migrants tend to desire, and how they arrive. Once proper knowledge of the migration crisis is obtained, it becomes more evident that migrants should be welcomed as Christ, which minimally means not being detained indefinitely, children not being separated from parents, and human persons created in God's image and likeness not being vilified in public, print, or anywhere in between.

In the middle term, Catholics need to support local, grassroots experiments in inclusive hospitality. Concretely, the most significant embodied and political act of the church that would flow from *memoria passionis* is the practice of sanctuary.[100] The practice of ecclesial sanctuary emerged in the 1980s in response to the influx of Central American migrants, particularly Salvadorans and Guatemalans, during the civil wars that consumed the region during that period. In response to the failure of civil authorities to provide legal refuge for these migrants (only 2.6 percent of Salvadorans and 1.8 percent of Guatemalans were granted formal refugee status), sanctuary churches (in the mid-1980s the number swelled to nearly 150 congregations) emerged as spaces of hospitality and protection.[101] The Department of Justice under Ronald Reagan responded to this practice by criminalizing those providing sanctuary and by prosecuting several activists associated with the movement. In the indictment of these activists, they were accused of running a "modern-day underground railroad that smuggled Central American natives across the Mexican border with Arizona."[102] Remarkably, the indictment links the work of the sanctuary churches to the work of the Underground Railroad, which provided asylum for former slaves as they escaped the manifestly immoral and unjust laws of the time.

Although this initial form of sanctuary practice dispersed with the end of the civil wars in Central America in the early 1990s, a "new" sanctuary movement emerged in response to the reforms to immigration policy in the 2000s. Specifically, in March 2006 Cardinal Roger Mahony, the archbishop of Los Angeles, instructed the clergy in his diocese to disregard the specific provisions of the congressional Border Protection, Terrorism, and Illegal Immigration Control Act of 2005, which criminalized the act of giving aid or humanitarian assistance without checking the legal status of the recipient. The subsequent battle between the Catholic Church, along with other Christian congregations, and Congress led to the organization of the new sanctuary movement.[103] A number of local Catholic parishes now (2019) serve as sanctuary churches, and yet the Catholic Church in the United States, as a collective body, has yet to announce itself as a sanctuary church.[104]

The long-term project is to reflect on what this ecclesial practice of sanctuary means for restructuring the whole of society. The question becomes: What does a sanctuary politics look like in response to the current crisis? As with abolitionism, the task is to contest the punitive features of the neoliberal security state while simultaneously describing the reforms necessary to build a society in which the detainment, punishment, and deportation of migrants is no longer the default response to migrants. First, this necessarily entails a reckoning with US interventionist foreign policy and its role in destabilizing the Central American region countless times over the past century (not to mention the Middle East, with Afghanistan, Iraq, and now Syria). Of course, blowback from American foreign policy in the region is not the sole cause of migration, but it has played a pivotal role. This is evidenced by the recent influx of migrants from Honduras, Guatemala, and El Salvador—all Central American countries that have experienced sustained periods of political destabilization in the wake of American-supported coups d'état or American-enabled civil wars.[105] Second, and consistent with the claims made earlier about transforming neoliberal economic policy in a more distributive direction, it is critical that Catholics advocate for more equitable trade policies and the protection of the labor rights of the undocumented. Third, it involves pointing to the contingency of border construction to illuminate the possibility of a different configuration. This entails a critique of the binary that forces us to choose between "border security" and "open borders." This binary is socially constructed and provides cover for processes of neoliberal securitization which seek to provide largely fictive safety for citizens through punitive "law and order" policies rather than economic reforms that improve their actual, material conditions.

The operation of a sanctuary politics is similar to that of abolitionism. We need to ask the same question of deportation that we asked of incarceration: Why have we chosen to treat the challenges associated with immigration through the procedures of neoliberal securitization? There is perhaps no better place to begin this process of interrogation than with Immigration and Customs Enforcement (ICE) agency. The United States' immigration and border enforcement has existed since the creation of the

Immigration and Naturalization Services (INS) in 1933. Importantly, the INS was housed in the Department of Labor from 1933 to 1940 and the Department of Justice from 1940 to 2003. In 2003, as a piece of the broader response to 9/11, the INS was split into three separate agencies: US Citizenship and Immigration Services (legal immigration), Customs and Border Protection (border enforcement), and ICE (tasked with monitoring and enforcing immigration law within the interior of the United States). All of these agencies are now housed within the Department for Homeland Security. The INS's move from the Departments of Labor and Justice to the Department of Homeland Security is representative of a shift from immigration viewed as a social good to a security threat to be actively managed (this shift was intensified after 9/11 when anti-immigrant views were animated by anti-Muslim and anti-Arab sentiment).

ICE's budget has grown over 100 percent from 2003 (3.3 billion) to 2018 (7.5 billion).[106] It now has over 20,000 ICE agents and over two hundred detention centers in the interior of the United States which detain an average of 44,361 people every day.[107] Of the 44,361 people detained each day in the United States approximately 18,000 (41 percent) are detained in private, for-profit detention centers. As with the prison-industrial complex, the detainment- and deportation-industrial complex coheres closely with neoliberal projects of privatization that profit from punishment.

The numbers of those detained has increased steadily under the Trump administration as a result of a shift in policy. Whereas the Obama administration focused on the detention and deportation of felons, the Trump administration has expanded the focus to include all undocumented immigrants. As the former acting director of ICE, Thomas Homan, testified before congress in 2017: "'If you're in this country illegally and you committed a crime by entering this country, you should be uncomfortable. . . . You should look over your shoulder, and you need to be worried.'"[108] The overarching goal of the Trump administration has been to create a climate of fear among undocumented immigrants. Because the US government does not possess the resources to remove all eleven million undocumented immigrants, the Trump administration has decided that the most effective means of expelling these populations is to create a climate in which fear of detention and involuntary removal is so extreme that undocumented immigrants view "voluntary" deportation as an act of rational self-interest. In the first eight months of Trump's presidency ICE arrests increased by 42 percent, contributing to this climate of fear among undocumented populations.[109]

In view of the genesis of ICE as a response to xenophobic and racialized fear after 9/11 and its current practice of invoking terror among vulnerable populations, pressing for the abolition of ICE should be viewed as a central feature of a sanctuary politics. It is important to recall here that ICE has existed for only sixteen years. Prior to its creation, the INS developed mechanisms for monitoring undocumented immigrants that did not reflexively resort to the criminalization and punishment of these populations (of course, we should not idealize those mechanisms either, but they were far more humane than the current approach adopted by ICE). Abolishing ICE, while also advocating for a shift in the approach of US Customs and Border Protection from policing, separating families, and expelling migrants to humanitarian ends of providing relief and protection for them, should be seen as a critical front in the attempt to dismantle neoliberal securitization and to build a politics of sanctuary in the United States.

Overall, neoliberal securitization is a contingent response that serves the interests of US businesses that profit from exploitable labor, politicians who utilize racial resentment to win elections, and the immigration industrial complex that profits from detention and deportation. Securitization is a major feature of the piety of neoliberal sacrifice and hinges on the construction of undocumented persons as "illegal," worthy of expulsion as the polar opposites to "human capital," the offering that the impersonal market finds acceptable. A holistic sanctuary politics desires mercy, not sacrifice, and aims to protect the rights of the stranger who bears the face of Christ by resisting the view that anyone should be labelled "illegal." The opposite of a politics of securitization is quite clearly a politics of sanctuary. Real freedom is not freedom from dangers, real or imagined, but freedom for enacting a merciful ethos of Christic hospitality.

The fact of the matter is that if the Catholic Church fails to embody a radical sanctuary politics, thus living out concretely its Christ-given mission of mercy, we have little hope that the United States will move in this direction. The Catholic Church is the largest single religious group in the United States, and only episodically has witnessed to a sanctuary politics.

In a recent poll, 45 percent of white Catholics responded that the United States has no responsibility to welcome refugees to the country (a remarkable 68 percent of white evangelicals registered the same opinion).[110] If the politics could become more consistent and widespread, a veritable cultural revolution could be accomplished. This would especially be the case if the Catholic Church could join with other Christian churches in fraternity and sorority.

The US Conference of Catholic Bishops forcefully and unambiguously argued in 2012 that the duties incumbent upon Catholics as outlined in CST must take precedence over secular laws:

> An unjust law cannot be obeyed. In the face of an unjust law, an accommodation is not to be sought, especially by resorting to equivocal words and deceptive practices. If we face today the prospect of unjust laws, then Catholics in America, in solidarity with our fellow citizens, must have the courage not to obey them. No American desires this. No Catholic welcomes it. But if it should fall upon us, we must discharge it as a duty of citizenship and an obligation of faith.[111]

This statement was released in response to the Affordable Care Act and the mandate that some Catholic institutions (schools and hospitals) provide contraceptive services. But, as Charles Camosy has argued, it should be rightfully applied to immigration policies in the United States.[112] There is precedent for this, when in 2006 Cardinal Mahoney instructed his clergy to engage in acts of civil disobedience in relation to provisions in the 2005 Border Protection, Terrorism, and Illegal Immigration Control Act. The current situation of detention and deportation is sufficiently dire that it calls for a similar—and more widespread—act of disobedience in relation to current ICE policies. Put simply, a Catholic sanctuary politics demands that the obligation of faith overrule a legal system predicated upon mercilessness.

Sanctuary is, at its roots, a theological notion. Certainly, sanctuary denotes a place of safety, but even more deeply it connotes a holy place. The sanctuary in a church is the prime site for *memoria passionis*, for the liturgical representation of the mystery of Christ's passion, death, and resurrection in preparation for God's people to share in consuming the body and blood of Jesus Christ at a common table. *Sanctuary* means a place of Christic inclusion, a place of radical hospitality. Sanctuary proclaims a challenge to Catholics to live up to the hospitality that Christ demands and that, in its concrete practice, the Eucharist rarely accomplishes. Sanctuary, like Eucharist (thanksgiving) demands a new politics, a politics of mercy. With sanctuary, properly applied, a true and living sacrifice (making-holy) can be accomplished, offering to the living God a holy ethos marked by mercy instead of offering to the lifeless market a corrupt ethos of expulsion as is the case with neoliberalism. Sanctuary politics as a politics of mercy would represent a thoroughgoing repentance from the merciless, racist ethos of neoliberalism, so that people in the United States and elsewhere may have life and have it abundantly (Jn 10:10).

Conclusion

For Holistic Mercy

We promised in the introduction that this book would be a critique of neoliberalism. The word *critique* derives from the same Greek verb (*krinein*) as the word *crisis*, which appears in this book's title and has been a key word since chapter 3. Crisis, in addition to meaning "terrible situation," means a time of decision, a crossroads. What we have argued in this book, amid our "critique" or drawing of the proper bounds of neoliberalism, is that we have reached a crossroads, where we have to decide whether all the sacrifices of neoliberalism are worth it: whether it is worth it for the rich to get richer while others either stand still or are expelled; whether it is worth it for political rationality to be narrowed into market valuation; whether it is worth it for culture to be deracinated and rendered merciless, all in the hopes that wealth will grow for all. *Even if it does*, is it all worth it? Or would we do better, even as a wager, as a utopian venture (recalling that neoliberalism is nothing if not utopian), to work toward neoliberalism's replacement by a politics of mercy? These are not questions of cost-benefit analysis but of truth, of how to live truthfully toward reality. We contend, in short, that mercy is a truer ethos than neoliberal sacrifice; shared mercy is deeper than shared sacrifice.

We began this book by rooting our argument of the social teachings of the three most recent popes. In chapter 1, we narrated how John Paul II introduced into CST a critique of economism, which originally meant reducing human work solely to its economic valence but grew to mean reducing virtually all of life to its economic aspects. We then showed how the social teachings of Benedict and Francis continued along this same line, whether, as with Benedict, the most proximate target was Marxism, or, with Francis, the economism critique aimed at neoliberal capitalism. After having identified this new form of capitalism, chapter 2 described its features in more detail. We showed that neoliberalism is a utopian form of political economy under which wealthy owners of capital wage class warfare on everyone else. Even more broadly, neoliberalism is a political rationality, a comprehensive ontology that regards all of reality as marketized or marketizable. We demonstrated that this political rationality ramifies into a marketized culture that defines the contours of everyday life as an ethos of mercilessness. Chapter 3 examined in detail four crises that are perpetuated and exacerbated by neoliberalism: environmental destruction, slum proliferation, mass incarceration, and mass deportation. We designated these crises as distinctively neoliberal in their enhanced willingness to sacrifice ecosystems and persons to the market, and in their redesigning of racism in an age of supposed color-blindness. The chapter concluded with Pope Francis's diagnosis of the culture of indifference, which we sharpened with his theological category of corruption. Chapter 4 unfolded a systematic theology of mercy that we directed specifically against the neoliberal ethos of mercilessness. We deemed it necessary to provide an overarching, holistic analysis of the Catholic message of mercy. Against neoliberalism's bedrock commitment to the market, we deployed Catholic belief in the Trinity, the one God whose merciful love is threefold, made manifest in the Creator's generosity, Jesus Christ's Sacred Heart, and the Spirit's life-giving indwelling in creation, especially in human hearts. Against the divisiveness of neoliberal human capital anthropology, we presented a neighbor anthropology and an innkeeper ecclesiology modeled on Jesus's parable of the Good Samaritan. And against the neoliberal ethos of mercilessness, we directed a meditation on the works of mercy and a plea that they be reimagined as a holistic politics. Chapter 5 returned to the neoliberal crises treated in chapter 3 in order to sketch Catholic responses to them in light of the theology of mercy. We mirrored the neoliberal playbook of holding to a bedrock principle and then finding a way to reshape society around it through short-term, middle-term, and long-term strategies. As our principles, we proposed the theological ideas of creation, *imago dei*, and freedom in Christ, the CST maxim of the universal destination of goods, and the coordinate practical principle of abolitionism to set our social vision. Then we proceeded through each crisis to recommend a program of conscientization, reform in civil society and public policy, and then civilizational transformation to redirect human energies away from environmental destruction, slum proliferation, mass incarceration, and mass deportation toward a global order of sustainability, dignified life, freedom, and hospitality. This would be called, once more, a politics of mercy.

If, as Catholics, we recognize the threat to the faith, the threat to creation, and the threat to human dignity that neoliberalism poses, it becomes imperative that we build and enact a bold cultural revolution against neoliberalism. Following Pope Francis, we insist that such a catholic movement should be polyhedric. Not all Catholics will perform all the works of mercy, whether in the short term as charity or the long term as politics. But working together, with the mind of Christ (Phil 2:2) and as Christ's body (1 Cor 12:12; Eph 4:12), we simply must contest neoliberalism mercifully. All works must, somehow, be represented. A politics of mercy must aim to ensure abundant life for the living, with hope for the restored subjectivity of the dead. Throughout this book, we have directed the church's message of mercy against neoliberalism, but as we close we should add to this an exhortation that the church apply *ad intra* the radicality of this gospel of mercy—which as good news may be bad news for a church that too often aligns itself with wealth and with history's victors. Christ's mercy requires that the church, *all* its members, not just the hierarchy, repent from its collusion with and profits from colonialism, structural racism, and neoliberalism, in its silences, its thoughts, its words, in what it has done and what it has failed to do. What *we* have done and failed to do.

In an address to celebrate the jubilee of mercy in the Americas, Pope Francis summarized the stark juxtaposition that we have developed throughout this book between a neoliberal, throwaway culture and a Catholic culture of mercy. He observed:

> We are part of a fragmented culture, a throwaway culture. A culture tainted by the exclusion of everything that might threaten the interests of a few. A culture that is leaving by the roadside the faces of the elderly, children, ethnic minorities seen as a threat. A culture that little by little promotes the comfort of a few and increases the suffering of many others. A culture that is incapable of accompanying the young in their dreams but sedates them with promises of ethereal happiness and hides the living memory of their elders. A culture that has squandered the wisdom of the indigenous peoples and has shown itself incapable of caring for the richness of their lands.
>
> All of us are aware, all of us know that we live in a society that is hurting; no one doubts this. We live in a society that is bleeding, and

the price of its wounds normally ends up being paid by the most vulnerable. But it is precisely to this society, to this culture, that the Lord sends us. He sends us and urges us to bring the balm of his presence. He sends us with one program alone: to treat one another with mercy. To become neighbors to those thousands of defenseless people who walk in our beloved American land by proposing a different way of treating them. A renewed way, trying to let our form of bonding be inspired by God's dream, by what he has done. A way of treating others based on remembering that all of us came from afar, like Abraham, and all of us were brought out of places of slavery, like the people of Israel.[1]

What Francis describes in this passage is not just a battle between throwaway culture and mercy, but between death and life. Out of the seven corporal works of mercy, the reader will notice that we have left out bury the dead. The chief promise of neoliberalism for most of us and for creation itself is death. This book rhetorically and substantively opposes that conclusion. We hope that the current global economic situation does not come down to the final work of mercy, bury the dead, having to be structurally implemented. We offer the works of mercy as a politics of hope that opens the space for the emergence of what would seem to be impossible. Because for Christianity, death is not the final word (1 Cor 15:55). The final word is life. The works of mercy comprise a struggle for life, for the gospel of life. And, for God, nothing is impossible (Lk 1:37, 18:27; Gen 18:14; Jer 32:17; Mt 19:26; Mk 10:27).

Acknowledgments

This book originated in a venture of team-teaching in the Department of Religious Studies at the College of the Holy Cross. Thank you to our department chair, Bill Reiser, SJ, who generously permitted us to experiment with our teaching so that we could explore these ideas in the classroom with our students, and to our colleagues for their continued support: Alan Avery-Peck; Bill Clark, SJ; Caner Dagli; Gary DeAngelis; John Gavin; Robert Green; Karen Guth; Mary Hobgood; Caroline Johnson Hodge; Alice Laffey; Mahri Leonard-Fleckman; Todd Lewis; Benny Liew; Joanne Pierce; Mary Roche; Ginny Ryan; and Mathew Schmalz. Thanks as well to the administration of the College of the Holy Cross, especially Philip L. Boroughs, president, and Margaret N. Freije, provost and dean, for granting us a sabbatical during the 2017/18 academic year and a Batchelor-Ford summer fellowship in 2018 to complete the first full draft of the manuscript. Thank you to the Committee on Faculty Scholarship and our department chair, William Reiser, SJ, for funds that paid for professional indexing. Thank you, finally, to our students in three different versions of a course on Catholicism and capitalism (spring 2015, fall 2015, spring 2017) for challenging our ideas and for making us articulate them more clearly and always back them with evidence.

Although this book originated in our work together at Holy Cross, our theological collaboration has deeper roots than that. We met in 2005 as doctoral students in systematic theology at the University of Notre Dame. We would like to thank, therefore, our teachers and classmates from Notre Dame, who laid the deep groundwork for the type of inquiry we do here, especially our dissertation directors, Cyril O'Regan and J. Matthew Ashley, who probably never saw this book coming.

Thank you to Fredric Nachbaur, director of Fordham University Press, who has supported this project with enthusiasm and admirable constancy. Thanks to John C. Seitz for welcoming our book into the series Catholic

Practice in North America. Thanks also to Will Cerbone for all his work in bringing this manuscript to press, Eric Newman for keeping us on task, and Michael Koch for doing an excellent job copyediting and refining the text. We would like to thank John Sniegocki, Matthew Shadle, and an anonymous reviewer for their constructive criticisms and helpful suggestions, which greatly improved the text.

Matt would like to thank Alice Cheng for her passion for this project, her willingness to debate and help refine many of the ideas in the book, and her tireless support. Thanks also to Tom and Judy Eggemeier for their constant encouragement and ongoing enthusiasm for my scholarship. Peter would like to thank his wife, partner, coparent, and best friend, Rochelle, and his children, Zephaniah, Gideon, Beatrice, and Malachi for, basically, putting up with me as Matt and I finished writing this book. For your steadfast love, grace, humor, and for keeping me realistic: thank you. Thanks, too, to Matthew and Paula Fritz, because of whose parenting I was first introduced to Catholic social teaching.

Notes

Introduction

1. Pope Francis, "Message of His Holiness Pope Francis for Lent 2016," October 4, 2015, accessed February 3, 2018, https://w2.vatican.va/content /francesco/en/messages/lent/documents/papa-francesco_20151004_messaggio -quaresima2016.html.

2. Francis, 2, 3.

3. Francis, 3.

4. Francis, 3.

5. Francis, 3.

6. Francis, 3.

7. Lest the reader deem such thinking idiosyncratic to Francis, we must note that Francis's predecessor, the great theologian-pope Benedict XVI, offered similar reflections in an Angelus message; see Benedict XVI, "Angelus," June 8, 2008, http://w2.vatican.va/content/benedict-xvi/en/angelus/2008 /documents/hf_ben-xvi_ang_20080608.html. All subsequent quotations in this paragraph come from this brief address, which is not divided into section numbers. Benedict calls Hosea 6:6, which Jesus glosses in Matthew 9:13, a "key word . . . that bring[s] us to the heart of Sacred Scripture." In this saying, Jesus "found himself," devoting himself to it and putting it into practice, "even at the cost of upsetting his People's leaders." Hosea's words, quoted and reimagined for his time by Jesus, synthesize, Benedict states, "the entire Christian message: true religion consists in love of God and neighbor." Such love gives value to worship. And like Francis, Benedict invokes Mary, calling upon her with the honorific "Mother of Mercy" and pleading for her help that Christians may place all hope in God, "who is infinite mercy."

8. See Springer, Birch, and MacLeavy, "An Introduction to Neoliberalism," 1–2: "Given the diversity of domains in which neoliberalism can be found, the term is frequently used somewhat indiscriminately and quite pejoratively to mean anything 'bad,' characterizing different social processes (e.g., privatiza-tion), institutions (e.g., free markets), and social actors (e.g., corporate power). While there is a strategic reason for such usage, particularly in terms of

mobilizing it as a 'radical political slogan,' such lack of specificity reduces its capacity as an analytic frame."

9. On this particular difficulty, see Kotz, *Rise and Fall of Neoliberal Capitalism*, 8–9.

10. See Mirowski, "The Movement that Dare Not Speak Its Name," 118–41.

11. Brown, "Who Is Not a Neoliberal Today?"

12. Monbiot, "Neoliberalism."

13. Monbiot.

14. Scruton, *Palgrave Macmillan Dictionary of Political Thought*, 472. This is a consistently held opinion often used to introduce neoliberalism. See, for example, Steger and Roy, *Neoliberalism*, 1–20.

15. Thomas Aquinas, *Summa theologiae*, Ia, q. 21. a. 4, corpus.

16. We forthrightly acknowledge a limitation of this work is that it focuses on the last three popes—John Paul II, Benedict, and Francis—as representative of Catholic social thought. This decision was strategic insofar as the most important debates surrounding political economy in Catholic theology have been in response to the papal encyclical tradition. To make the argument about how the Catholic tradition should respond to neoliberalism, we deemed it necessary to first chart how the popes have already responded (however incipiently) and to explore resources within their encyclicals, writings, and public speeches for a more direct and substantive confrontation with neoliberalism. Of course, this decision could be criticized from any number of angles, not least among them a feminist critique of the decision to take the writings of three popes as representative of what is a diverse and pluralistic tradition of Catholic social thought. Women's experiences are, in our book, admittedly an underdeveloped area. A more thorough treatment of the crises of neoliberalism that we explore later on would have to include more extensive engagement with feminist theologies and criticisms of capitalism. Although we do not explicitly take up this issue in the text, we do think that offering a sustained Catholic critique of neoliberalism converges with the central concerns of contemporary Catholic feminist theology. For instance, Elisabeth Schüssler Fiorenza has argued recently that neoliberalism should serve as the primary object of critique for feminist theology. She observes: "I see *the* major task of theology and religion as creating and sustaining a different vision of hope in the face of the dehumanization and exploitation of neoliberalism. Creating a vision of a different world of justice, care, and well-being is the task of religion" (emphasis added). See Schüssler Fiorenza, "Articulating a Different Future." See also, Schüssler Fiorenza, *Congress of Wo/men*, 103–5. For a feminist theological critique of contemporary capitalism, see Firer Hinze, *Glass Ceilings and Dirt Floors*.

17. See, for example, Pope John Paul II, *Centesimus Annus*, 43.

18. In chapter 5, it may seem that we abandon this questioning posture somewhat, inasmuch as we begin to sketch a Catholic alternative to neoliberalism and its attendant crises. But the reader should understand that this sketching is merely that, and that we do not intend to provide a complete program for action and social organization but a series of proposals meant to ignite debate and experiments in practice. We want to underscore the provisional character of these proposals. Following Benedict XVI, we are suspicious of attempts to achieve this-worldly eschatological fulfillment. Nevertheless, we are equally suspicious of those who refuse to attempt to approximate God's love and mercy more adequately in this world.

19. Brown, *Edgework*, 5–6. Subsequent quotations in this paragraph come from these same pages.

20. Brooks, *Conservative Heart*, makes such an argument with respect to poverty reduction. For an alternative take on this question, see Hickel, *Divide*.

21. Even though R. R. Reno does not use the term *neoliberalism*, he makes this argument in "The Spirit of Democratic Capitalism."

22. Brown, *Undoing the Demos*, 10 and 31.

23. Martijn Konings and Quinn Slobodian are two recent authors who have called into question a critique of neoliberalism as economism. They criticize theorists who see neoliberalism as a kind of blind faith in markets, which is often referred to as "market fundamentalism." They emphasize that, far from being a blind faith, which would be associated with a revival of laissez-faire economics, neoliberalism is instead a constructivist project. It does not leave markets alone but does everything politically and culturally to ensure the operation and proliferation of markets. Neoliberalism is, in short, very hands on. See Konings, *Capital and Time*, and Slobodian, *Globalists*. When we use *economism* in this book, we use it in the sense of the dissemination of market values and practices to every dimension of life. This is consistent with John Paul II and Francis, with some analogues in Benedict XVI (see chapter 1).

24. Slobodian, *Globalists*, 87, 269.

1. Catholic Social Thought against Economism

1. For a much more comprehensive treatment of this tradition, all the way up to Pope Francis and including not just popes but numerous other voices, see Shadle, *Interrupting Capitalism*.

2. For more background on CST, see Massaro, SJ, *Living Justice*; McCarthy, *Heart of Catholic Social Teaching*; Clark, *Vision of Catholic Social Thought*; US Conference of Catholic Bishops, *Compendium on the Social Doctrine of the Church*; and O'Brien and Shannon, *Catholic Social Thought*.

3. Pope Leo XIII, *Rerum Novarum: On Capital and Labor*, May 15, 1891, hereafter *RN*.

4. In particular, Leo observes: "It has come to pass that working men have been surrendered, isolated and helpless, to the hardheartedness of employers and the greed of unchecked competition. . . . [A] small number of very rich men have been able to lay upon the teeming masses of the laboring poor a yoke little better than that of slavery itself" (*RN*, 3).

5. Pope Pius XI, *Quadragesimo Anno: On Reconstruction of the Social Order*, May 15, 1931, hereafter *QA*.

6. Pius XI observes: "Just as the unity of human society cannot be founded on an opposition of classes, so also the right ordering of economic life cannot be left to a free competition of forces."

7. Pope John XXIII, *Mater et Magistra: On Christianity and Social Progress*, May 15, 1961, hereafter *MM*.

8. Pope Paul VI, *Populorum Progressio: On the Development of Peoples*, March 26, 1967, hereafter *PP*.

9. Pope John Paul II, *Redemptor Hominis*, March 4, 1979.

10. Pope John Paul II, *Dives in Misericordia*, November 30, 1980, hereafter *DM*.

11. Pope John Paul II, *Laborem Exercens*, September 14, 1981, hereafter *LE*; idem, *Sollicitudo Rei Socialis*, December 30, 1987, hereafter *SRS*; idem, *Centesimus Annus*, May 1, 1991, hereafter *CA*.

12. Pope John Paul II, "Homily."

13. Pope John Paul II .

14. See *LE*, 13, where John Paul posits economism as the initial practical, then theoretical, error that led to the development of dialectical materialism (a synonym, for him, for Marxism).

15. We are stating this rather matter-of-factly, although much more could be said. On the intricacy of John Paul's argumentation here, and his displacement of the concepts "labor" and "capital" as they are used in class analysis, see Lamoureux, "Commentary on *Laborem exercens* (*On Human Work*)," 397.

16. It is in close dialogue with a philosophical trajectory by the same name represented by the German phenomenologists Max Scheler and Edith Stein, but John Paul takes this philosophy sharply in a Christological direction, following Thomas Aquinas. The classic expression of his personalism is John Paul II (Karol Wojtyla), *Acting Person*. John Paul's personalism has been a constant object of scholarly interest, from early in his pontificate through the present day. See, for example, Lawler, *Christian Personalism of John Paul II*, and, as an example of some of the latest research, the *Journal of Interdisciplinary Studies* 29 (2017), special issue "The Future of Religion: Reenchantment of the

World?," which is almost entirely devoted to John Paul II's personalism and cultural vision.

17. Curran, Himes, and Shannon, "Commentary," 415.

18. Curran, Himes, and Shannon.

19. John Paul frequently refers to the logic of "blocs," always condemning both East and West as "ideological" and sinful (subjecting the world to "structures of sin"); see SRS, 10, 20, 22, 24, 36, 37, 39n65.

20. Specifically, John Paul sets out to ask whether "the sad reality of today might not be, at least in part, the result of a too narrow idea of development, that is, a mainly economic one" (SRS 15).

21. John Paul succeeds this statement with a reference to Matthew 25, Jesus's parable about divine, end-time judgment based on the standard of mercy to "the least of these."

22. John Paul II, *Reconciliatio et Paenitentia*, 16. The following sentences all refer to this same section in the apostolic exhortation.

23. *CA*, 63 is the final section, which includes a catena of scriptural quotations playing on the title, *Rerum Novarum* (the new things).

24. John Paul II, "Talk to the Representatives of the Academic and Cultural World."

25. John Paul II, *Ecclesia in America*.

26. See the preface to Ratzinger, *Co-Workers of the Truth*. The following quotations are from this same preface.

27. "The modern age, particularly from the nineteenth century on, has been dominated by various versions of a philosophy of progress whose most radical form is Marxism." Benedict XVI, *Deus Caritas Est*, 31. Cyril O'Regan provides a helpful synopsis of Benedict's engagement with the dominant species of secularized eschatology. See O'Regan, "Benedict the Augustinian," 27.

28. For relevant secondary literature on Benedict XVI's approach to the economy, see Pabst, *Crisis of Global Capitalism*; Casarella, *Jesus Christ*; Curran, *Catholic Social Teaching*; Christiansen, "Metaphysics and Society"; Clark, "Caritas in Veritate"; and Beretta, "Development Driven by Hope and Gratuitousness."

29. Ratzinger, "Church and Economy," and *Eschatology*, 3.

30. See Ratzinger, *Church, Ecumenism, and Politics*, 189.

31. Ratzinger, *Values in a Time of Upheaval*, 17.

32. At various points in his writings, Benedict avers that in addition to its other problems Marxism simply had an inadequate economic theory in that it "failed in what was most its own—as a theory of economics—and it is no longer to be taken seriously as science today." Ratzinger, *Turning Point for Europe?*, 96. In *Without Roots* he puts it this way: "the communist systems

collapsed under the weight of their own fallacious economic dogmatism."
Ratzinger, *Without Roots*, 73.

33. Ratzinger, "Church and Economy," 202.

34. In "Truth and Freedom," Benedict puts it this way: "they took refuge in
mythology: the new structure, they claimed, would bring forth a new man—for,
as a matter of fact, Marxism's promises could work only with new men who are
entirely different from what they are now. If the moral character of Marxism lies
in the imperative of solidarity and the idea of the indivisibility of freedom, there
is an unmistakable lie in its proclamation of the new man, a lie that paralyzes
even its inchoate ethics." Benedict XVI, *Essential Pope Benedict XVI*, 343.

35. Ratzinger, *Values in a Time of Upheaval*, 145.

36. Ratzinger, *Eschatology*, 13.

37. Ratzinger, *A Turning Point for Europe?*, 88.

38. Ratzinger, *Values in a Time of Upheaval*, 16.

39. Within Marxist discourse "the future is an idol that devours the
present." Ratzinger, *Values in a Time of Upheaval*, 18.

40. Ratzinger, *Eschatology*, 3.

41. O'Regan, "Benedict the Augustinian," 30.

42. Joseph Ratzinger, as Prefect of Congregation for the Doctrine of the
Faith, "Instruction on Certain Aspects of the 'Theology of Liberation,'"
August 6, 1984. http://www.vatican.va/roman_curia/congregations/cfaith
/documents/rc_con_cfaith_doc_19840806_theology-liberation_en.html.

43. Ratzinger, *Values in a Time of Upheaval*, 17.

44. In "Relativism: The Central Problem for Faith Today," Benedict
observes of the failure of Marxism: "the nonfulfillment of this hope brought a
great disillusionment with it, which is still far from being assimilated. Therefore, it seems probable to me that new forms of the Marxist conception of the
world will appear in the future. For the moment, we cannot but be perplexed:
the failure of the only scientifically based system for solving human problems
could only justify nihilism or, at the least, total relativism." Benedict XVI,
Essential Pope Benedict XVI, 228.

45. Ratzinger, "Church and Economy," 200.

46. Ratzinger, 200.

47. Ratzinger, 200.

48. The market "must draw its moral energies from other subjects that are
capable of generating them" (*CV*, 35).

49. Ratzinger, "Church and Economy," 204, emphasis added.

50. Ratzinger, 203.

51. The phrase the "dictatorship of relativism" appears a number of times in
his writings, most famously in his homily on the eve of his election to the
papacy on April 18, 2005. Ratzinger, "Homily (Pro Eligendo Romano Pontifice)."

52. Benedict XVI, *Values in a Time of Upheaval*, 144.

53. Benedict XVI, "Address at the Inaugural Session." Subsequent references in this paragraph are to this same section.

54. He stated, specifically, "no one can accept the precepts of neoliberalism and consider themselves a Christian." Bergoglio, *Dialogos*, 7.

55. For theological commentary on Francis's approach to the economy, see Massaro, *Mercy in Action*; Doak, "Evangelizing in an Economy of Death"; Tornielli and Galeazzi, *This Economy Kills*; Rourke, *Roots*; and Cloutier, "The Theological Roundtable."

56. Thomas Aquinas, *Summa Theologiae* 2a–2ae, q. 30, a. 4, ad 1, our translation.

57. Francis is not unique in this respect. Such idolatry critique in the neoliberal era begins with John Paul II, and as we saw with Benedict's view of the state, he includes idolatry critique, too. In *Centesimus Annus*, John Paul initiates this trajectory by offering incisive commentary on the relationship between the market and idolatry in CA: "Certainly the mechanisms of the market offer secure advantages: they help to utilize resources better; they promote the exchange of products; above all they give central place to the person's desires and preferences, which, in a contract, meet the desires and preferences of another person. Nevertheless, these mechanisms carry the risk of an 'idolatry' of the market, an idolatry which ignores the existence of goods which by their nature are not and cannot be mere commodities" (*CA*, 40). For a broader discussion of Francis on idolatry, see Cavanaugh, "Return of the Golden Calf."

58. Pope Francis, "Address to the New Non-Resident Ambassadors."

59. Pope Francis, "General Audience."

60. It is important to note here that the then Archbishop Jorge Cardinal Bergoglio explicitly names neoliberalism as an approach to the economy that defends the autonomy of the market and its logic: "the social and economic crisis, and the consequent increase in poverty, has its causes in policies inspired by those forms of neo-liberalism that consider profits and the laws of the market absolute." Pope Francis, *Only Love Can Save Us*, 108.

61. For Francis, one of the problems is that advocates of contemporary capitalism often "defend the absolute autonomy of the marketplace and financial speculation" (*EG*, 56).

62. Francis observes of the economy: "when it falls into the hands of speculators, everything is ruined. With the speculator, the economy loses face and loses its faces. It is a faceless economy. An abstract economy. Behind the speculator's decisions there are no people, and therefore we do not see the people who are to be dismissed and cut out. When the economy loses contact with the faces of concrete people, it itself becomes a faceless economy and

therefore a ruthless economy." Francis, "Pastoral Visit of the Holy Father Francis."

63. For an analysis of Francis's criticisms of trickle-down economics, see *Vatican Insider*, "The 'Trickle-Down Theory the Pope Frowns Upon."

64. Francis observes: "There was the promise that once the glass had become full it would overflow and the poor would benefit. But what happens is that when it's full to the brim, the glass magically grows, and thus nothing ever comes out for the poor." Davies, "Pope Says He Is Not a Marxist."

65. Francis, "Address of the Holy Father (Bolivia)."

66. Francis, "General Audience." As with Benedict's criticism of Marxism as a sacrificial ideology, Francis describes capitalism as a form of idolatry that "sacrifice(s) human lives on the altar of money and profit." In both cases, it is a theological error that generates an ethos of sacrifice. Pope Francis, "Address of the Holy Father (Paraguay)."

67. Francis, "Address of the Holy Father (Paraguay)."

68. Francis, "Address of the Holy Father (Bolivia)."

69. Francis, "Message (First World Day of the Poor)."

70. Francis, "Address of the Holy Father (Bolivia)."

71. "Solidarity is a spontaneous reaction by those who recognize that the social function of property and the universal destination of goods are realities which come before private property. The private ownership of goods is justified by the need to protect and increase them, so that they can better serve the common good; for this reason, solidarity must be lived as the decision to restore to the poor what belongs to them. These convictions and habits of solidarity, when they are put into practice, open the way to other structural transforma-tions and make them possible. Changing structures without generating new convictions and attitudes will only ensure that those same structures will become, sooner or later, corrupt, oppressive and ineffectual" (*LS*, 189).

72. *LS*, 189.

73. Francis, "General Audience (Poverty and Mercy)." Further quotations in this paragraph are from this source.

74. See also Francis, "Address to the New Non-Resident Ambassadors to the Holy See."

75. Francis, "General Audience (Poverty and Mercy)."

76. For the self-ascription of neoconservative, see Weigel, "The Neoconser-vative Difference." For a critique of this group as "neoconservative" appropria-tors of John Paul II, see Sniegocki, "The Social Ethics of John Paul II."

77. There is a growing literature on the collaboration of neoconservatives and neoliberals. Of remarkable importance is Cooper, *Family Values*.

78. Novak, *Toward a Theology of the Corporation*, 12–18; see especially 15n20, which derides the naiveté of one of John Paul's 1979 homilies.

79. Michael Novak, "Beyond *Populorum Progressio*."

80. Weigel, "Camels and Needles," 98.

81. Novak, "Introduction to *Centesimus Annus*," 331.

82. Weigel, "Blessings on Capitalism at Its Best"; Michael Novak, "Wisdom from the Pope"; and Weigel, "Enduring Importance of *Centesimus Annus*," *First Things*, June 22, 2011. See also Neuhaus, "The Pope Affirms the 'New Capitalism.'"; and Sirico, "Reading *Centesimus Annus*."

83. Weigel makes this plea in "Neoconservative Difference," 162n36, among many other places. See chapter 2 on how neoliberals have consistently used the cipher "freedom" for an economic agenda that sharply limits freedom for the majority of those it will supposedly benefit.

84. For Novak's condemnation of prior papal thinking for its being stuck in a "traditional" social mindset as opposed to embracing "modern, differentiated, pluralist society," see Novak, *Toward a Theology of the Corporation*, 14.

85. Novak, "Economic Heresies of the Left."

86. Novak, "Pope of Caritapolis."

87. *CA* includes John Paul's criticisms of the social welfare state, on the grounds of the principle of subsidiarity (48). See our treatment of this same section of *CA* in chapter 3.

88. Weigel, "Discusses Pope Francis's U.S. Visit."

89. Novak, "Agreeing with Pope Francis."

90. Dolan, "The Pope's Case for Virtuous Capitalism."

91. Weigel, "Pope's Encyclical."

92. Hahn, "Rocco Buttiglione." Buttiglione is author of the influential *Karol Wojtyla*. For the critical edition of the work Buttiglione recommends, along with related texts, see Hayek, *Studies on the Abuse and Decline of Reason*. This volume of Hayek's collected works includes his impassioned defense of "individualism."

93. Todd Whitmore made such a suggestion with respect to Novak many years ago, offering that Novak's reading of John Paul II was so at variance with the pope's teaching as to constitute dissent. See Whitmore, "John Paul II."

2. Neoliberal Capitalism

1. Sniegocki, *Catholic Social Teaching and Economic Globalization*.

2. Hayek, "Intellectuals and Socialism," 384.

3. Recent years have seen an outpouring of major publications this history; see, for example, Stedman Jones, *Masters of the Universe*; Mirowski and Plehwe, *Road from Mont Pélerin*; Kotz, *Rise and Fall of Neoliberal Capitalism*; MacLean, *Democracy in Chains*; and Slobodian, *Globalists*.

4. Stedman Jones, *Masters of the Universe*, 6.

5. Stedman Jones, 7.

6. Stedman Jones , 8.

7. See Slobodian, *Globalists*, 14.

8. Slobodian, 5–7. Slobodian also criticizes on these pages the descriptor "unfettered," which critics habitually apply to the neoliberal market. Pope Francis does, at times, do this, but with his critique of the idolatry of money (see our comments on sacrifice below), he hits upon a critique more in line with Slobodian's corrections.

9. Slobodian, 6.

10. Slobodian, 13.

11. Slobodian, 15.

12. Slobodian, 16.

13. Slobodian, 18.

14. Slobodian, 82–87.

15. Slobodian, 86–87. Slobodian writes here of the "Geneva School" of neoliberalism whose luminaries included Ludwig von Mises, Friedrich Hayek, Lionel Robbins, Wilhelm Röpke, and Michael Heilperin. Although Slobodian is careful as a historian not to conflate varied schools of neoliberalism, and we want to take similar care, we recognize, as does he (hence his project) that the Geneva School was widely influential on neoliberalism and certain key commitments of this school became bedrock for neoliberals generally. This is especially true of the epistemological cast of neoliberalism, and in large measure is true of its "theological" character. For the sake of concision, then, we take Slobodian's descriptions of the Geneva School to be reasonably adequate for explicating neoliberalism as a broader theoretical and political enterprise.

16. Slobodian, 87, 269–70.

17. Slobodian, 89.

18. Slobodian, 133.

19. Slobodian, 125.

20. Slobodian, 137.

21. Slobodian, 44–46, 144, 257–58.

22. Although some details of Harvey's approach have been contested by Mirowski and others, Harvey's central claim that the utopian orientation of neoliberalism was driven by a politics of class warfare has been confirmed in recent historical scholarship. Slobodian offers a similar narrative, as do Duménil and Lévy. See Slobodian, *Globalists*, and Duménil and Lévy, *Crisis of Neoliberalism*.

23. Harvey, *Brief History*, 19.

24. Harvey, 19.

25. Harvey, 3. We disagree slightly with Harvey on this point and argue that neoliberalism has been utopian all the way down, inasmuch as it has

remained consistent in its willingness to sacrifice human persons and the earth in the interest of the impersonal market. Nevertheless, we agree with recent defenses of his history of neoliberalism (from Dardot and Laval and Cahill and Konings) as a class warfare project that creates wealth through dispossession. We discuss this idea below.

26. Risager, "Neoliberalism Is a Political Project."

27. Harvey and Slobodian both emphasize the pivotal importance of the World Trade Organization's founding in 1995, as it represents a crowning achievement of neoliberalism, namely a globalist body tasked with encasing the economy (Slobodian) and governing the global interests of capital (Harvey). See Slobodian, *Globalists*, 223, and Harvey, *Brief History*, 93.

28. Harvey, *Brief History*, 39.

29. Harvey, 49.

30. Harvey, 21.

31. Harvey, 44.

32. Harvey, 40.

33. Harvey, 23.

34. This is the central thesis of Klein, *Shock Doctrine*. See also Loewenstein, *Disaster Capitalism*.

35. Harvey, *Brief History*, 7.

36. Harvey, 6.

37. Harvey, 7.

38. Overall, Harvey remarks, "State after state, from the new ones that emerged from the collapse of the Soviet Union to old-style social democracies and welfare states such as New Zealand and Sweden, have embraced, sometimes voluntarily and sometimes in response to coercive pressures, some version of neoliberal theory." Harvey, *Brief History*, 3.

39. Harvey, 29.

40. Harvey, 65.

41. Harvey, 159.

42. Harvey, *Rebel Cities*, 159–60.

43. For more on this notion, see Harvey, *New Imperialism*, 137–82.

44. See John Paul II, *SRS*, 21–22; Francis, "Address of the Holy Father (Bolivia)."

45. Harvey, *Brief History*, 160–64.

46. Harvey, 165–75.

47. The Marxist engagement with neoliberalism is vast and generally interprets neoliberalism as an intensified form of capitalism. See Harvey, *New Imperialism*; Duménil and Lévy, *Crisis of Neoliberalism*; and Callinicos, *Bonfire of Illusions*.

48. Harvey, *Brief History*, 202.

49. Harvey observes that neoliberalism "has pervasive effects on ways of thought to the point where it has become incorporated into the common-sense way many of us interpret, live in, and understand the world." Harvey, *Brief History*, 3. But Harvey does not really explain how this happened. He offers a detailed exposition of how it emerged as an approach to political economy in the North Atlantic world (ideologically) and in the Global South (coercively), but he does not sufficiently engage the question of how it became the common sense of the world in the twenty-first century. As we will show later in this chapter, Brown and Mirowski approach this question through their engagements with neoliberalism.

50. Francis, "Address of the Holy Father (Bolivia)."

51. It is generally agreed at this point that there are two dominant frameworks for thinking about neoliberalism: the Marxist framework and the Foucauldian one. With regard to the former, Harvey is a central voice. With respect to the latter, Brown has distinguished herself as a leading thinker. For more on Foucault's approach to neoliberalism and neoliberal rationality, see Peck, *Constructions of Neoliberal Reason*; Dardot and Laval, *New Way of the World*; and Barry and Osborne, *Foucault and Political Reason*. On the so-called Foucault controversy, whether Foucault was in fact sympathetic with elements of neoliberalism, see Zamora and Behrent, *Foucault and Neoliberalism*.

52. As Brown observes, it is important to understand that there exist diverse interpretations of neoliberalism and a lot depends "on whether you define neoliberalism as a modification of economic liberalism, of what you call laissez-faire capitalism, or whether you define neoliberalism as a modification of liberal governance, or what Foucault calls governmentality, which is more about the way that societies, societies and subjects, are constituted and governed by a particular form of political reason." Brown, "Conversation with Wendy Brown."

53. For example, "Political rationalities posit ontological qualities and relations of citizens, laws, rights, economy, society, and states—qualities and relations inhering in orders of reason such as liberalism, Christianity, Roman law, and so on, which may combine awkwardly, but nonetheless all become salient parts of that by which worlds are ordered, humans act, and governments rule." Brown, *Undoing the Demos*, 116.

54. Brown, *Undoing the Demos*, 117.

55. Brown, 35–36. See also Brown, 104: "We are dealing not merely with an absurd and false account of human motives and conduct, a misrepresentation of who we are and what sustains us, but with the production of the 'real' through this depiction of purposes, conduct, and ends."

56. Brown, "Conversation with Wendy Brown"; see also Brown, *Undoing the Demos*, 30.

57. Brown, *Undoing the Demos*, 31.

58. Brown, 31–32.

59. "Market principles frame every sphere of activity, from mothering to mating, from learning to criminality, from planning one's family to planning one's death." Brown, *Undoing the Demos*, 67.

60. Brown, 17.

61. Obama, "Inaugural Address"; Obama, "State of the Union Address."

62. Brown, *Undoing the Demos*, 24.

63. Brown, 24–25.

64. Brown, 25–26.

65. Brown, 26.

66. Brown, 27.

67. Brown, 27.

68. Brown, 25.

69. For a concise, pithy commentary on this phenomenon, see Monbiot, "Neoliberalism: The Deep Story."

70. Brown, "Apocalyptic Populism."

71. Brown.

72. Jamie Peck calls this feature of neoliberalism "a self-contradictory form of regulation-in-denial." Peck, *Constructions of Neoliberal Reason*, xiii.

73. Brown, "Apocalyptic Populism."

74. Bessner and Sparke, "Don't Let His Trade Policy Fool You."

75. We will elaborate on our case that neoliberalism is a racial phenomenon in chapter 3. See Fraser, "End of Progressive Neoliberalism."

76. Brown, *Undoing the Demos*, 40.

77. Foucault, *Birth of Biopolitics*, 219.

78. Schultz, *Investment in Human Capital*; Becker, *Human Capital*. For Foucault on Schultz and Becker, see Foucault, *Birth of Biopolitics*, 220.

79. *Economist*, "Gary Becker's Concept of Human Capital (Six Big Ideas)."

80. Khan Academy, "Human Capital," video, accessed February 9, 2018, https://www.khanacademy.org/economics-finance-domain/core-finance /investment-vehicles-tutorial/investment-consumption/v/human-capital.

81. Foucault, *Birth of Biopolitics*, 222.

82. Foucault, 224–25.

83. Foucault, 226.

84. Feher, "Self-Appreciation," 24, 27.

85. Feher, 34.

86. Feher, 34.

87. We will discuss this further later in this chapter, but for now, see Mirowski, *Never Let a Serious Crisis Go to Waste*, 107.

88. Burnside, "Investing in a Brilliant New YOU™."

89. See Brown, *Undoing the Demos*, 70.

90. For Brown's suggestions for revisions of Foucault on neoliberalism in an age of finance's dominance, see Brown, *Undoing the Demos*, 70–78. Regarding the perversity of neoliberal financialization of human life and death in the form of so-called viatical settlements, see Mirowski, *Never Let a Serious Crisis Go to Waste*, 125–26.

91. Brown, *Undoing the Demos*, 37.

92. Brown, "University and Its Worlds." See also Brown, *Undoing the Demos*, 22.

93. Brown, *Undoing the Demos*, 71.

94. Brown, 71.

95. Brown, 71.

96. Brown, 134.

97. Brown, 134 and 37.

98. Most notable and influential has been Judith Butler, for whom "precarity" (the flipside of neoliberal "austerity") has become a central concern over the past few years. See Butler and Athanasiou, *Dispossession*; and Butler, *Notes*. See also Lorey, *State of Insecurity*.

99. Brown, *Undoing the Demos*, 72.

100. Brown, 72.

101. Brown, 38.

102. Brown, 38.

103. Brown, 39.

104. We say that these perspectives do not necessarily conflict, because some scholars have combined features of both in their work. Exemplary in this respect is Lazzarato, "Neoliberalism in Action," which revises Foucault in light of financialization and insists upon the need to analyze the restoration of capital's (class) power in neoliberal "enterprise society."

105. Harvey has mildly criticized approaches inspired by Foucault: "A version of this is Foucault's governmentality argument, which sees neoliberalizing tendencies already present in the eighteenth century. But if you just treat neoliberalism as an idea or a set of limited practices of governmentality, you will find plenty of precursors. What is missing here is the way in which the capitalist class orchestrated its efforts during the 1970s and early 1980s. I think it would be fair to say that at that time—in the English-speaking world anyway—the corporate capitalist class became pretty unified." Risager, "Neoliberalism Is a Political Project."

106. For a succinct case by two other geographers regarding how to navigate the "generic" character of neoliberalism while retaining sensitivity to its variegated local forms, see Peck and Tickell, "Neoliberalizing Space."

107. Mirowski was not the first to focus on neoliberalism and everyday life, although his chapter on everyday neoliberalism has proven most influential since its publication a few years ago. For a slightly earlier example, see

Braedley and Luxton, *Neoliberalism and Everyday Life*, whose contributors examine various aspects of statecraft, culture, race, gender, health care, child care, and much more, mostly within the Canadian context, as all these are shaped by neoliberalism.

108. Mirowski, *Never Let a Serious Crisis Go to Waste*, 119.

109. Mirowski, 119.

110. Mirowski, 119.

111. Lazzarato, *Making of Indebted Man*, esp. chap. 1.

112. On infinite debt, see Lazzarato, *Making of Indebted Man*, 77–81; and Lazzarato, *Governing by Debt*, 83–90. Any car owner knows the economic pressure to remain perpetually in debt, which comes in the form of panicked emails coming from one's car dealership as one approaches paying off one's auto loan, urging one to purchase a new vehicle and maintain the stream of monthly payments.

113. Mirowski, *Never Let a Serious Crisis Go to Waste*, 124.

114. It has become commonplace to clarify that "feeling" in this case does not mean "emotion," but the affective substratum of daily life. Theologians should be familiar with something like this from study of Friedrich Schleiermacher (1768–1834). For Williams's formulation of "structures of feeling," see Williams, *Marxism and Literature*, 128–35. Because of its clear applicability to neoliberalism, which operates at the visceral level and not just at the levels of economy, politics, and society, this idea of Williams has been revived in earnest over the past decade. See, for example, Ventura, *Neoliberal Culture*, 1–4 and passim; and Wilson, *Neoliberalism*, 25, 94–95.

115. Friedman, *Capitalism and Freedom*, 119.

116. With regard to the Clintons and Obama, we refer to them as figureheads of a general sense of "colorblindness" and lack of class awareness in late neoliberalism. The seeds are sown for such cultural bleaching in Hayek and Friedman, who take great pains to remove layers of social differentiation as part of the ideological legitimation of neoliberalism. "Social justice," according to Hayek, is a misguided political slogan that attempts to undermine the proper moral disposition of people in a free society. It distracts people from their duty to submit to market valuation, instead positing a fictitious "distributor" who should guarantee equality. It is a hoax confabulated by "special interests," which is Hayek's euphemism for disadvantaged groups, to make those who are successful in the market feel bad. Everyone starts off on an even playing field, and advance or fall inasmuch as they devote themselves to the market and its judgments (Hayek, *Mirage of Social Justice*, 97). Like Hayek, Friedman treats "social responsibility" as something too amorphous to be real, a "subversive doctrine." Chapter 7, "Capitalism and Discrimination," in *Capitalism and Freedom* shows that Friedman assumes that all people start off with the economic "game" on a relatively level playing field, assuming the

government has not somehow handicapped them through intervention such as "fair employment practice commissions." Even were one to find oneself in a situation of oppression, exploitation, or discrimination, capitalism allows for freedom from coercion, because there is always another job, another product, another place for each person; the market provides. See Friedman, *Capitalism and Freedom*, 133, 100–18.

117. Konings, "Rethinking Neoliberalism and the Subprime Crisis," 120.

118. Here we combine Konings's analysis with Wilson, *Neoliberalism*, 3–5 and passim, which avers that the neoliberal ethos of competition turns people into "self-enclosed individualists." For the source of this idea, see Keating, *Transformation Now!*, 171.

119. Konings, "Rethinking Neoliberalism," 120.

120. Mirowski, *Never Let a Serious Crisis Go to Waste*, 131–38.

121. Mirowski, 131–32.

122. On predatory lending not existing (according to neoliberals), see Mirowski, 122.

123. Among these is a much-publicized example from higher education in Indiana, where so-called "income-share agreements" have become a new way for investors to turn students into investments. Beckie Supiano from the *Chronicle for Higher Education* explains, "Under an income-share agreement, or ISA, an investor pays for all or part of a student's education upfront. In return, the student gives the investor a certain percentage of his or her income for a set number of years." See Supiano, "Guide to Income-Share Agreements." Regarding the contemporary return of debtors' prisons, see Benns and Strode, "Debtors' Prison."

124. Mirowski, *Never Let a Serious Crisis Go to Waste*, 138.

125. Mirowski, 46.

126. Here is a representative sample: McCarthy, "Reality Television," 17–42; Couldry, "Reality TV"; McCurria, "Desperate Citizens and Good Samaritans"; Best, "Raymond Williams"; and Redden, "Is Reality TV Neoliberal?" The connection was, perhaps, first substantively made in Andrejevic, *Reality TV*.

127. Mirowski, *Never Let a Serious Crisis Go to Waste*, 134.

128. Mirowski, 130.

129. Mirowski, 135.

130. Mirowski, 136.

131. Mirowski, 154.

3. Sacrifice, Race, and Indifference

1. Francis, *Evangelii Gaudium*, 202; Francis, "Address of the Holy Father (Bolivia)"; Knight, "Pope Francis."

2. Sassen, *Expulsions*.

3. Sassen, 3.

4. Sassen, 2, 149–50. See also Kolbert, *Sixth Extinction*.

5. Harvey, "Neoliberalism as Creative Destruction," 22. For a broader elaboration of this definition, see Harvey, *Brief History of Neoliberalism*.

6. Schumpeter, *Capitalism, Socialism, and Democracy*, esp. 81–87.

7. Schumpeter, 82–83. See, for example, a *New York Times* column fêting Schumpeter: Reier, "Half a Century Later."

8. Klein, *This Changes Everything*, 301–5.

9. Lerner, *Sacrifice Zones*, 2.

10. Klein, *This Changes Everything*, 161–87.

11. Acosta, "Extractivism and Neoextractivism," 61–86. See also Gómez-Barris, *Extractive Zone*.

12. Gómez-Barris, 62.

13. Gómez-Barris, 63.

14. Klein, *This Changes Everything*, 169.

15. Klein, 169.

16. For this phrase, see Acosta, "Posextractivismo."

17. Crutzen and Stoermer, "Anthropocene," 17–18.

18. See Moore, *Anthropocene or Capitalocene*; and Street, "How to Stop Capitalism's Deadly War with Nature."

19. Mirowski, *Never Let a Serious Crisis Go to Waste*, 334.

20. Mirowski, 336.

21. Mirowski, 337–38.

22. Mirowski, 338.

23. Mirowski, 338.

24. Mirowski, 338.

25. Klein, *This Changes Everything*, 267.

26. For more on the aspirant profitability of geoengineering, see Klein, 256–90.

27. Mirowski, *Never Let a Serious Crisis Go to Waste*, 355.

28. As many authors have argued, neoliberalism has been particularly adept at profiting from environmental crises, crises often exacerbated or caused by the market commitments of neoliberal ideology. See Klein, *Shock Doctrine*; Klein, *Battle for Paradise*; and Fletcher, "Capitalizing on Chaos."

29. Parr, *Radical Politics*; and Elliott, *Natural Catastrophe*.

30. *Guardian*, "Obama Focuses on Green Economy in Speech before Congress."

31. Ecological economists have argued that there is a fundamental tension between economic growth—even green economic growth—and the need to significantly reduce emission levels. See, for example, Jackson, *Prosperity without Growth*; Daly, *Beyond Growth*; Speth, *Bridge at the End of the World*; and Victor, *Managing without Growth*.

32. Francis argues further that this lie "is an attempt to legitimize the present model of distribution, where a minority believes that it has the right to consume in a way which can never be universalized, since the planet could not even contain the waste products of such consumption" (*LS*, 50).

33. Klein, "Capitalism vs. the Climate." For a more extensive discussion of "big green" as well as the relationship between neoliberalism and climate change, see Klein, *This Changes Everything*.

34. The contemporary discussion of slums was kicked off by a 2003 report by the United Nations Human Settlements Program (UN-Habitat), in which it was estimated that 32 percent of the world's urban population lived in slums. See UN-Habitat, *Challenge of Slums*, v.

35. Davis, *Planet of Slums*.

36. Davis, 121–22.

37. Auyero and Swistun, *Flammable*, 18.

38. See UN-Habitat, "Housing and Slum Upgrading."

39. Brenner and Theodore, "Cities and the Geographies," 367.

40. Brenner and Theodore, 373–74.

41. Brenner and Theodore, 374.

42. Nijman, "Against the Odds," 74.

43. Brenner and Theodore, "Cities and the Geographies," 370.

44. See Nijman's summary of the vast literature on critiques of NGOs in "Against the Odds," 74–75.

45. Brenner and Theodore, "Cities and the Geographies," 369, 371. The phrase "slums and skyscrapers" comes from a 2015 public lecture by David Harvey. See Harvey, "Slums and Skyscrapers."

46. Brenner and Theodore, "Cities and the Geographies," 369. For a study that highlights the contrast between global aspirations and local capacities, see Weinstein, "'One-Man Handled.'"

47. Glaeser, *Triumph of the City*; and de Soto, *Mystery of Capital*.

48. For example, de Soto seems to think that if slums were divided up among owners and "adequately recorded" in property documents, then this land could be converted to capital, invested and invested in, and all would eventually be well. See de Soto, *Mystery of Capital*, 5.

49. Marx, Stoker, and Suri, "The Economics of Slums in the Developing World."

50. See Sassen, *Expulsions*, ch. 1.

51. On push-and-pull factors with regard to slum growth, see Mahabir, Crooks, Croitoru, and Agouris, "The Study of Slums as Social and Physical Constructs," 403–4.

52. On land-grabbing and its neocolonial, financialized attributes, see Liberti, *Land-Grabbing*; on the relationship between urban power centers, land

grabs, urbanization, and slums, see Leon, "Role of Global Cities in Land Grabs."

53. The polymorphic and polysemous reality of slums necessarily involves abstraction, imagination, and theoretical choices based on the empirical data available. See Rao, "Slum as Theory"; and Roy, "Slumdog Cities." The type of theoretical caveats Rao and Roy pose cohere with similar cautions set forth in studies such as Jeffrey W. Paller's study of political activity in Ghana's slums; people who live in slums should not be viewed simply through the lens of disaster, since realities on the ground often prove more positive than one might think. See Paller, "From Urban Crisis to Political Opportunity." While we agree that the fully apocalyptic option for discussing slums should be put off the table, we also deem it equally perilous to ignore the negativity of slum life, especially when this ignorance bolsters neoliberal narratives about the primacy and salutariness of markets.

54. Gilbert, "Extreme Thinking about Slums and Slumdwellers."

55. Chandran, "What's a Slum?" This article is part of a five-part series by Thomson Reuters called "Slumscapes," Place, October 10, 2016, accessed May 15, 2018, http://www.thisisplace.org/i/?id=ece2998b-2847-4e52-ba7e -f67b0422c49c.

56. Chandran.

57. Iyer, Macomber, and Arora, "Dharavi."

58. This has been pithily and helpfully captured in a video produced by UC Berkeley sociologist Ananya Roy and her associates. See Roy and the #Global-POV Project, "Are Slums the Urban Future."

59. As just one example, a study on health inequalities in Rio de Janeiro found that life expectancy is far lower in slums than in wealthy parts of the city. Men in the richest parts of the city live on average 12.8 years longer than men in slums. See Szwarcwald, Corrêa da Mota, Damacena, and Sardinha Pereira, "Health Inequalities in Rio de Janeiro, Brazil."

60. Roy, Capitalism, 7–8, 46–47.

61. Datta, "Intimate City."

62. Robinson, Black Marxism. For other works dealing with racial capitalism and racial neoliberalism, see Kelley, "What Did Cedric Robinson Mean by Racial Capitalism?"; Melamed, Represent and Destroy; Bhattacha-ryya, Racial Capitalism; Wang, Carceral Capitalism; Roberts and Mahtani, "Neoliberalizing Race, Racing Neoliberalism"; Roberts, "Race and Neoliber-alism"; Inwood, "Neoliberal Racism"; Hohle, Racism in the Neoliberal Era; and Mele, "Neoliberalism, Race, and the Redefining of Urban Development."

63. Kelly, "What Did Cedric Robinson Mean by Racial Capitalism?"

64. See Lowe, Intimacies of Four Continents, 149–50.

65. See Gilmore, "Globalization and US Prison Growth"; Wacquant, "Class, Race, and Hyperincarceration in Revanchist America"; and Johnson, "The Urban Precariat"; Clarno, "The Constitution of State/Space."

66. Goldberg, *Threat of Race.*

67. Wacquant, *Punishing the Poor,* 2.

68. Clarno, *Neoliberal Apartheid,* 204–5.

69. Piven and Cloward, *Regulating the Poor.*

70. Sassen, *Expulsions,* 68.

71. Camp, *Incarcerating the Crisis,* 3; and Alexander, *New Jim Crow,* 60.

72. Democrats contributed decisively to this process as well. Bill Clinton's administration was as instrumental as Reagan in building the mass incarceration system in the United States. For the broader history that stretches back to the presidencies of John F. Kennedy and Lyndon Johnson, see Hinton, *From the War on Poverty to the War on Crime* and Murakawa, *First Civil Right.*

73. Lopez, *Dog Whistle Politics.*

74. Alexander, *New Jim Crow,* 180.

75. Wacquant, "Class, Race, and Hyperincarceration," 74.

76. Piven and Cloward, *Regulating the Poor.* See also Wacquant, *Punishing the Poor,* 290.

77. Gottschalk, *Caught,* 46. In *Golden Gulag,* Ruth Wilson Gilmore contends that the dramatic rise in incarceration in California was a response to four surpluses: finance capital, labor, land, and state capacity. See Gilmore, *Golden Gulag.*

78. Wacquant explains, "Incarceration has de facto become America's largest government program for the poor." Wacquant, *Prisons of Poverty,* 69.

79. Davis, *Are Prisons Obsolete?,* 16.

80. Harvey, *Seventeen Contradictions* and *Enigma of Capital.*

81. Wacquant, *Punishing the Poor,* 299.

82. Davis, "Hell Factories in the Field."

83. Aviram, *Cheap on Crime,* 99.

84. Quoted in Gopnik, "Caging of America."

85. Mukherjee, "Impacts of Private Prison Contracting."

86. This is the argument made by Pflaff, *Locked In.*

87. Parenti, *Lockdown America,* 230.

88. See Sawyer, "How Much Do Incarcerated People Earn in Each State?"

89. For a broader, multifaceted discussion of this phenomenon, see Herivel and Wrigth, *Prison Profiteers.*

90. Nakamura, "Trump Administration Moving Quickly."

91. Lind, "The Disastrous."

92. Golash-Boza, *Deported*, 263. Golash-Boza observes that by 2014, six years into Obama's presidency, his administration had deported more undocumented immigrants—two million—than the total of deportations prior to 1997. Golash-Boza, "The Parallels between Mass Incarceration and Mass Deportation," 485.

93. Chomsky, *They Take Our Jobs!*, 87.

94. Ngai, *Impossible Subjects*, 227.

95. Cacho, *Social Death*, 123. See also, Chacon and Davis, "Neoliberalism."

96. Mize and Swords, *Consuming Mexican Labor*.

97. Genova, *Working the Boundaries*.

98. Genova, "Migrant 'Illegality' and Deportability."

99. Golash-Boza, *Deported*, 5.

100. Lopez, *Dog Whistle Politics*, 120–25.

101. Brown, *Walled States*, 8–9. See also Vallet, *Borders, Fences and Walls* and Jones, *Border Walls*.

102. See Chacón and Davis, *No One is Illegal*; Fernandes, *Targeted*; and Golash-Boza, "The Immigration Industrial Complex."

103. Robbins, "Little-Known Immigration Mandate."

104. Pérez-Peña, "Contrary to Trump's Claims."

105. Doty and Wheatley, "Private Detention," 430–38.

106. At the international level, a recent *Financial Times* article argued that refugee camps represent an "untapped" resource for private sector investment. See, John Aglionby, "World Bank Urges Private Sector Interest in Refugee Camps," May 5, 2018, accessed June 26, 2019, https://www.ft.com/content /e2d6588a-5042-11e8-b3ee-41e0209208ec?list=intlhomepage.

107. Chomsky, *Undocumented*.

108. Khosravi, *After Deportation*, 4.

109. Pope Francis, "Homily: Mass at Santa Cruz, Bolivia," July 9, 2015, accessed March 2, 2019, https://zenit.org/articles/pope-francis-homily-at-mass -in-santa-cruz-bolivia/,

110. Francis, *Way of Humility*, 9–56. Thanks are due to Matthew Ashley for first alerting us to this essay of Bergoglio's and its possible significance for our book.

111. See Francis, 15–16.

112. Francis, 11.

113. Francis, 11–12.

114. Francis, 23.

115. Francis, 24–25.

116. Francis, 34.

117. Francis, 38.

118. Francis, 39.

119. Francis, 41, 13.

120. Francis, 39.

121. Francis, 39.

122. Francis, 40.

123. Francis, 45.

124. Francis, 45–46.

125. Francis, 46.

126. Francis, 46.

127. Francis, 47.

128. Francis, 12–13, 47.

129. See Francis, 47.

130. Although it is a project very different from ours in style and substance, we affirm much of the contribution of Kotsko, *Neoliberalism's Demons.*

4. A Theology of Mercy

1. We take a similar stance to Philip Mirowski, who says that neoliberalism is "a general philosophy of market society, and not some narrow set of doctrines restricted to economics." See Mirowski, "Neoliberalism."

2. There are two marks of distinction here: Catholic and anti-neoliberal. Both of these are crucial to addressing the situation in which we find ourselves today. Neoliberalism must be met frontally, and, for Catholics, it must be met out of the chief root of Catholicism, which is the revelation of God's mercy in the life of Jesus Christ. Some may well argue that the politics of mercy we sketch in chapter 5 is not "distinctively Catholic" enough, insofar as this politics could smoothly coordinate with and, in fact, draws many of its ideas and strategies from "secular" sources. We do not endorse such a position, since we see redemption in Christ extending, at least *in potentia*, to all, so the "distinctiveness" of Christ's mark in the world is more pluriform than some like to think. To put things more plainly, as Jesus does, those who are not against us are for us (Mk 9:40; Lk 9:50).

3. We regard our approach as similar to that recently prosecuted by Kathryn Tanner in her Gifford Lectures (2016). There she delves into Protestant theology not to discover, for example, explicit ways that Christian teaching opposes supposed capitalist vices (e.g., greed) but to find how Protestant Christianity and finance-dominated capitalism conflict with one another *in toto*, from discourse through practice to the whole of life. We do something analogous, in a Catholic vein. These lectures have recently been published as Tanner, *Christianity and the New Spirit of Capitalism.* The original lectures can be viewed online as Tanner, "Christianity and the New Spirit of Capitalism," Gifford Lectures, University of Edinburgh, May 2–12, 2016, accessed February 12, 2018, https://www.giffordlectures.org/lectures/christianity-and-new-spirit-capitalism.

4. Hayek, *Law, Legislation, and Liberty*, 94.

5. Hayek, 95.

6. Hayek, 75, 93.

7. Hayek, 64, 78.

8. Slobodian, *Globalists*, 87, 269.

9. Francis, "Angelus." The excerpt is from this Angelus.

10. Kasper, *Mercy*, 83–129.

11. Kasper, 10. While he has been criticized in some sectors for attributing this catastrophic failure to a deficiency in the "traditional metaphysical starting point of the doctrine of God" (11), we do not deem it necessary here to engage in a defense of metaphysics, a defense of Kasper's criticism of metaphysics, or any permutation of such defense or criticism. For a widely read public debate between Kasper and one of his critics, Daniel Moloney, on this count, see Moloney, "What Mercy Is"; and Kasper, "Cardinal Kasper Responds to First Things Review of 'Mercy.'"

12. See Kasper, *Mercy*, 90, 119–20.

13. Kasper, 91.

14. Kasper, 92.

15. Kasper, 93.

16. Kasper, 94.

17. One could detect here, were one so inclined, a tinge of theodicy in John Paul's remarks. Neither John Paul nor we, however, are so inclined. His point is not to explain the problem of evil, constructing a theoretical theodicy. Rather, his aim and ours is to explicate the meaning of mercy, which consists in a recognition of value even where value would seem to have been severely eroded. This is the point that is essential to a theology of mercy that resists neoliberalism as we discuss it here.

18. Kasper, *Mercy*, 111–17.

19. Kasper, 112.

20. John Paul II, "Letter on the 100th Anniversary of the Consecration of the Human Race."

21. John Paul II.

22. John Paul II, 2.

23. Kasper, *Mercy*, 114.

24. Francis, "Address to the New Non-Resident Ambassadors to the Holy See," emphasis added.

25. John Paul II, "Letter (11 June 1999)," 3.

26. Kasper, *Mercy*, 94.

27. Kasper, 94.

28. John Paul II, *Dominum et Vivificantem*. Hereafter *DV*.

29. The NAB has "convince"; the *ET* of *DV* has "convict." The Greek is "*elenxei*."

30. This is a running theme in *DV*; see especially *DV* 32.

31. Slobodian, *Globalists*, 87.

32. Slobodian, 84.

33. Benedict XVI (Ratzinger), *Introduction to Christianity*, 172–73.

34. Ratzinger, *Introduction to Christianity*, 183.

35. Benedict XVI, "Angelus."

36. Benedict XVI.

37. Francis, "Message on the Occasion of the World Meeting of Popular Movements." The rest of the references in this paragraph are to this message.

38. Francis, "Angelus."

39. Francis, "Angelus." In a similar vein, Francis used one of his general audiences in 2014 to relate the parable of the Good Samaritan to the sacrament of Anointing of the Sick. See Francis, "General Audience (St. Peter's Square)."

40. For a more thorough plumbing of the Christological depths of Francis's social teaching, see Clark, "Pope Francis."

41. Francis, "Te Deum Homily"; our translation.

42. On Bergoglio's efforts, along with President Eduardo Duhalde, to rebuild civil society in the aftermath of the depression, see Ivereigh, *Great Reformer*, 268–71. The 2003 Te Deum address was delivered on the inaugural day of the next president, Nestor Kirchner.

43. Francis, "Te Deum Homily."

44. "We are accustomed to a culture of indifference and we must strive and ask for the grace to create a culture of encounter, of a fruitful encounter, of an encounter that restores to each person his or her own dignity as a child of God, the dignity of a living person. We are accustomed to this indifference, when we see the disasters of this world or small things: 'What a shame, poor people, look how they are suffering,' and then we carry on. An encounter. And if I don't look, it's not enough to see, no, (we must) look—if I don't stop, if I don't look, if I don't touch, if I don't speak, I cannot have an encounter and I cannot help to build a culture of encounter." Francis, "Morning Reflection." "In this 'stepping out' it is important to be ready for encounter. For me this word is very important. Encounter with others. Why? Because faith is an encounter with Jesus, and we must do what Jesus does: encounter others. We live in a culture of conflict, a culture of fragmentation, a culture in which I throw away what is of no use to me, a culture of waste." He concludes that "with our faith we must create a 'culture of encounter.'" Francis, "Address of the Holy Father: Vigil of Pentecost."

45. Francis, *Misericordiae Vultus*.

46. Francis, "General Audience (February 26, 2014)."

47. Francis, *Misericordiae Vultus*, 14.

48. Kasper, *Mercy*, 157.

49. Francis, "A Big Heart Open to God."

50. Kasper, *Mercy*, 159.

51. Kasper, 159.

52. Kasper, *Mercy*, 160–61. For a brief history of the new evangelization, there is no better source than Benedict XVI's homily in which he announced the formation of the Pontifical Council for Promoting the New Evangelization: Benedict XVI, "Homily (First Vespers)."

53. Kasper, *Mercy*, 160.

54. Kasper, 160.

55. Kasper, 161. John Paul II opened his pontificate with a homily that included the exhortation, "do not be afraid," and he frequently repeated this phrase throughout his papacy. His words in this inaugural homily are worth quoting: "Brothers and sisters, do not be afraid to welcome Christ and accept his power. Help the Pope and all those who wish to serve Christ and with Christ's power to serve the human person and the whole of mankind. Do not be afraid. Open wide the doors for Christ. To his saving power open the boundaries of States, economic and political systems, the vast fields of culture, civilization and development. Do not be afraid. Christ knows 'what is in man'. He alone knows it." John Paul II, "Homily of His Holiness John Paul II."

56. Kasper, *Mercy*, 161.

57. Kasper, 164.

58. Kasper, 165.

59. Pope Francis, *Misericordiae Vultus*, 17.

60. Kasper, *Mercy*, 166.

61. Kasper, 165.

62. Kasper, 165.

63. Feminist sacramental theology can lead such critical inquiry. Natalie Watson helpfully registers this impulse when she writes, "Feminist theology needs to reconsider the sacraments even though they have in the past represented the alienation of women from the church." Watson, *Introducing Feminist Ecclesiology*, 79. Focused as it is on the formula of absolution, which can only be pronounced by a priest, who can only be male, inevitably raises questions of participation, exclusion, power, and indeed how the sacramental mercy of the church is put into practice on the ground (i.e., Susan Ross's example that women are often doing "all but" key sacramental actions). See Ross, *Extravagant Affections*, 74. An ecclesiology centered on mercy should involve serious examination of these intra-ecclesial critical questions, which fit in lockstep with the examination of conscience entailed by the sacrament of penance.

64. Second Vatican Council, *Lumen Gentium: Dogmatic Constitution on the Church*, November 21, 1964, 8. For a longer theological meditation on this and other apposite lines in *Lumen Gentium*, see Rahner, "Sinful Church," 270–93.

65. See Thomas Aquinas, *Summa theologiae* Ia–IIae, q. 30, a. 1, corpus.

66. Daniel M. Bell Jr.'s own critique of contemporary capitalism in his *The Economy of Desire* culminates in his own recommendation of the works of mercy as a way to form and to put into practice (and to form by putting into practice) what he calls a Christian "economy of desire." We concur with what Bell has to say with regard to turning the works of mercy against today's global capitalist economy. But we take the works of mercy in a different direction by reimagining them as a politics of mercy. See this chapter and chapter 5 for more detail on what we mean about the politics of mercy. See also Bell, *Economy of Desire*, 187–213.

67. Keenan, *Works of Mercy*.

68. Lists of the works of mercy abound and vary slightly. We base ours, with minor modification on Day, "Scandal of the Works of Mercy," in *Selected Writings*, 98.

69. Day, "We Go on Record," in *Selected Writings*, 313.

70. Day, "Love Is the Measure," in *Selected Writings*, 98.

71. Day, "Room for Christ," in *Selected Writings*, 97.

72. Day, *Long Loneliness*, 186.

73. See Day, "Aims and Purposes," in *Selected Writings*, 91.

74. See Day, 91: "Food for the body is not enough. There must be food for the soul. Hence the leaders of the work, and as many as we can induce to join us, must go daily to Mass, to receive food for the soul. And as our perceptions are quickened, and as we pray that our faith be increased, we will see Christ in each other, and we will not lose faith in those around us, no matter how stumbling their progress is." Because of statements (and practices) like this, Margaret Pfeil argues that Day's focus on the works of mercy was a form of "liturgical asceticism." Pfeil, "Love and Poverty."

75. Francis, *Misericordia et Misera*.

76. Harvey, *Seventeen Contradictions*, 286–87.

77. For a sharply critical analysis of this phenomenon, see Giridharadas, *Winners Take All*.

78. For a helpful introductory overview, see Nelson, *Sin*, 105–15. Kristin Heyer has recently added rich reflections pertinent to this question. Heyer defines social sin in its broadest sense as "the unjust structures, distorted consciousness, and collective actions and inaction that facilitate injustice and dehumanization." Heyer, *Kinship Across Borders*, 37. She rightly notes that "until recent decades, the Catholic moral tradition has neglected, if not resisted, a social understanding of sin due in part to an individualistic, act-oriented approach in traditional moral theology and a legalistic approach to questions of social justice" (37). This approach endures in John Paul II inasmuch as his teaching on social sin, for the praiseworthy reason of trying to

preserve personal responsibility at all levels, amounts almost exclusively to social sin being an aggregation of individuals' sins (Heyer calls this a "derivative notion" [40]).

79. Heyer, 42.

80. For a relevant treatment of concupiscence using Karl Rahner as a guide, see Fritz, *Freedom Made Manifest*, chs. 1 and 4. For Rahner's own correction of Neothomist views of concupiscence, see Rahner, "Theological Concept."

81. Sobrino, *Principle of Mercy*.

82. Sobrino, 69–82.

83. Sobrino, 71.

84. Sobrino, 73.

85. Sobrino, "The Samaritan Church and the Principle of Mercy" in *Principle of Mercy*, 15–26.

86. Sobrino, 16.

87. Sobrino, 18.

88. Sobrino, 20.

89. Sobrino, 21.

90. Sobrino, 18. For an excellent article on Sobrino's continuity with but also development of the Catholic tradition on mercy in a structural direction, see Walatka, "Principle of Mercy." Kevin Ahern, in concert with Sobrino, has written about how the gift of God's grace—always gratuitous (unmerited), ever healing of human sinfulness, and forever raising those on whom it rests to a new life of participation in the Trinitarian nature—enlivens the work of Catholic justice organizations worldwide. Ahern, *Structures of Grace*, esp. ch. 6.

91. Mirowski, *Never Let a Serious Crisis Go to Waste*, 332.

92. Friedman, *Capitalism and Freedom*, xiv.

5. The Politics of Mercy against Neoliberal Sacrifice

1. Francis, "Address of the Holy Father (Bolivia)."

2. Francis.

3. Francis.

4. Francis, "Address of the Holy Father (Kenya)."

5. In *Laudato Si'* Francis follows John Paul II when he writes: "the principle of the subordination of private property to the universal destination of goods, and thus the right of everyone to their use, is a golden rule of social conduct and 'the first principle of the whole ethical and social order'" (*LS*, 93).

6. See the treatment of Quinn Slobodian in chapter 2. In his account we see that neoliberals perform a sleight of hand with regard to the phrase "private property." Here we can elaborate just a bit more. Even though neoliberalism's popular apologists will discuss private property as a good (a contention with

which CST would agree), they do not let on that what neoliberals really mean by private property and what they mean to defend as private property is not personal possessions needed for life, but the higher order assets of corporations and the wealthy.

7. Keenan, *Works of Mercy*, 49.

8. Benedict XVI, "Message of His Holiness Benedict XVI for the Nineteenth World Day of the Sick."

9. Additionally, in a speech on "Environment and Health" in 1997, John Paul II argued that it is absolutely critical that Catholics attend to the environment when they reflect on the promotion of health in society.

10. Francis, "Message of his Holiness on World Day of Prayer for the Care of Creation."

11. John Paul II, "Peace with God."

12. John Paul II, 8.

13. Benedict XVI, "Message of His Holiness for World Day of Peace."

14. As formulated in the *Compendium of the Social Doctrine of the Church*, the doctrine of creation and the universal destination of goods are inherently connected: "The principle of the universal destination of goods is an affirmation both of God's full and perennial lordship over every reality and of the requirement that the goods of creation remain ever destined to the development of the whole person and of all humanity" (#177).

15. Armstrong, "Cardinal George Pell Criticizes Pope Francis."

16. European Water Movement, "Overexploitation of Ground Water."

17. Chazan, "French Town of Vittel." For a broader discussion of similar local movements, see Naomi Klein, *This Changes Everything*, 293–336.

18. Other significant efforts include attempts to preserve the Brazilian rainforest by local indigenous groups and the protest at Standing Rock led by Native Americans to resist the construction of the Dakota Pipeline. See "'Keep It Local' Approach to Protecting the Rainforest Can Be More Effective Than Government Schemes," University of Cambridge Research, September 12, 2017, accessed March 9, 2019, https://www.cam.ac.uk/research/news/keep-it -local-approach-to-protecting-the-rainforest-can-be-more-effective-than -government-schemes; and Klein, "Lesson from Standing Rock."

19. Indian physicist, author, and activist Vandana Shiva has been perhaps the most vocal opponent of the patenting of life, which has become a commonplace in industrial agriculture. For a brief explanation of the perversity of the patenting of life (a legal practice that all people, especially Catholics, should find offensive and impermissible), see the "Seed Freedom Report," Navdanya, accessed March 7, 2019, http://www.navdanya.org/site/living-seed/seed -manifesto.

20. Francis, "Address of the Holy Father (Bolivia)."

21. Aronoff, "Denial by a Different Name." See also Riley, "Just 100 Companies."

22. Klein, *This Changes Everything*, 129.

23. Harvey and Doherty, "China Demands Developed Countries 'Pay their Debts' on Climate Change."

24. Pogge, *World Poverty and Human Rights*, 202.

25. Pogge, "An Egalitarian Law of Peoples," 220.

26. *The Catechism of the Catholic Church* notes that "political authority has the right and duty to regulate the legitimate exercise of the right to ownership for the sake of the common good" (#2406), http://www.vatican.va/archive/ccc _css/archive/catechism/p3s2c2a7.htm.

27. Wooden, "Destroying Creation."

28. Francis, *LS*, 95, and Connolly, *Facing the Planetary*, 9.

29. Second Vatican Council, *Gaudium et Spes*.

30. Second Vatican Council, 9.

31. Notably, Benedict continues by relating this defense of human dignity to defense of creation, saying that "we must recognize our grave duty to hand the earth on to future generations in such a condition that they too can worthily inhabit it and continue to cultivate it" (*CV*, 50).

32. Benedict XVI, "Address of His Holiness Benedict XVI."

33. Moyn, *Not Enough*, xii. Moyn observes: "The real trouble about human rights, when historically correlated with market fundamentalism, is not that they promote it but that they are unambitious in theory and ineffectual in practice in the face of market fundamentalism's success. Neoliberalism has changed the world, while the human rights movement has posed no threat to it. The tragedy of human rights is that they have occupied the global imagination but have so far contributed little of note, merely nipping at the heels of the neoliberal giant whose path goes unaltered and unresisted" (216).

34. Moyn, 217–18.

35. Pope Francis, Twitter, April 28, 2014.

36. He has discussed these most prominently in his addresses to the World Meeting of Popular Movements. See Francis, "Discurso del Santo Padre"; and Francis, "Discurso del Santo Padre Francisco."

37. Francis, "Address of the Holy Father (Bolivia)."

38. Francis, "Address of the Holy Father (Kenya)."

39. Francis.

40. Francis.

41. Pontifical Council for Justice and Peace, "Compendium of the Social Doctrine of the Church," 177.

42. In his infamous "*Caritas in Veritate* in Gold and Red," George Weigel determined that Benedict XVI and his predecessors—John XXIII in *Mater et*

Magistra and Paul VI in *Populorum Progressio* who have advocated for a global political authority—have pursued nothing more than a "fantasy." He counsels that they engage the "canons of Christian realism" more seriously (as Weigel himself apparently has) to remedy this fantastical thinking.

43. Oxfam International, "Reward Work, Not Wealth."

44. Oxfam International, "5 Shocking Facts."

45. Sobrino, "On the Way to Healing."

46. Francis, "Address to Participants in the International Forum on 'Migration and Peace.'"

47. Massingale, *Racial Justice*, 43.

48. Second Vatican Council, *Gaudium et Spes*, 8, 29, 58, 64, 92.

49. For a very helpful compendium of these documents, see Nothwehr, *That They May Be One*.

50. US Conference of Catholic Bishops, "Brothers and Sisters to Us."

51. Quoted in Massingale, "James Cone," 701.

52. Schlumpf, "Bishop Lays Out Plan for Eradicating this Plague of Racism."

53. Massingale, "James Cone," 712.

54. Cone, "Theological Challenge."

55. Massingale, "James Cone," 700.

56. Cone, "Theologians and White Supremacy."

57. Massingale, *Racial Justice*, 77.

58. US Conference of Catholic Bishops, *Welcoming the Stranger Among Us*.

59. US Conference of Catholic Bishops, "Catholic Church's Position on Immigration Reform."

60. Anthea Butler, "Catholic Church's Last Major Effort."

61. Winters, "US Bishops Present United Front."

62. See US Conference of Catholic Bishops, *Open Wide Our Hearts*, 30 and 21–22.

63. US Conference of Catholic Bishops, 21.

64. US Conference of Catholic Bishops, 10–14. Whereas *Welcoming the Stranger Among Us: Unity in Diversity* only used the term *racism* four times, *Open Wide Our Hearts* does much better on this front and invokes the term *racism* eighty-three times.

65. US Conference of Catholic Bishops, *Open Wide Our Hearts*, 3.

66. US Conference of Catholic Bishops, 28.

67. Copeland, "White Supremacy."

68. Disappointingly and perplexingly, this verse is not cited in *Open Wide Our Hearts*, the most recent official ecclesial document on racism.

69. One could object, of course, that Gal 3:28 and these other pericopes have the upshot of insisting that one must have faith in Christ, thus there is

some exclusivity to being in Christ (namely one has to make an act of faith to be included in the "no Jew/Greek, etc.," but this reading grates against the facts and presupposes a human standard of justice. The response to this objection is, "You are thinking not as God does, but as humans do" (Mk 8:33; Mt 16:23).

70. See, for example, the USCCB's webpages on the corporal and spiritual works of mercy, where race and racism are conspicuously absent: http://www .usccb.org/beliefs-and-teachings/how-we-teach/new-evangelization/jubilee-of -mercy/the-corporal-works-of-mercy.cfm.

71. As Angela Davis puts it, abolitionism "is not only, or not even primarily, about abolition as a negative process of tearing down, but it is also about building up, about creating new institutions." Davis, *Abolition Democracy*, 73.

72. Francis, "Visit to the Penitentiary (Cereso N. 3)."

73. But in the twentieth century, Dorothy Day laments, "What a neglected work of mercy, visiting the prisoner. 'When were you in Prison, Lord, and we did not visit you?' It is a hard picture Christ presents. He did not forgive this ignorance. 'Inasmuch as you did not visit these prisoners ye did not visit Me.' 'But they are guilty, they are the scum of the earth, they are the refuse, they are the offscourings. They drink, they take dope, they are prostitutes. They are vicious themselves and they make others vicious. They even sell drugs to little children. They are where they belong. Prison is too good for them. We can't pamper them.' 'I have come to call them to repentance. I have come to be with publicans and sinners. I have come for the lost sheep. I am more there with these most miserable ones than with the judges sitting on the high seats.' This is not sentimentality. This is truth." Day, "Where Are the Poor?"

74. Keenan, *Works of Mercy*, 19–20.

75. Harris, *Pound of Flesh*.

76. Francis, "Mass of the Lord's Supper."

77. Francis.

78. Francis, "Address of the Holy Father (Visit to Curran-Fromhold)."

79. The US Catholic bishops have steadily lobbied congress on various pieces of legislation intended to reform sentencing in the criminal justice system, but there has been no direct confrontation with the racialized character of the prison industrial complex in the United States.

80. Davis, *Are Prisons Obsolete?*, 9–21.

81. Davis, *Freedom Is a Constant Struggle*, 22.

82. Davis, *Abolition Democracy*, 73. See also Wacquant, "From Slavery to Mass Incarceration."

83. Davis, "Incarcerated Women," 26.

84. Davis, *Abolition Democracy*, 75.

85. Davis, 96.

86. See, for example, Davis, "Recognizing Racism."

87. Davis, *Are Prisons Obsolete?*, 10.

88. Davis, *Freedom Is a Constant Struggle*, 6.

89. Davis, *Abolition Democracy*, 85.

90. Benedict XVI, *Values in a Time of Upheaval*, 144. Additionally, while the tendency among the US Catholic bishops has been to call for prison reform, we argue that once the connection between slavery and mass incarceration is established (as Davis and others have done), it becomes necessary to demand a more radical response to it as an institution of structural racism. Neither slavery nor Jim Crow should have been met with calls to reform the structures but rather to abolish them. So too with the prison industrial complex as the descendent of slavery and Jim Crow as institutionalized forms of racism in American history.

91. Davis exhorts: "there must be an alternative to capitalism. Today, the tendency to assume that the only version of democracy available to us is capitalist democracy poses a challenge. We must be able to disentangle our notions of capitalism and democracy so to pursue truly egalitarian models of democracy." Davis, *Abolition Democracy*, 6.

92. Gilmore, "Ruth Gilmore Interview by Andalusia Knoll."

93. Keenan, *Works of Mercy*, 24.

94. Frye, Horner, and Baker, *Rule of St. Benedict*.

95. Vatican News, "Pope at Mass: Be Free from Fear of Migrants and Refugees," February 15, 2019, accessed March 7, 2019, https://www .vaticannews.va/en/pope/news/2019-02/pope-francis-mass-sacrofano-migrants -refugees.html.

96. Metz, *Memoria Passionis*.

97. See Kinzer, *Overthrow*.

98. Francis, "Address to the Participants in the Plenary."

99. Chomsky, "Americans Wanted to Keep Immigrants."

100. On the New Sanctuary Movement, see Carbine, "Artisans of a New Humanity," 175–77; and, on the broader movement, see Garcia, "Dangerous Times Call for Risky Responses."

101. Paik, "Abolitionist Futures."

102. US Court of Appeals for the Ninth Circuit, 871 F.2d 1436 (9th Cir. 1989), argued and submitted December 9, 1988, decided March 30, 1989, https://law .justia.com/cases/federal/appellate-courts/F2/871/1436/44380/.

103. See newsanctuarymovement.org.

104. Feuerherd, "Churches Upfront about Legal Risks."

105. See Sassen, "A Massive Loss of Habitat," on the recent spike in migrants from Honduras, Guatemala, and El Salvador as a result of political instability and violence.

106. National Immigration Forum, "Fact Sheet."

107. Hang, "What Does It Mean to Abolish ICE?"; and Ackerman and Rawnsley, "800 Million."

108. Foer, "How Trump Radicalized ICE."

109. Foer.

110. Hartig, "Republicans Turn more Negative."

111. Jeffrey, "U.S. Bishop Prepare Catholics for Civil Disobedience."

112. Camosy, "Is It Time for Catholic Churches to Become Sanctuary Churches?"

Conclusion: For Holistic Mercy

1. Francis, "Video Message of His Holiness Pope Francis."

Bibliography

Acosta, Alberto. "Extractivism and Neoextractivism: Two Sides of the Same Curse." In *Beyond Development: Alternative Visions from Latin America*, edited by Miriam Lang and Dunia Mokrani, translated by Sara Shields, Rosemary Underhay, 61–86. Amsterdam: Transnational Institute, 2013.

———. "Postextractivismo: del discurso a la práctica—Reflexiones para la acción," *International Development Policy: Revue internationale de politique de développement* 9 (2017). DOI: 10.4000/poldev.2496.

Ackerman, Spencer, and Adam Rawnsley. "800 Million in Taxpayer Money Went to Private Prisons Where Migrants Work for Pennies." *Daily Beast*, December 27, 2018. https://www.thedailybeast.com/dollar800-million-in -taxpayer-money-went-to-private-prisons-where-migrants-work-for-pennies.

Ahern, Kevin. *Structures of Grace: Catholic Organizations Serving the Global Common Good*. Maryknoll, NY: Orbis, 2015.

Alexander, Michelle. *The New Jim Crow: Mass Incarceration in the Age of Colorblindness*. New York: New Press, 2012.

Andrejevic, Mark. *Reality TV: The Work of Being Watched*. Lanham, MD: Rowman and Littlefield, 2004.

Aronoff, Kate. "Denial by a Different Name," *Intercept*, April 17, 2018. https:// theintercept.com/2018/04/17/climate-change-denial-trump-germany/.

Armstrong, Kerrie. "Cardinal George Pell Criticizes Pope Francis over Climate Change," *Sydney Morning Herald*, July 19, 2015. https://www.smh.com.au /world/cardinal-george-pell-criticises-pope-francis-over-climate-change -stance-20150719-gifhjt.html

Auyero, Javier, and Deborah Alejandra Swistun. *Flammable: Environmental Suffering in an Argentine Shantytown*. New York: Oxford University Press, 2009.

Aviram, Hadar. *Cheap on Crime: Recession-Era Politics and the Transformation of American Punishment*. Berkeley: University of California Press, 2015.

Barry, Andrew, and Thomas Osborne, eds. *Foucault and Political Reason: Liberalism, Neo-Liberalism, and the Rationalities of Government*. New York: Routledge Press, 2016.

Becker, Gary. *Human Capital: A Theoretical and Empirical Analysis, with Special Reference to Education*. Chicago: University of Chicago Press, 1964.

Bell, Daniel Jr. *The Economy of Desire: Christianity and Capitalism in a Postmodern World*. Grand Rapids, MI: Baker Academic, 2012.

Benedict XVI [Joseph Ratzinger]. "Address at the Inaugural Session of the Fifth General Conference of the Bishops of Latin American and the Caribbean." May 13, 2007. https://w2.vatican.va/content/benedict-xvi/en/speeches/2007/may/documents/hf_ben-xvi_spe_20070513_conference-aparecida.html.

——. "Address of His Holiness Benedict XVI (Bungaroo, Sydney Harbor)." July 17, 2008. http://w2.vatican.va/content/benedict-xvi/en/speeches/2008/july/documents/hf_ben-xvi_spe_20080717_barangaroo.html.

——. "Angelus." June 8, 2008. http://w2.vatican.va/content/benedict-xvi/en/angelus/2008/documents/hf_ben-xvi_ang_20080608.html.

——. *Caritas in Veritate*. June 29, 2009. http://w2.vatican.va/content/benedict-xvi/en/encyclicals/documents/hf_ben-xvi_enc_20090629_caritas-in-veritate.html.

——. "Church and Economy." *Communio* 13, no. 3 (Fall 1986): 199–204.

——. *Church, Ecumenism, and Politics: New Essays in Ecclesiology*. New York: Crossroad, 1988.

——. *Co-Workers of the Truth: Meditations for Every Day of the Year*. Edited by Sister Irene Grassl, translated by Sister Mary Frances McCarthy SND, and Reverend Lothar Krauth. San Francisco: Ignatius Press, 1992.

——. *Deus Caritas Est*. December 25, 2005. http://w2.vatican.va/content/benedict-xvi/en/encyclicals/documents/hf_ben-xvi_enc_20051225_deus-caritas-est.html.

——. *Eschatology: Death and Eternal Life*. Washington, DC: Catholic University of America Press, 1988.

——. *The Essential Pope Benedict XVI*. Edited by John F. Thornton and Susan B. Varenne. New York: Harper One, 2008.

——. "Homily (First Vespers, the Solemnity of Sts. Peter and Paul, in Rome)." June 28, 2010. http://w2.vatican.va/content/benedict-xvi/en/homilies/2010/documents/hf_ben-xvi_hom_20100628_vespri-pietro-paolo.html.

——. "Homily (Pro Eligendo Romano Pontifice)." April 18, 2005. http://www.vatican.va/gpII/documents/homily-pro-eligendo-pontifice_20050418_en.html.

——. "Instruction on Certain Aspects of the 'Theology of Liberation.'" August 6, 1984. http://www.vatican.va/roman_curia/congregations/cfaith/documents/rc_con_cfaith_doc_19840806_theology-liberation_en.html.

——. *Introduction to Christianity*. Translated by J. R. Foster, with a new preface translated by Michael J. Miller. San Francisco: Ignatius Press, 2004.

——. "Message of His Holiness Benedict XVI for the Nineteenth World Day of the Sick." February 11, 2011. https://w2.vatican.va/content/benedict-xvi

/en/messages/sick/documents/hf_ben-xvi_mes_20101121_world-day-of-the
-sick-2011.html.

———. "Message of His Holiness for World Day of Peace." January 1, 2019.
https://w2.vatican.va/content/benedict-xvi/en/messages/peace/documents
/hf_ben-xvi_mes_20091208_xliii-world-day-peace.html.

———. *Spe Salvi*. November 30, 2007. http://w2.vatican.va/content/benedict
-xvi/en/encyclicals/documents/hf_ben-xvi_enc_20071130_spe-salvi.html.

———. *A Turning Point for Europe?* San Francisco: Ignatius Press, 2010.

———. *Values in a Time of Upheaval*. San Francisco: Ignatius Press, 2006.

———. *Without Roots: The West, Relativism, Christianity, Islam*. San Francisco:
Basic Books, 2006.

Benns, Whitney, and Blake Strode. "Debtors' Prison in 21st-Century America."
Atlantic, February 23, 2016. https://www.theatlantic.com/business/archive
/2016/02/debtors-prison/462378/.

Beretta, Simona. "Development Driven by Hope and Gratuitousness: The
Innovative Economics of Benedict XVI." In *Explorations in the Theology of
Benedict XVI*, 187–214. Notre Dame, IN: University of Notre Dame Press,
2012.

Bergoglio, Jorge Mario. *See* Francis, Pope.

Bessner, Daniel, and Matthew Sparke. "Don't Let His Trade Policy Fool You:
Trump is a Neoliberal." *Washington Post*, March 22, 2017. https://www
.washingtonpost.com/posteverything/wp/2017/03/22/dont-let-his-trade
-policy-fool-you-trump-is-a-neoliberal/?utm_term=.53b265f0e842.

Best, Beverly. "Raymond Williams and the Structure of Feeling of Reality TV."
International Journal of Humanities and Social Science 2, no.7 (2012):
192–201.

Bhattacharyya, Gargi. *Racial Capitalism: Questions of Reproduction and Survival*.
Lanham, MD: Rowman and Littlefield, 2018.

Braedley, Susan, and Meg Luxton, eds. *Neoliberalism and Everyday Life*.
Montreal: McGill-Queen University Press, 2010.

Brenner, Neil, and Nik Theodore, "Cities and the Geographies of 'Really
Existing Neoliberalism.'" *Antipode* 34, no. 3 (2002): 349–79.

Brooks, Arthur. *The Conservative Heart: How to Build a Fairer, Happier, and More
Prosperous America*. New York: Broadside Books, 2017.

Brown, Wendy. "Apocalyptic Populism." *Eurozine*, August 30, 2017. http://www
.eurozine.com/apocalyptic-populism/.

———. *Edgework: Critical Essays on Knowledge and Politics*. Princeton, NJ:
Princeton University Press, 2005.

——— "Who Is Not a Neoliberal Today?" Interview by Jacob Hamburger.
Tocqueville 21, January 18, 2018. https://tocqueville21.com/interviews/wendy
-brown-not-neoliberal-today/.

———. *Undoing the Demos: Neoliberalism's Stealth Revolution*. New York: Zone Books, 2015.

———. "The University and Its Worlds: A Panel Discussion (with Achille Mbembe, Judith Butler, and David Theo Goldberg)." YouTube, May 26, 2016. https://www.youtube.com/watch?v=s07xFdD-ivQ.

———. *Walled States, Waning Sovereignty*. New York: Zone Books, 2010.

Burnside, Sarah. "Investing in a Brilliant New YOU™: The Rise and Tyranny of the 'Personal Brand.'" *Guardian*, April 15, 2014. https://www.theguardian.com/commentisfree/2014/apr/15/investing-in-a-brilliant-new-youtm-the-rise-and-tyranny-of-the-personal-brand.

Butler, Anthea. "The Catholic Church's Last Major Effort on Racism was in 1979. Charlottesville Woke it Up." *Washington Post*, August 23, 2017. https://www.washingtonpost.com/news/acts-of-faith/wp/2017/08/23/the-u-s-catholic-churchs-last-major-effort-on-racism-was-in-1979-charlottesville-woke-it-up/?utm_term=.efcbeca63e58.

Butler, Judith. *Notes Toward a Performative Theory of Assembly*. Mary Flexner Lectures of Bryn Mawr College. Cambridge, MA: Harvard University Press, 2015.

Butler, Judith, and Athena Athanasiou. *Dispossession: The Performative in the Political*. Malden, MA: Polity Books, 2013.

Buttiglione, Rocco. *Karol Wojtyla: The Thought of the Man Who Became John Paul II*. Foreword by Michael Novak. Grand Rapids, MI: William B. Eerdmans, 1997.

Callinicos, Alex. *Bonfire of Illusions: The Twin Crises of the Liberal World*. Boston, MA: Polity, 2010.

Camosy, Charles C. "Is It Time for Catholic Churches to Become Sanctuary Churches?" *Crux*, February 24, 2017. https://cruxnow.com/commentary/2017/02/24/time-catholic-churches-become-sanctuaries/.

Camp, Jordan T. *Incarcerating the Crisis: Freedom Struggles and the Rise of the Neoliberal State*. Oakland: University of California Press, 2017.

Cacho, Lisa Marie. *Social Death: Racialized Rightlessness and the Criminalization of the Unprotected*. New York: New York University Press, 2012.

Carbine, Rosemary P. "'Artisans of a New Humanity': Re-Visioning the Public Church in a Feminist Perspective." In *Frontiers in Catholic Feminist Theology*, edited by Susan Abraham and Elena Procario-Foley, 173–92. Minneapolis: Fortress Press, 2009.

Casarella, Peter J., ed. *Jesus Christ: The New Face of Social Progress*. Grand Rapids, MI: William B. Eerdmans, 2015.

Cavanaugh, William T. "Return of the Golden Calf: Economy, Idolatry, and Secularization since *Gaudium et spes*." *Theological Studies* 76, no. 4 (2015): 698–717.

Chacon, Justin Akers, and Mike Davis, "Neoliberalism Consumes the 'Mexican Miracle.'" In *No One Is Illegal: Fighting Racism and State violence on the U.S.-Mexico Border*, 109–14. Chicago: Haymarket, 2006.

Chandran, Rina. "What's a Slum? India's Dharavi Defies Label with Thriving Informal Economy." Place, October 11, 2016. http://www.thisisplace.org/i/?id=7f6614e4-b139-4db2-9dd7-e0cf4f38f2d3.

Chazan, David. "French Town of Vittel Suffering Water Shortages as Nestle Accused of 'Overusing' Resources." *Telegraph*, April 26, 2018. https://www.telegraph.co.uk/news/2018/04/26/french-town-vittel-suffering-water-shortages-nestle-accused/.

Chomsky, Aviva. "Americans Wanted to Keep Immigrants Out Long Before Donald Trump Was Even Born." *Nation*, September 13, 2016. https://www.thenation.com/article/america-wanted-to-keep-immigrants-out-long-before-donald-trump-was-even-born/.

———. *They Take Our Jobs! And 20 Other Myths about Immigration*. Boston, MA: Beacon Press, 2018.

———. *Undocumented: How Immigration Became Illegal*. Boston, MA: Beacon Press, 2014.

Christiansen, Drew, SJ. "Metaphysics and Society: A Commentary on *Caritas in Veritate*." *Theological Studies* 71, no. 1 (2010): 3–28.

Clark, Meghan. "*Caritas in Veritate*." In *Modern Catholic Social Teaching: Commentaries and Interpretations*, edited by Kenneth R. Himes, OFM Washington DC: Georgetown University Press, 2018.

———. "Pope Francis and the Christological Dimensions of Solidarity in Catholic Social Teaching." *Theological Studies* 80, no. 1 (2019): 102–22.

———. *The Vision of Catholic Social Thought: The Virtue of Solidarity and the Praxis of Human Rights*. Minneapolis: Fortress Press, 2014.

Clarno, Andy. "The Constitution of State/Space and the Limits of 'Autonomy' in South Africa and Palestine/Israel." In *Sociology and Empire*, edited by George Steinmetz, 588–626. Durham, NC: Duke University Press, 2013.

———. *Neoliberal Apartheid: Palestine/Israel and South Africa after 1994*. Chicago: University of Chicago Press, 2017.

Cloutier, David, "The Theological Roundtable: Pope Francis and American Economics." *Horizons* 42, no. 1 (June 2015): 122–55.

Cone, James. "Theologians and White Supremacy: An Interview with James Cone." *America*, November 20, 2006. https://www.americamagazine.org/arts-culture/2006/11/20/theologians-and-white-supremacy-interview-james-h-cone.

———. "A Theological Challenge to the American Catholic Church." In *Speaking the Truth: Ecumenism, Liberation, and Black Theology*, 130–37. Grand Rapids, MI: Eerdmans, 1986.

Connolly, William. *Facing the Planetary: Entangled Humanism and the Politics of Swarming.* Raleigh, NC: Duke University Press, 2017.

Cooper, Melinda. *Family Values: Between Neoliberalism and the New Social Conservatism.* Brooklyn: Zone Books, 2017.

Copeland, M. Shawn. "White Supremacy and Anti-Black Logics in the Making of U.S. Catholicism." In *Anti-Blackness and Christian Ethics*, edited by Vincent M. Lloyd and Andrew Prevot, 61–75. Maryknoll, NY: Orbis, 2017.

Couldry, Nick. "Reality TV, or the Secret Theater of Neoliberalism." *Review of Education, Pedagogy, and Cultural Studies* 30, no. 1 (2008): 1–13.

Crutzen, Paul J., and Eugene F. Stoermer. "The Anthropocene." *Global Change Newsletter*, no. 41 (May 2000): 17–18.

Curran, Charles E., Kenneth R. Himes, OFM, and Thomas A. Shannon. *Catholic Social Teaching and Pope Benedict XVI.* Washington, D.C.: Georgetown University Press, 2014.

———. "Commentary on *Sollicitudo rei socialis (On Social Concern).*" In *Modern Catholic Social Teaching: Commentaries and Interpretations*, edited by Kenneth R. Himes, 415–35. Washington, DC: Georgetown University Press, 2005.

Daly, Herman. *Beyond Growth: The Economics of Sustainable Development.* Boston, MA: Beacon Press, 1996.

Dardot, Pierre, and Christian Laval. *The New Way of the World: On Neoliberal Society.* Translated by Gregory Elliot. New York: Verso, 2017.

Datta, Ayona. "The Intimate City: Violence, Gender, and Ordinary Life in the Slums." *Urban Geography* 37, no. 3 (2016): 323–42.

Davies, Lizzie. "Pope Says He Is Not a Marxist, But Defends Criticism of Capitalism." *Guardian*, December 15, 2013, https://www.theguardian.com/world/2013/dec/15/pope-francis-defends-criticism-of-capitalism-not-marxist.

Davis, Angela. *Abolition Democracy: Beyond Empire, Prisons, and Torture.* New York: Seven Stories Press, 2005.

———. *Are Prisons Obsolete?* New York: Seven Stories Press, 2010.

———. *Freedom Is a Constant Struggle: Ferguson, Palestine, and the Foundation of a Movement.* Chicago: Haymarket, 2016.

———. "Incarcerated Women: Transformed Strategies," *Black Renaissance/Renaissance Noir* 1, no.1 (1996): 21–34.

———. "Recognizing Racism in an Era of Neoliberalism." In *The Meaning of Freedom and Other Difficult Dialogues*, 165–78. San Francisco: City Lights, 2009.

Davis, Mike. "Hell Factories in the Field: A Prison-Industrial Complex." *Nation*, February 20, 1995.

———. *Planet of Slums.* New York: Verso, 2006.

Day, Dorothy. *The Long Loneliness.* New York: Harper and Row, 1952.

——. *Selected Writings: By Little and By Little*. Edited by Robert Ellsberg. Maryknoll, NY: Orbis Books, 2005.

——. "Where Are the Poor? They Are in Prisons, Too," Catholic Worker, July–August 1955. http://www.catholicworker.org/dorothyday/articles/241 .html.

de Soto, Hernando. *The Mystery of Capital: Why Capitalism Triumphs in the West and Fails Everywhere Else*. New York: Basic Books, 2000.

Doak, Mary. "Evangelizing in an Economy of Death." In *Pope Francis and the Future of Catholicism: Evangelii Gaudium and the Papal Agenda*, edited by Gerard Mannion, 179–202. New York: Cambridge University Press, 2017.

Dolan, Timothy. "The Pope's Case for Virtuous Capitalism." *Wall Street Journal*, May 22, 2014, https://www.wsj.com/articles/cardinal-timothy-dolan-the -popes-case-for-virtuous-capitalism-1400799968.

Doty, Roxanne, and Elizabeth Wheatley. "Private Detention and the Immigration Industrial Complex." *International Political Sociology* 7, no. 4 (2013): 426–43.

Duménil, Gérard, and Dominique Lévy, *The Crisis of Neoliberalism*. Cambridge, MA: Harvard University Press, 2013.

Economist, "Gary Becker's Concept of Human Capital (Six Big Ideas)." August 3, 2017. https://www.economist.com/news/economics-brief/21725757 -becker-made-people-central-focus-economics-second-our-series-big.

Elliott, Brian. *Natural Catastrophe: Climate Change and Neoliberal Governance*. Edinburgh: Edinburgh University Press, 2016.

European Water Movement, "The Overexploitation of Ground Water in the Southern Western Vosges by Nestlé Waters and the Ermitage Cheese Dairy." http://europeanwater.org/actions/country-city-focus/663-the -overexploitation-of-ground-water-in-the-south-western-vosges-by-nestle -waters-and-ermitage.

Feher, Michel. "Self-Appreciation; or, the Aspirations of Human Capital." Translated by Ivan Ascher. *Public Culture* 21, no. 1 (2009): 21–41.

Fernandes, Deepa. *Targeted: Homeland Security and the Business of Immigration*. New York: Seven Stories Press, 2010.

Feuerherd, Peter. "Churches Upfront about Legal Risks When Providing Immigrants Sanctuary." *National Catholic Reporter*, February 21, 2017. https://www.ncronline.org/news/parish/churches-upfront-about-legal-risks -when-providing-immigrants-sanctuary.

Firer Hinze, Christine. *Glass Ceilings and Dirt Floors: Women, Work, and the Global Economy*. New York: Paulist, 2015.

Fletcher, Robert. "Capitalizing on Chaos: Climate Change and Disaster Capitalism." Ephemera, n.d. http://www.ephemerajournal.org/contribution /capitalizing-chaos-climate-change-and-disaster-capitalism.

Foer, Franklin. "How Trump Radicalized ICE." *Atlantic*, September 2018. https://www.theatlantic.com/magazine/archive/2018/09/trump-ice/565772/.

Foucault, Michel. *Birth of Biopolitics: Lectures at the College de France, 1978–1979.* Edited by Michel Senellart and Graham Burchell. New York: Palgrave Macmillan, 2008.

Francis, Pope [Jorge Mario Bergoglio]. "Address of the Holy Father (Kangemi Slum in Nairobi, Kenya)." November 27, 2015. http://w2.vatican.va/content /francesco/en/speeches/2015/november/documents/papa-francesco _20151127_kenya-kangemi.html.

———. "Address of the Holy Father (Meeting with Representatives of Civil Society, Paraguay)," July 11, 2015. https://w2.vatican.va/content/francesco /en/speeches/2015/july/documents/papa-francesco_20150711_paraguay -societa-civile.html.

———. "Address of the Holy Father (Second World Meeting of Popular Movements, Bolivia)." July 9, 2015. http://w2.vatican.va/content/francesco /en/speeches/2015/july/documents/papa-francesco_20150709_bolivia -movimenti-popolari.html.

———. "Address of the Holy Father (Visit to Curran-Fromhold Correctional Facility)." September 27, 2015. http://w2.vatican.va/content/francesco/en /speeches/2015/september/documents/papa-francesco_20150927_usa -detenuti.html.

———. "Address of the Holy Father: Vigil of Pentecost with the Ecclesial Movements." May 18, 2013. http://w2.vatican.va/content/francesco/en /speeches/2013/may/documents/papa-francesco_20130518_veglia-pentecoste .html.

———. "Address to the New Non-Resident Ambassadors to the Holy See: Kyrgyzstan, Antigua and Barbuda, Luxembourg, and Botswana." May 16, 2013, http://w2.vatican.va/content/francesco/en/speeches/2013/may /documents/papa-francesco_20130516_nuovi-ambasciatori.html.

———. "Address to Participants in the International Forum on 'Migration and Peace.'" February 21, 2017. http://w2.vatican.va/content/francesco/en /speeches/2017/february/documents/papa-francesco_20170221_forum -migrazioni-pace.html.

———. "Address to the Participants in the Plenary of the Pontifical Council for the Pastoral Care of Migrants and Itinerant People." May 24, 2013. https://w2.vatican.va/content/francesco/en/speeches/2013/may/documents /papa-francesco_20130524_migranti-itineranti.html.

———. "Angelus." July 10, 2016. https://w2.vatican.va/content/francesco/en /angelus/2016/documents/papa-francesco_angelus_20160710.html.

———. "A Big Heart Open to God: An Interview with Pope Francis." Interviewed by Antonio Spadaro, SJ. *America*, September 30, 2013. https://www

.americamagazine.org/faith/2013/09/30/big-heart-open-god-interview-pope
-francis.

———. *Dialogos entre Juan Pablo II y Fidel Castro*. Buenos Aires: Editorial de
Ciencia y Cultura, 1998.

———. "Discurso del Santo Padre (Expo Feria, Santa Cruz de la Sierra,
Bolivia)." July 9, 2015. http://w2.vatican.va/content/francesco/es/speeches
/2015/july/documents/papa-francesco_20150709_bolivia-movimenti
-popolari.html.

———. "Discurso del Santo Padre Francisco a los Participantes en el Encuentro
Mundial de Movimientos Populares (Aula Pablo VI, Vatican)." November 5,
2016. http://w2.vatican.va/content/francesco/es/speeches/2016/november
/documents/papa-francesco_20161105_movimenti-popolari.html.

———. *Evangelii Gaudium*. November 24, 2013. http://w2.vatican.va/content
/francesco/en/apost_exhortations/documents/papa-francesco_esortazione
-ap_20131124_evangelii-gaudium.html.

———. "General Audience." June 5, 2013. https://w2.vatican.va/content
/francesco/en/audiences/2013/documents/papa-francesco_20130605
_udienza-generale.html.

———. "General Audience (Poverty and Mercy)." May 18, 2016. https://w2
.vatican.va/content/francesco/en/audiences/2016/documents/papa-francesco
_20160518_udienza-generale.html.

———. "General Audience (St. Peter's Square)." February 26, 2014. https://w2
.vatican.va/content/francesco/en/audiences/2014/documents/papa-francesco
_20140226_udienza-generale.html.

———. *Laudato Si'*. May 24, 2015. http://w2.vatican.va/content/francesco/en
/encyclicals/documents/papa-francesco_20150524_enciclica-laudato-si.html.

———. "Mass of the Lord's Supper: Homily of His Holiness Pope Francis."
http://w2.vatican.va/content/francesco/en/homilies/2018/documents/papa
-francesco_20180329_omelia-coena-domini.html.

———. "Message (First World Day of the Poor)." November 19, 2017. https://w2
.vatican.va/content/francesco/en/messages/poveri/documents/papa
-francesco_20170613_messaggio-i-giornatamondiale-poveri-2017.html.

———. "Message of his Holiness on World Day of Prayer for the Care of
Creation." http://w2.vatican.va/content/francesco/en/messages/pont
-messages/2016/documents/papa-francesco_20160901_messaggio-giornata
-cura-creato.html.

———. "Message of His Holiness Pope Francis for Lent 2016." https://w2
.vatican.va/content/francesco/en/messages/lent/documents/papa-francesco
_20151004_messaggio-quaresima2016.html.

———. "Message on the Occasion of the World Meeting of Popular Movements, Modesto, California." February 10, 2017. https://w2.vatican.va

/content/francesco/en/messages/pont-messages/2017/documents/papa
-francesco_20170210_movimenti-popolari-modesto.html.

———. *Misericordia et Misera: Apostolic Letter at the Conclusion of the Extraordinary Jubilee of Mercy.* November 20, 2016. https://w2.vatican.va/content
/francesco/en/apost_letters/documents/papa-francesco-lettera-ap_20161120
_misericordia-et-misera.html.

———. *Misericordiae Vultus: Bull of Indiction of the Extraordinary Jubilee of Mercy.* April 11, 2015. http://w2.vatican.va/content/francesco/en/bulls
/documents/papa-francesco_bolla_20150411_misericordiae-vultus.html.

———. "Morning Reflection in the Chapel of the Domus Sanctae Marthae: For a Culture of Encounter." September 13, 2016. http://w2.vatican.va/content
/francesco/en/cotidie/2016/documents/papa-francesco-cotidie_20160913
_for-a-culture-of-encounter.html.

———. *Only Love Can Save Us: Letters, Homilies, and Talks of Cardinal Jorge Bergoglio.* Translated by Gerard Seromik. Huntington, IN: Our Sunday Visitor, 2013.

———. "Pastoral Visit of the Holy Father Francis to the Archdiocese of Genoa (27 May 2017)—Meeting with the World of Work at the Ilva Factory (transcript of questions and answers)." May 27, 2017. https://press.vatican.va
/content/salastampa/en/bollettino/pubblico/2017/05/27/170527a.html.

———. "Te Deum Homily." May 25, 2003. http://www.arzbaires.org.ar/inicio
/homilias/homilias2003.htm#Tedeum25/5/2003.

———. *The Way of Humility: Corruption and Sin and On Self-Accusation.* Translated by Helena Scott. San Francisco: Ignatius, 2013.

———. "Video Message of His Holiness Pope Francis on the Occasion of the Celebration of the Extraordinary Jubilee of Mercy in the Americas." August 27–30, 2016. https://w2.vatican.va/content/francesco/en/messages
/pont-messages/2016/documents/papa-francesco_20160827_videomessaggio
-giubileo-misericordia-americhe.pdf.

———. "Visit to the Penitentiary (Cereso N. 3) of Ciuadad Juárez." https://w2
.vatican.va/content/francesco/en/speeches/2016/february/documents/papa
-francesco_20160217_messico-detenuti.html.

Fraser, Nancy. "The End of Progressive Neoliberalism." *Dissent* 64, no. 2 (2017): 130–40.

Friedman, Milton. *Capitalism and Freedom.* Chicago: University of Chicago Press, 2002.

Fritz, Peter Joseph. *Freedom Made Manifest: Rahner's Fundamental Option and Theological Aesthetics.* Washington, DC: Catholic University of America Press, 2019.

Frye, Timothy, Timothy Horner, and Imogene Baker, eds. *The Rule of St. Benedict* Collegeville, MN: Liturgical Press, 1981.

Garcia, Maria Cristina. "'Dangerous Times Call for Risky Responses': Latino
    Immigration and Sanctuary, 1981–2001." In *Latino Religions and Activism in
    the United States*, edited by Gaston Espinosa, Virgil Elizondo, and Jesse
    Miranda, 159–73. New York: Oxford University Press, 2005.

Genova, de Nicholas. "Migrant 'Illegality' and Deportability in Everyday Life."
    Annual Review of Anthropology 31 (2002): 419–47.

———. *Working the Boundaries: Race, Space, and "Illegality" in Mexican Chicago.*
    Durham, NC: Duke University Press, 2005.

Gilbert, Alan. "Extreme Thinking about Slums and Slumdwellers: A Critique."
    SAIS Review of International Affairs 29, no. 1 (Winter–Spring 2009): 35–48.

Gilmore, Ruth Wilson. "Globalization and US Prison Growth: From Military
    Keynesianism to Post-Keynesian Militarism." *Race and Class* 40, nos. 2–3
    (1998–99): 171–88.

———. *Golden Gulag: Prisons, Surplus, Crisis, and Opposition in Globalizing
    California.* Berkeley: University of California Press, 2007.

———. "Ruth Gilmore Interview by Andalusia Knoll," A-Infos, April 6, 2009.
    http://www.ainfos.ca/09/apr/ainfos00080.html.

Giridharadas, Anand, *Winners Take All: The Elite Charade of Changing the World.*
    New York: Knopf, 2018.

Glaeser, Edward L. *Triumph of the City: How Our Greatest Invention Makes Us
    Richer, Smarter, Greener, Healthier, and Happier.* New York: Penguin Press,
    2011.

Golash-Boza, Tanya. *Deported: Immigrant Policing, Disposable Labor, and Global
    Capitalism.* New York: New York University Press, 2015.

———. "The Immigration Industrial Complex: Why We Enforce Immigration
    Policies Destined to Fail." *Sociology Compass* 3, no. 2 (2009): 295–309.

———. "The Parallels between Mass Incarceration and Mass Deportation: An
    Intersectional Analysis of State Repression." *Journal of World Systems
    Research* 22, no. 2 (2016): 484–509.

Goldberg, David Theo. *The Threat of Race: Reflections on Racial Neoliberalism.*
    Malden, MA: Wiley-Blackwell, 2008.

Gómez-Barris, Macarena. *The Extractive Zone: Ecologies and Decolonial
    Perspectives.* Raleigh, NC: Duke University Press, 2017.

Gopnik, Adam. "The Caging of America." *New Yorker*, January 30, 2012.

Gottschalk, Marie. *Caught: The Prison State and the Lockdown of American
    Politics.* Princeton, NJ: Princeton University Press, 2016.

Guardian. "Obama Focuses on Green Economy in Speech before Congress."
    February 25, 2009. https://www.theguardian.com/world/2009/feb/25
    /barack-obama-green-economy-environment.

Hahn, Nicholas G. III. "Rocco Buttiglione: The RealClearReligion Interview,"
    RealClearReligion, September 25, 2014. http://www.realclearreligion.org

/articles/2014/09/25/rocco_buttiglione_the_realclearreligion_interview
.html.

Hang, Julianne. "What Does It Mean to Abolish ICE?" *Nation*, July 11, 2018.
https://www.thenation.com/article/mean-abolish-ice/.

Harris, Alexes. *A Pound of Flesh: Monetary Sanctions as a Punishment for the
Poor*. New York: Russell Sage, 2016.

Hartig, Hannah. "Republicans Turn more Negative Toward Refugees as
Number Admitted to U.S. Plummets." Pew Research, May 24, 2018.
http://www.pewresearch.org/fact-tank/2018/05/24/republicans-turn-more
-negative-toward-refugees-as-number-admitted-to-u-s-plummets/.

Harvey, David. *A Brief History of Neoliberalism*. New York: Oxford, 2005.

———. *The Enigma of Capital: And the Crises of Capitalism*. New York: Oxford
University Press, 2011.

———. "Neoliberalism as Creative Destruction." *Annals of the American
Academy of Political and Social Science*, no. 610 (March 2007): 22–44.

———. *The New Imperialism*. New York: Oxford University Press, 2003.

———. *Rebel Cities: From the Right to the City to the Urban Revolution*. New York:
Verso, 2012.

———. *Seventeen Contradictions and the End of Capitalism*. New York: Oxford
University Press, 2015.

———. "Slums and Skyscrapers: Space, Housing, and the City Under Neoliberalism." Video. Davidharvey.org (blog), July 2015. http://davidharvey.org
/2015/07/video-david-harvey-slums-skyscrapers-space-housing-and-the-city
-under-neoliberalism/.

Harvey, Fiona, and Ben Doherty. "China Demands Developed Countries 'Pay
their Debts' on Climate Change." *Guardian*, December 13, 2018. https://
www.theguardian.com/science/2018/dec/13/china-demands-developed
-countries-pay-their-debts-on-climate-change.

Hayek, F. A. *The Collected Works of F. A. Hayek*. Vol. 13: *Studies on the Abuse and
Decline of Reason: Texts and Documents*. Edited by Bruce Caldwell. Chicago:
University of Chicago Press, 2010.

———. "The Intellectuals and Socialism." In *The Intellectuals: A Controversial
Portrait*, edited by George B. de Huszar, 371–84. Glencoe, IL: Free Press, 1960.

———. *Law, Legislation, and Liberty*. Vol. 2: *The Mirage of Social Justice*.
Chicago: University of Chicago Press, 1976.

Herivel, Tara, and Paul Wright, eds. *Prison Profiteers: Who Makes Money from
Mass Incarceration*. New York: New Press, 2009.

Heyer, Kristin. *Kinship Across Borders: A Christian Ethic of Immigration*. Washington, DC: Georgetown University Press, 2012.

Hickel, Jason. *The Divide: Global Inequality from Conquest to Free Markets*. New
York: W. W. Norton, 2018.

Hinton, Elizabeth. *From the War on Poverty to the War on Crime*. Cambridge, MA: Harvard University Press, 2017.

Hohle, Randolph. *Racism in the Neoliberal Era: A Meta-History of White Power*. New York: Routledge Press, 2017.

Inwood, Joshua FJ. "Neoliberal Racism: The 'Southern Strategy' and the Expanding Geographies of White Supremacy." *Social and Cultural Geography* 16, no. 4 (2015): 407–23.

Iyer, Lakshmi, John D. Macomber, and Namrata Arora. "Dharavi: Developing Asia's Largest Slum." *Harvard Business Review*, July 21, 2009.

Ivereigh, Austin. *The Great Reformer: Francis and the Making of a Radical Pope*. New York: Picador, 2015.

Jackson, Timothy. *Prosperity without Growth*. New York: Routledge, 2011.

Jeffrey, Terence, P. "U.S. Bishop Prepare Catholics for Civil Disobedience May Need to Witness to the Truth by Resistance." *Catholic News Service*, May 27, 2012. https://www.cnsnews.com/news/article/us-bishops-prepare-catholics -civil-disobedience-we-may-need-witness-truth-resisting-law.

John XXIII. *Mater et Magistra: On Christianity and Social Progress*. May 15, 1961. http://w2.vatican.va/content/john-xxiii/en/encyclicals/documents/hf_j-xxiii _enc_15051961_mater.html.

John Paul II [Karol Wojtyla]. *The Acting Person: A Contribution to Phenomeno- logical Anthropology*. Analecta Husserliana 10. Edited by Anna-Teresa Tymieniecka. Dordrecht: Kluwer, 1979.

———. "Celebration of the World Day of Peace." January 1, 1990. https://w2 .vatican.va/content/john-paul-ii/en/messages/peace/documents/hf_jp-ii_mes _19891208_xxiii-world-day-for-peace.html.

———. *Centesimus Annus: On the Hundredth Anniversary of* Rerum Novarum. May 1, 1991. http://w2.vatican.va/content/john-paul-ii/en/encyclicals /documents/hf_jp-ii_enc_01051991_centesimus-annus.html.

———. *Dives in Misericordia*. November 30, 1980. http://w2.vatican.va/content /john-paul-ii/en/encyclicals/documents/hf_jp-ii_enc_30111980_dives-in -misericordia.html.

———. *Dominum et Vivificantem: On the Holy Spirit in the Life of the Church and the World*. May 18, 1986. http://w2.vatican.va/content/john-paul-ii/en /encyclicals/documents/hf_jp-ii_enc_18051986_dominum-et-vivificantem .html.

———. "Ecclesia in America." June 22, 1999. http://w2.vatican.va/content /john-paul-ii/en/apost_exhortations/documents/hf_jp-ii_exh_22011999 _ecclesia-in-america.html.

———. "Environment and Health." March 1997. https://w2.vatican.va/content /john-paul-ii/en/speeches/1997/march/documents/hf_jp-ii_spe_19970324 _ambiente-salute.html.

———. "Homily of His Holiness John Paul II for the Inauguration of His Pontificate." October 22, 1978. https://w2.vatican.va/content/john-paul-ii/en/homilies/1978/documents/hf_jp-ii_hom_19781022_inizio-pontificato.html.

———. Homily: Holy Mass at Yankee Stadium." October 2, 1979. https://w2.vatican.va/content/john-paul-ii/en/homilies/1979/documents/hf_jp-ii_hom_19791002_usa-new-york.html.

———. Laborem Exercens. September 14, 1981. http://w2.vatican.va/content/john-paul-ii/en/encyclicals/documents/hf_jp-ii_enc_14091981_laborem-exercens.html.

———. "Letter on the 100th Anniversary of the Consecration of the Human Race to the Divine Heart of Jesus," June 11, 1999. http://w2.vatican.va/content/john-paul-ii/en/letters/1999/documents/hf_jp-ii_let_19990611_consagrazione-sacro-cuore.html.

———. "Peace with God the Creator, Peace with All of Creation." December 8, 1989. http://w2.vatican.va/content/john-paul-ii/en/messages/peace/documents/hf_jp-ii_mes_19891208_xxiii-world-day-for-peace.html.

———. Reconciliatio et Paenitentia: Apostolic Exhortation on Reconciliation and Penance in the Mission of the Church Today. December 2, 1984. http://w2.vatican.va/content/john-paul-ii/en/apost_exhortations/documents/hf_jp-ii_exh_02121984_reconciliatio-et-paenitentia.html.

———. Redemptor Hominis. March 4, 1979. http://w2.vatican.va/content/john-paul-ii/en/encyclicals/documents/hf_jp-ii_enc_04031979_redemptor-hominis.html.

———. Sollicitudo Rei Socialis. December 30, 1987. http://w2.vatican.va/content/john-paul-ii/en/encyclicals/documents/hf_jp-ii_enc_30121987_sollicitudo-rei-socialis.html.

———. "Talk to the Representatives of the Academic and Cultural World in the University of Riga, Latvia." September 9, 1993. https://w2.vatican.va/content/john-paul-ii/it/speeches/1993/september/documents/hf_jp-ii_spe_19930909_ateneo-riga.html.

———. Veritatis Splendor. August 6, 1993. http://w2.vatican.va/content/john-paul-ii/en/encyclicals/documents/hf_jp-ii_enc_06081993_veritatis-splendor.html.

Johnson, Cedric. "The Urban Precariat, Neoliberalization, and the Soft Power of Humanitarian Design." Journal of Developing Societies 27, nos. 3–4 (2011): 445–75.

Jones, Reece. Border Walls: Security and the War on Terror in the United States, India, and Israel. New York: Zed Books, 2012.

Kasper, Walter. "Cardinal Kasper Responds to First Things Review of 'Mercy.'" First Things, March 23, 2015. https://www.firstthings.com/web-exclusives/2015/03/cardinal-kasper-responds-to-first-things-review-of-mercy.

———. *Mercy: The Essence of the Gospel and the Key to Christian Life*. Translated by William Madges. New York: Paulist Press, 2014.

Keating, Ana Louise. *Transformation Now!: Toward a Post-Oppositional Politics of Change*. Champaign: University of Illinois Press, 2012.

Keenan, James. *The Works of Mercy*. Lanham, MD: Rowman and Littlefield, 2017.

Kelley, Robin D. G. "What Did Cedric Robinson Mean by Racial Capitalism?" *Boston Review*, January 12, 2017. http://bostonreview.net/race/robin-d-g-kelley-what-did-cedric-robinson-mean-racial-capitalism.

Khosravi, Shahram. *After Deportation: Ethnographic Perspectives*. Cham, Switzerland: Palgrave Macmillan, 2018.

Kinzer, Stephen. *Overthrow: America's Century of Regime Change from Hawaii to Iraq*. New York: Times Books, 2007.

Klein, Naomi. *The Battle for Paradise: Puerto Rico Takes on the Disaster Capitalists*. Chicago: Haymarket Books, 2018.

———. "Capitalism vs. the Climate." *Nation*, November 9, 2011. https://www.thenation.com/article/capitalism-vs-climate.

———. *This Changes Everything: Capitalism vs. the Climate*. New York: Simon and Schuster, 2015.

———. "The Lesson from Standing Rock: Organizing and Resistance Can Win," *Nation*, December 4, 2016. https://www.thenation.com/article/the-lesson-from-standing-rock-organizing-and-resistance-can-win/.

———. *The Shock Doctrine: The Rise of Disaster Capitalism*. New York: Picador, 2007.

Knight, Nika. "Pope Francis: Capitalism Is 'Terrorism Against All of Humanity,'" Common Dreams, August 2, 2016. https://www.commondreams.org/news/2016/08/02/pope-francis-capitalism-terrorism-against-all-humanity.

Kolbert, Elizabeth. *The Sixth Extinction: An Unnatural History*. New York: Henry Holt, 2014.

Konings, Martijn. *Capital and Time: For a New Critique of Neoliberal Reason*. Stanford, CA: Stanford University Press, 2018.

———. "Rethinking Neoliberalism and the Subprime Crisis: Beyond the Re-regulation Agenda." *Competition and Change* 13, no. 2 (2009): 108–27.

Kotsko, Adam. *Neoliberalism's Demons: On the Political Theology of Late Capital*. Stanford, CA: Stanford University Press, 2018.

Kotz, David. *The Rise and Fall of Neoliberal Capitalism*. Cambridge, MA: Harvard University Press, 2015.

Lamoureux, Patricia A. "Commentary on *Laborem exercens* (*On Human Work*)." In *Modern Catholic Social Teaching: Commentaries and Interpretations*, edited by Kenneth R. Himes, 389–414. Washington, DC: Georgetown University Press, 2005.

Lawler, Ronald David, OFM. *The Christian Personalism of John Paul II.* Chicago: Franciscan Herald Press, 1982.

Lazzarato, Marizio. *Governing by Debt.* Translated by Joshua David Jordan. Pasadena, CA: Semiotext(e), 2013.

———. *The Making of Indebted Man.* Translated by Joshua David Jordan. Los Angeles: Semiotext(e), 2012.

———. "Neoliberalism in Action: Inequality, Insecurity, and the Reconstitution of the Social." *Theory, Culture and Society* 26, no. 6 (2009): 109–33.

Leo XIII. *Rerum Novarum: On Capital and Labor.* May 15, 1891. http://w2.vatican .va/content/leo-xiii/en/encyclicals/documents/hf_l-xiii_enc_15051891 _rerum-novarum.html.

Leon, Joshua K. "The Role of Global Cities in Land Grabs." *Third World Quarterly* 36, no. 2 (2015): 257–73.

Lerner, Steven. *Sacrifice Zones: The Front Lines of Toxic Chemical Exposure in the United States.* Cambridge, MA: MIT Press, 2010.

Liberti, Stefano. *Land-Grabbing: Journeys in the New Colonialism.* Translated by Enda Flannelly. New York: Verso, 2013.

Lind, Dara. "The Disastrous, Forgotten 1996 Law that Created Today's Immigration Problem." *Vox,* April 28, 2016. https://www.vox.com/2016/4/28 /11515132/iirira-clinton-immigration.

Loewenstein, Antony. *Disaster Capitalism: Making a Killing Out of Catastrophe.* New York: Verso, 2015.

Lopez, Ian Hanley. *Dog Whistle Politics: How Coded Racial Appeals have Reinvented Racism and Wrecked the Middle Class.* New York: Oxford University Press, 2015.

Lorey, Isabel, *State of Insecurity: Government of the Precarious.* Translated by Aileen Derieg. New York: Verso, 2015.

Lowe, Lisa. *The Intimacies of Four Continents.* Chapel Hill, NC: Duke University Press, 2015.

MacLean, Nancy. *Democracy in Chains: The Deep History of the Radical Right's Stealth Plan for America.* New York: Viking, 2017.

Mahabir, Ron, Andrew Crooks, Arie Croitoru, and Peggy Agouris. "The Study of Slums as Social and Physical Constructs: Challenges and Emerging Research Opportunities." *Regional Studies, Regional Science* 3, no. 1 (2016): 399–419.

Marx, Benjamin, Thomas Stoker, and Tanveet Suri. "The Economics of Slums in the Developing World." *Journal of Economic Perspectives* 27, no. 4 (Fall 2013): 187–210.

Massaro, Thomas. *Living Justice: Catholic Social Teaching in Action.* Lanham, MD: Rowman and Littlefield, 2011.

———. *Mercy in Action: The Social Teachings of Pope Francis.* Lanham, MD: Rowman and Littlefield, 2018.

Massingale, Bryan. "James Cone and Recent Catholic Episcopal Teaching on Racism." *Theological Studies* 61 (2000): 700–30.

———. *Racial Justice and the Catholic Church*. Maryknoll, NY: Orbis, 2010.

McCarthy, Anna. "Reality Television: A Neoliberal Theater of Suffering." *Social Text* 25, no. 4 (2007): 17–42.

McCarthy, David Matzko, ed. *The Heart of Catholic Social Teaching: Its Origin and Contemporary Significance*. Grand Rapids, MI: Brazos Press, 2009.

McCurria, John. "Desperate Citizens and Good Samaritans: Neoliberalism and Makeover Reality TV." *Television and New Media* 9, no. 4 (2008): 305–32.

Melamed, Jodi. *Represent and Destroy: Rationalizing Violence in the New Racial Capitalism*. Minneapolis: University of Minnesota, 2011.

Mele, C. "Neoliberalism, Race, and the Redefining of Urban Development." *International Journal of Urban and Regional Research* 37, no. 2 (March 2013): 598–617.

Metz, Johann Baptist. *Memoria Passionis: Ein Provozierendes Gedächtnis in Pluralisticher Gesellschaft*. Freiburg: Herder, 2006.

Mirowski, Philip. "Neoliberalism: The Movement that Dare Not Speak Its Name." *American Affairs Journal* 2, no. 1 (Spring 2018): 118–41.

———. *Never Let a Serious Crisis Go to Waste: How Neoliberalism Survived the Financial Meltdown*. New York: Verso Press, 2013.

Mirowski, Philip, and Dieter Plehwe. *The Road from Mont Pèlerin: The Making of the Neoliberal Thought Collective*. Cambridge, MA: Harvard University Press, 2015.

Mize, Ronald L., and Alicia C. S. Swords. *Consuming Mexican Labor: From the Bracero Program to NAFTA*. Toronto: University of Toronto Press, 2010.

Moloney, Daniel P. "What Mercy Is: A Review of *Mercy*." *First Things*, March 2015. https://www.firstthings.com/article/2015/03/what-mercy-is.

Monbiot, George. "Neoliberalism: The Deep Story that Lies Beneath Donald Trump's Triumph." *Guardian*, November 14, 2016. https://www.theguardian .com/commentisfree/2016/nov/14/neoliberalsim-donald-trump-george-monbiot.

———. "Neoliberalism: The Ideology at the Root of All Our Problems." *Guardian*, April 15, 2016. https://www.theguardian.com/books/2016/apr/15 /neoliberalism-ideology-problem-george-monbiot.

Moore, Jason W., ed. *Anthropocene or Capitalocene? Nature, History, and the Crisis of Capitalism*. Oakland, CA: PM Press, 2016.

Moyn, Samuel. *Not Enough: Human Rights in an Unequal World*. New Haven, CT: Yale University Press, 2018.

Mukherjee, Anita. "Impacts of Private Prison Contracting on Inmate Time Served and Recidivism." SSRN, August 20, 2017. https://ssrn.com/abstract=2523238.

Murakawa, Naomi. *The First Civil Right: How Liberals Built Prison America*. New York: Oxford University Press, 2014.

Nakamura, David. "Trump Administration Moving Quickly to Build Up Nationwide Deportation Force." *Washington Post*, April 12, 2017. https://www.washingtonpost.com/politics/trump-administration-moving-quickly-to-build-up-nationwide-deportation-force/2017/04/12/7a7f59c2-1f87-11e7-be2a-3a1fb24d4671_story.html.

National Immigration Forum, "Fact Sheet: Immigration and Customs Enforcement." July 20, 2018. https://immigrationforum.org/article/fact-sheet-immigration-and-customs-enforcement-ice/.

Nelson, Derek. *Sin: A Guide for the Perplexed*. New York: T&T Clark, 2011.

Neuhaus, Richard John. "The Pope Affirms the 'New Capitalism.'" *Wall Street Journal*, May 2, 1991.

Ngai, Mae. *Impossible Subjects: Illegal Aliens and the Making of Modern America*. Princeton, NJ: Princeton University Press, 2004.

Nijman, Jan. "Against the Odds: Slum Rehabilitation in Neoliberal Mumbai." *Cities* 25, no. 1 (2008): 73–85.

Nothwehr, Dawn M., ed. *That They May Be One: Catholic Social Teaching on Racism, Tribalism, and Xenophobia*. Maryknoll, NY: Orbis Books, 2008.

Novak, Michael. "Agreeing with Pope Francis." *National Review*, December 7, 2013. https://www.nationalreview.com/2013/12/agreeing-pope-francis-michael-novak/.

———. "Beyond *Populorum Progressio*: John Paul II's 'Economic Initiative.'" *Crisis Magazine*, March 1, 1988. https://www.crisismagazine.com/1988/beyond-populorum-progressio-john-paul-iis-economic-initiative.

———. "Economic Heresies of the Left." *First Things*, June 29, 2009. https://www.firstthings.com/web-exclusives/2009/06/economic-heresies-of-the-left.

———. "Introduction to *Centesimus Annus*." *A Free Society Reader: Principles for the New Millennium*, edited by Michael Novak, William Brailsford, and Cornelius Heesters, 331–32. Lanham, MD: Lexington Books, 2000.

———. "The Pope of Caritapolis." *First Things*, July 7, 2009. https://www.firstthings.com/blogs/firstthoughts/2009/07/the-pope-of-caritapolis.

———. *Toward a Theology of the Corporation*. Washington, DC: AEI Press, 1990.

———. "Wisdom from the Pope." *Washington Post*, May 7, 1991.

O'Brien, David, and Thomas Shannon. *Catholic Social Thought: The Documentary Heritage*. Maryknoll, NY: Orbis Books, 2010.

O'Regan, Cyril. "Benedict the Augustinian." In *Explorations in the Theology of Benedict XVI*, edited by John Cavadini, 21–62. Notre Dame, IN: University of Notre Dame Press, 2012.

Obama, Barack. "Inaugural Address." January 21, 2013. https://obamawhitehouse.archives.gov/the-press-office/2013/01/21/inaugural-address-president-barack-obama.

———. "State of the Union Address." February 13, 2013. https://
obamawhitehouse.archives.gov/photos-and-video/video/2013/02/12/2013
-state-union-address-0#transcript.

Oxfam International. "5 Shocking Facts about Extreme Global Inequality and
How to Even It Up." N.d. https://www.oxfam.org/en/even-it/5-shocking-facts
-about-extreme-global-inequality-and-how-even-it-davos.

———. "Reward Work, Not Wealth." January 2018. https://www.oxfam.org
/sites/www.oxfam.org/files/file_attachments/bp-reward-work-not-wealth
-220118-summ-en.pdf.

Pabst, Adrian, ed. *The Crisis of Global Capitalism: Pope Benedict XVI's Social
Encyclical and the Future of Political Economy*. New York: James Clarke,
2012.

Paik, A. Naomi, "Abolitionist Futures and the US Sanctuary Movement." *Race
and Class* 59, no. 2 (2017): 3–25.

Paller, Jeffrey. "From Urban Crisis to Political Opportunity: Africa's Slums." In
Africa Under Neoliberalism, edited by Nana Poku and Jim Whitman, 76–95.
New York: Routledge, 2018.

Parenti, Christian. *Lockdown America: Police and Prisons in the Age of Crisis*.
New York: Verso Books, 2008.

Parr, Adrian. *The Radical Politics of Environmentalism*. New York: Columbia
University Press, 2017.

Paul VI. *Populorum Progressio: On the Development of Peoples*. March 26, 1967.
http://w2.vatican.va/content/paul-vi/en/encyclicals/documents/hf_p-vi_enc
_26031967_populorum.html.

Peck, Jamie. *Constructions of Neoliberal Reason*. New York: Oxford University
Press, 2013.

Peck, Jamie, and Adam Tickell. "Neoliberalizing Space." *Antipode* 34, no. 3
(2002): 380–404.

Pérez-Peña, Richard. "Contrary to Trump's Claims, Immigrants Less Likely to
Commit Crimes." *New York Times*, January 26, 2017. https://www.nytimes
.com/2017/01/26/us/trump-illegal-immigrants-crime.html.

Pfeil, Margaret, "Love and Poverty: Dorothy Day's Twofold Diakonia," *Journal
of Moral Theology* 1, no. 2 (June 2012): 61–71.

Pflaff, John. *Locked In: The True Causes of Mass Incarceration and How to Achieve
Real Reform*. New York: Basic Books, 2017.

Pius XI. *Quadragesimo Anno: On Reconstruction of the Social Order*. May 15, 1931.
http://w2.vatican.va/content/pius-xi/en/encyclicals/documents/hf_p-xi_enc
_19310515_quadragesimo-anno.html.

Piven, Frances Fox and Richard Cloward, *Regulating the Poor: The Functions of
Public Welfare*. New York: Vintage Books, 1993.

Pogge, Thomas. "An Egalitarian Law of Peoples." *Philosophy and Public Affairs* 23, no. 3 (1994): 195–224.

———. *World Poverty and Human Rights: Cosmopolitan Responsibilities and Reforms*. New York: Polity, 2008.

Pontifical Council for Justice and Peace. "Compendium of the Social Doctrine of the Church." June 29, 2004. http://www.vatican.va/roman_curia /pontifical_councils/justpeace/documents/rc_pc_justpeace_doc_20060526 _compendio-dott-soc_en.html#Origin%20and%20meaning.

Rahner, Karl. "The Sinful Church in the Decrees of Vatican II." In *Concerning Vatican Council II: Theological Investigations 6*, translated by Karl H. and Boniface Kruger, 270–93. Baltimore, MD: Helicon Press, 1969.

———. "The Theological Concept of *Concupiscentia*." In *God, Christ, Mary, and Grace: Theological Investigations 1*, translated by Cornelius Ernst, OP, 347–82 Baltimore, MD: Helicon, 1961.

Rao, Vyjayanthi. "Slum as Theory: The South Asian City and Globalization." *International Journal of Urban and Regional Research* 30, no. 1 (2006): 225–32.

Ratzinger, Joseph. *See* Benedict XVI.

Redden, Guy. "Is Reality TV Neoliberal?" *Television and New Media*. 19, no. 5 (2018): 399–414.

Reier, Sharon. "Half a Century Later, Economist's 'Creative Destruction' Theory Is Apt for the Internet Age: Schumpeter: The Prophet of Boom and Bust." *New York Times*, June 10, 2000. http://www.nytimes.com/2000 /06/10/your-money/half-a-century-later-economists-creative-destruction -theory-is.html.

Riley, Tess. "Just 100 Companies Responsible for 71% of Global Emissions, Study Says." Guardian, July 10, 2017. https://www.theguardian.com /sustainable-business/2017/jul/10/100-fossil-fuel-companies-investors -responsible-71-global-emissions-cdp-study-climate-change.

Reno, R. R. "The Spirit of Democratic Capitalism." *First Things*, October 2017. https://www.firstthings.com/article/2017/10/the-spirit-of-democratic -capitalism.

Risager, Bjarke Skærlund. "Neoliberalism Is a Political Project: An Interview with David Harvey," *Jacobin*, July 23, 2016. https://www.jacobinmag.com /2016/07/david-harvey-neoliberalism-capitalism-labor-crisis-resistance/.

Robbins, Ted. "Little-Known Immigration Mandate Keeps Detention Beds Full." NPR, November 19, 2013. https://www.npr.org/2013/11/19/245968601 /little-known-immigration-mandate-keeps-detention-beds-full.

Roberts, David J. "Race and Neoliberalism." In *Handbook of Neoliberalism*, edited Simon Springer, Kean Birch, and Julie MacLeavy, 209–16. New York: Routledge Press, 2016.

Roberts, David J., and Minelle Mahtani. "Neoliberalizing Race, Racing Neoliberalism: Placing 'Race' in Neoliberal Discourses." *Antipode: A Radical Journal of Geography* 42, no. 2 (March 2010): 248–57.

Robinson, Cedric. *Black Marxism: The Making of the Black Radical Tradition.* Chapel Hill: University of North Carolina Press, 2000.

Ross, Susan A. *Extravagant Affections: A Feminist Sacramental Theology.* New York: Continuum, 2001.

Rourke, Thomas. *The Roots of Pope Francis's Social and Political Thought: From Argentina to the Vatican.* Lanham: Rowman and Littlefield, 2016.

Roy, Ananya. "Slumdog Cities: Rethinking Subaltern Urbanism." *International Journal of Urban and Regional Research* 35, no. 2 (2011): 223–38.

Roy, Ananya, and the #GlobalPOV Project, "Are Slums the Urban Future." YouTube, June 31, 2013. https://www.youtube.com/watch?v=1xk7dr3VG6s.

Roy, Arundhati. *Capitalism: A Ghost Story.* Chicago: Haymarket Books, 2014.

Sassen, Saskia. *Expulsions: Brutality and Complexity in the Global Economy.* Cambridge, MA: Harvard University Press, 2014.

———. "A Massive Loss of Habitat." *Sociology of Development* 2, no. 2 (2016): 204–33.

Sawyer, Wendy. "How Much Do Incarcerated People Earn in Each State?" Prison Policy Initiative, April 10, 2017. https://www.prisonpolicy.org/blog /2017/04/10/wages/.

Second Vatican Council. *Gaudium et Spes: Pastoral Constitution on the Church in the Modern World.* December 7, 1965. http://www.vatican.va/archive/hist _councils/ii_vatican_council/documents/vat-ii_const_19651207_gaudium -et-spes_en.html.

Shadle, Matthew A. *Interrupting Capitalism: Catholic Social Thought and the Economy.* New York: Oxford University Press, 2018.

Schlumpf, Heidi. "Bishop Lays Out Plan for Eradicating this Plague of Racism." *National Catholic Reporter*, February 15, 2018. https://www.ncronline.org /news/parish/bishop-lays-out-plans-eradicating-plague-racism.

Schultz, Theodore. *Investment in Human Capital: The Role of Education and Research.* New York: Free Press, 1971.

Schumpeter, Joseph A. *Capitalism, Socialism, and Democracy.* New York: Harper, 1942.

Schüssler Fiorenza, Elisabeth. "Articulating a Different Future: An Interview with Elisabeth Schüssler Fiorenza." Interviewed by Caroline Matas. *Harvard Divinity Bulletin*, Spring/Summer 2017. https://bulletin.hds.harvard.edu /articles/springsummer2017/articulating-different-future.

———. *Congress of Wo/men: Religion, Gender, and Kyriarchal Power.* Cambridge, MA: Feminist Studies in Religion Books, 2017.

Scruton, Roger. *The Palgrave Macmillan Dictionary of Political Thought*. 3rd ed. New York: Palgrave Macmillan, 2007.

Sirico, Robert. "Reading *Centesimus Annus*," *Religion and Liberty* 11, no. 3 (July 20, 2010). https://acton.org/pub/religion-liberty/volume-11-number-3 /reading-centesimus-annus.

Slobodian, Quinn. *Globalists: The End of Empire and the Birth of Neoliberalism*. Cambridge, MA: Harvard University Press, 2018.

Sniegocki, John. *Catholic Social Teaching and Economic Globalization: The Quest for Alternatives*. Milwaukee: Marquette University Press, 2009.

———. "The Social Ethics of John Paul II: A Critique of Neoconservative Interpretations." *Horizons* 33, no. 1 (2006): 7–32.

Sobrino, Jon, SJ. "On the Way to Healing: Humanizing a 'Gravely Ill World.'" *America*, October 29, 2014. https://www.americamagazine.org/issue/way -healing.

———. *The Principle of Mercy: Taking the Crucified People from the Cross*. Translated by Robert R. Barr. Maryknoll, NY: Orbis, 1994.

Speth, James Gustave. *The Bridge at the End of the World: Capitalism, the Environment, and Crossing from Crisis to Sustainability*. New Haven, CT: Yale University Press, 2008.

Springer, Simon, Kean Birch, and Julie MacLeavy, "An Introduction to Neoliberalism." In *The Handbook of Neoliberalism*, edited by Simon Springer, Kean Birch, and Julie MacLeavy, 1–14. New York: Routledge, 2016.

Stedman Jones, Daniel. *Masters of the Universe: Hayek, Friedman, and the Birth of Neoliberalism*. Princeton, NJ: Princeton University Press, 2014.

Steger, Manfred B., and Ravi K. Roy, *Neoliberalism: A Very Short Introduction*. New York: Oxford University Press, 2010.

Street, Paul. "How to Stop Capitalism's Deadly War with Nature." Truthdig, September 16, 2016. http://www.truthdig.com/report/item/how_to_stop _capitalisms_deadly_war_with_nature_20160913.

Szwarcwald, Célia Landman, Jurema Corrêa da Mota, Giseli Nogueira Damacena, and Tatiana Guimarães Sardinha Pereira, "Health Inequalities in Rio de Janeiro, Brazil: Lower Healthy Life Expectancy in Socioeconom- ically Disadvantaged Areas." *American Journal of Public Health*, 101, no. 3 (March 2011): 517–23.

Supiano, Beckie. "A Guide to Income-Share Agreements, Which Some See as a Better Way to Finance College." *Chronicle for Higher Education*, April 14, 2015. https://www.chronicle.com/article/A-Guide-to-Income-Share/229321.

Tanner, Kathryn. *Christianity and the New Spirit of Capitalism*. New Haven, CT: Yale University Press, 2019.

Tornielli, Andrea, and Giacomo Galeazzi. *This Economy Kills: Pope Francis on Capitalism and Social Justice*. Collegeville: Liturgical Press, 2015.

UN-Habitat, *The Challenge of Slums: Global Report on Human Settlements.*
Sterling, VA: Earthscan Publications, 2003.

———. "Housing and Slum Upgrading," Unhabitat.org. https://unhabitat.org
/urban-themes/housing-slum-upgrading/.

US Conference of Catholic Bishops. "Brothers and Sisters to Us." 1979.
http://www.usccb.org/issues-and-action/cultural-diversity/african-american
/brothers-and-sIsters-to-us.cfm.

———. "Catholic Church's Position on Immigration Reform." August 2013.
http://www.usccb.org/issues-and-action/human-life-and-dignity
/immigration/churchteachingonimmigrationreform.cfm.

———. *Compendium on the Social Doctrine of the Church.* Washington, DC:
United States Conference of Catholic Bishops, 2005.

———. *Open Wide Our Hearts: The Enduring Call to Love.* Pastoral Letter on
Racism. November 15, 2018. http://www.usccb.org/issues-and-action
/human-life-and-dignity/racism/upload/open-wide-our-hearts.pdf.

———. *Strangers No Longer: Together on the Journey of Hope.* January 23, 2003.
http://www.usccb.org/issues-and-action/human-life-and-dignity
/immigration/strangers-no-longer-together-on-the-journey-of-hope.cfm.

———. *Welcoming the Stranger Among Us: Unity in Diversity.* November 15,
2000. http://www.usccb.org/issues-and-action/cultural-diversity/pastoral
-care-of-migrants-refugees-and-travelers/resources/welcoming-the-stranger
-among-us-unity-in-diversity.cfm.

Vatican Insider (La Stampa), "The 'Trickle-Down Theory the Pope Frowns
Upon." July 16, 2015. http://www.lastampa.it/2015/07/16/vaticaninsider/eng
/the-vatican/the-trickledown-theory-the-pope-frowns-upon
-JIMvFup2gIVKc4jXGileHN/pagina.html.

Vallet, Elizabeth, ed. *Borders, Fences and Walls: State of Insecurity?* Burlington,
VT: Ashgate, 2014.

Ventura, Patricia. *Neoliberal Culture: Living with American Neoliberalism.*
Burlington, VT: Ashgate, 2012.

Victor, Peter. *Managing without Growth: Slower by Design, Not Disaster.*
Northampton, MA: E. Elgar, 2014.

Wacquant, Loïc. "Class, Race, and Hyperincarceration in Revanchist America."
Dædalus 139, no. 3 (2010): 74–90.

———. "From Slavery to Mass Incarceration: Rethinking the 'Race Question'
in the US." *New Left Review* 13, no. 1 (2002): 41–60.

———. *Prisons of Poverty.* Minneapolis: University of Minnesota Press, 2009.

———. *Punishing the Poor: The Neoliberal Government of Social Insecurity.*
Durham, NC: Duke University Press, 2009.

Walatka, Todd, "The Principle of Mercy: Jon Sobrino and the Catholic
Theological Tradition." *Theological Studies* 77, no. 1 (2016): 96–117.

Wang, Jackie. *Carceral Capitalism*. New York: Semiotext(e), 2018.

Watson, Natalie. *Introducing Feminist Ecclesiology*. New York: Bloomsbury, 2002.

Weigel, George. "Blessings on Capitalism at Its Best." *Los Angeles Times*, May 3, 1991.

———. "Camels and Needles, Talents and Treasure: American Catholicism and the Capitalist Ethic." In *Freedom and Its Discontents: Catholicism Confronts Modernity*, 77–99. Washington, DC: Ethics and Public Policy Center, 1991.

———. *Caritas in Veritate* in Gold and Red." *National Review*, July 7, 2009. https://www.nationalreview.com/2009/07/caritas-veritate-gold-and-red -george-weigel/.

———. "The Enduring Importance of *Centesimus Annus*." *First Things*. June 22, 2011.

———. "George Weigel Discusses Pope Francis's U.S. Visit." Ethics and Public Policy Center, September 17, 2015. https://eppc.org/publications/george -weigel-discusses-pope-franciss-u-s-visit/.

———. "The Neoconservative Difference: A Proposal for the Renewal of Church and Society." In *Being Right: Conservative Catholics in America*, edited Mary Jo Weaver and R. Scott Appleby, 138–62. Bloomington: Indiana University Press, 1995.

———. "The Pope's Encyclical, at Heart, Is About Us, Not Trees and Snail Darters." *National Review*, July 18, 2015, http://www.nationalreview.com /article/419933/popes-encyclical-heart-about-us-not-trees-and-snail-darters -george-weigel.

Weinstein, Liza. "'One-Man Handled': Fragmented Power and Political Entrepreneurship in Growing Mumbai." *International Journal of Urban and Regional Research* 38, no. 1 (2014): 14–35.

Whitmore, Todd David. "John Paul II, Michael Novak, and the Differences Between Them." *Annual of the Society of Christian Ethics* 21 (2001): 215–32.

Williams, Raymond. *Marxism and Literature*. New York: Oxford University Press, 1977.

Wilson, Julie. *Neoliberalism*. New York: Routledge, 2017.

Winters, Michael Sean. "US Bishops Present United Front on First Day of General Assembly." National Catholic Reporter, November 14, 2017. https://www.ncronline.org/news/opinion/distinctly-catholic/us-bishops -present-united-front-first-day-general-assembly.

Wooden, Cindy. "Destroying Creation is Destroying a Gift of God, Pope says at Audience." CNS News, May 21, 2014. http://www.catholicnews.com /services/englishnews/2014/destroying-creation-is-destroying-a-gift-of-god -pope-says-at-audience.cfm.

Wojtyla, Karol. *See* John Paul II.

Zamora, Daniel and Michael C. Behrent, eds. *Foucault and Neoliberalism*. Boston, MA: Polity, 2015.

Index

MATTHEW T. EGGEMEIER is associate professor in the Department of Religious Studies at the College of the Holy Cross, where he teaches courses on Catholic social teaching, political theology, and liberation theology. He is the author of *A Sacramental-Prophetic Vision: Christian Spirituality in a Suffering World* (Collegeville, MN: Liturgical Press, 2014) and *Against Empire: Ekklesial Resistance and the Politics of Radical Democracy*, Theopolitical Visions series (Eugene, OR: Cascade Books, 2020).

PETER JOSEPH FRITZ is associate professor in the Department of Religious Studies at the College of the Holy Cross in Worcester, Massachusetts. He has taught varied courses in modern Catholic theology, the history of Christianity since the Reformation, Catholic social teaching, theological aesthetics, and theology and art. He is author of *Karl Rahner's Theological Aesthetics* (Washington, DC: Catholic University of America Press, 2014) and *Freedom Made Manifest: Rahner's Fundamental Option and Theological Aesthetics* (Washington, DC: Catholic University of America Press, 2019).

CATHOLIC PRACTICE IN NORTH AMERICA

James T. Fisher and Margaret M. McGuinness (eds.), *The Catholic Studies Reader*

Jeremy Bonner, Christopher D. Denny, and Mary Beth Fraser Connolly (eds.), *Empowering the People of God: Catholic Action before and after Vatican II*

Christine Firer Hinze and J. Patrick Hornbeck II (eds.), *More than a Monologue: Sexual Diversity and the Catholic Church. Volume I: Voices of Our Times*

J. Patrick Hornbeck II and Michael A. Norko (eds.), *More than a Monologue: Sexual Diversity and the Catholic Church. Volume II: Inquiry, Thought, and Expression*

Jack Lee Downey, *The Bread of the Strong: Lacouturisme and the Folly of the Cross, 1910–1985*

Michael McGregor, *Pure Act: The Uncommon Life of Robert Lax*

Mary Dunn, *The Cruelest of All Mothers: Marie de l'Incarnation, Motherhood, and Christian Tradition*

Dorothy Day and the Catholic Worker: The Miracle of Our Continuance. Photographs by Vivian Cherry, Text by Dorothy Day, Edited, with an Introduction and Additional Text by Kate Hennessy

Nicholas K. Rademacher, *Paul Hanly Furfey: Priest, Scientist, Social Reformer*

Margaret M. McGuinness and James T. Fisher (eds.), *Roman Catholicism in the United States: A Thematic History*

Gary J. Adler Jr., Tricia C. Bruce, and Brian Starks (eds.), *American Parishes: Remaking Local Catholicism*

Stephanie N. Brehm, *America's Most Famous Catholic (According to Himself): Stephen Colbert and American Religion in the Twenty-First Century*

Jill Peterfeso, *Womanpriest: Tradition and Transgression In the Contemporary Roman Catholic Church*

John C. Seitz and Christine Firer Hinze (eds.), *Working Alternatives: American and Catholic Experiments in Work and Economy*

Matthew T. Eggemeier and Peter Joseph Fritz, *Send Lazarus: Catholicism and the Crises of Neoliberalism*

www.ingramcontent.com/pod-product-compliance
Lightning Source LLC
Chambersburg PA
CBHW032120020426
42334CB00016B/1015